ON THE
THEORY AND MEASUREMENT OF
TECHNOLOGICAL CHANGE

ON THE THEORY AND MEASUREMENT OF TECHNOLOGICAL CHANGE

BY

MURRAY BROWN

George Washington University

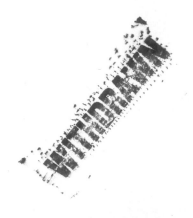

CAMBRIDGE

AT THE UNIVERSITY PRESS

1966

PUBLISHED BY
THE SYNDICS OF THE CAMBRIDGE UNIVERSITY PRESS

Bentley House, 200 Euston Road, London, N.W.1
American Branch: 32 East 57th Street, New York, N.Y. 10022
West African Office: P.M.B. 5181, Ibadan, Nigeria

Printed in Great Britain at the University Printing House, Cambridge
(Brooke Crutchley, University Printer)

LIBRARY OF CONGRESS CATALOGUE
CARD NUMBER: 66-10349

TO BOBBIE

PREFACE

Perhaps it is precipitate to offer a book on production functions when recent developments in the field have been so spirited and novel. In fact, they have been so rapid and novel that classical production analysis may well include the most recent articles on the subject. But, give or take a year or two, the production economics done between 1956 and 1963 can be duly regarded as an intellectual watershed. Hence, even given the novel developments in the area, a volume dealing with most of the contributions, yet with no pretence to completeness, surely can be justified. This is not meant to imply that the book is simply an historical survey of the period. It is that to some extent, since one of its purposes is to provide material for the non-specialist who wishes to enter the field. But in addition, it has a point of view, or rather two points of view: one is an econometric orientation, the desire to state theory in a form which is readily amenable to the measurement of the relevant quantities; and the other is a particular way of looking at technological progress. Since there are many characterizations of this troublesome phenomenon, some readers are sure to have some difficulty in accepting my point of view. My wholesale justification of it is simply that it flows readily from traditional economic analysis and that it has proven useful in understanding certain tricky problems.

The book was begun in 1962 in Rotterdam while I was a Ford Fellow at the Econometric Institute. The members of the Institute kindly permitted me to sound out my initial ideas and offered valuable comments. Also, while in Rotterdam, Alfred Conrad gave unstintingly of his time from which the manuscript benefited immensely. Subsequently, I had the advantage of discussions with my former colleagues at the Office of Business Economics of the U.S. Department of Commerce, of comments from Michael McCarthy, of the detailed critique of the entire manuscript by Richard Nelson to whom especial gratitude is due, of comments and encouragement given by Adolph Lowe

and Hans Neisser, and of criticisms from Raford Boddy. After a
point the development of the manuscript assumed a dynamics of
its own so that I did not always make use of their remarks. But
to all these people I give my thanks.

Grateful acknowledgement is also made of the Ford Fellowship
and a Social Science Research Council Grant, which enabled
me to complete the manuscript.

M. B.

October 1964

    of substitution world*   *page* 43

    The form of the CES production function   45

    Neoclassical properties of the CES production
    function   46

    Imperfect competition in a CES world   51

    Technological change in a CES world   54

    Neutral technological progress   54

    Changes in the marginal rate of substitution due to
    technological progress   55

    The impact of non-neutral technological progress
    on CES production   56

    Limitations of the CES production function   59

    Summary   61

5   *Long-run, short-run, and secular production processes*   63

    Long- and short-run production   65

    A model of short- and long-run production
    processes   68

    Production in the secular period   72

    The transition period   74

    Summary   75

6   *Embodied technological progress*   77

    Solow's embodied technological change model   78

    The old and new view of capital stock   81

    Conclusions   90

PART II   FRAMEWORKS FOR THE MEASUREMENT OF
          TECHNOLOGICAL PROGRESS

7   *Productivity indexes, the Solow model and the Salter
    method: three measures of technological progress* 95

    Productivity ratios and the measurement of
    technological progress   96

    The multifactor productivity ratio   98

1

INTRODUCTION

There has occurred in the post-World War II period an increasing awareness in economic thought concerning the importance and implications of technological progress. Not since classical economics has it been found by non-Marxist economists to play such a crucial role in the determination of production movements and in the distribution of income. This is probably attributable to the evidence that is being amassed in which the contribution to economic growth of variable technologies is found to be as important as—or in some cases even more important than— the traditional labour and capital factors.

The upsurge in the attention given to technological change can be dated in 1956 with the appearance of an article by Moses Abramowitz.† There, he found that almost the entire increase in net product *per capita* was associated with the rise in something other—subsequently called the 'Residual'—than the inputs of the physical capital stock and the services of labour. He proffers the guarded challenge:

This result is surprising in the lopsided importance which it appears to give to [the Residual] and it should be, in a sense, sobering, if not discouraging, to students of economic growth. Since we know little about the causes of [the Residual], the indicated importance of this element may be taken to be some sort of measure of our ignorance about the causes of economic growth in the United States and some sort of indication of where we need to concentrate our attention.‡

After the appearance of the Abramowitz article, evidence on the importance of the Residual accumulated.§ The studies which

† 'Resource and Output Trends in the United States Since 1870', *Papers and Proceedings of the American Economic Association*, vol. 46 (May 1956), pp. 5–23.
‡ *Ibid.* p. 11.
§ R. Solow, 'Technical Change and the Aggregate Production Function', *The Review of Economics and Statistics*, vol. 39 (August 1957), pp. 312–20; J. Kendrick, *Productivity Trends in the United States* (Princeton, National Bureau of Economic Research, 1961), pp. 65 ff.; B. F. Massell, 'Capital Formation and Technological Change in United States Manufacturing', *The Review of Economics and Statistics*, vol. 42 (May 1960), pp. 182–8; M. Brown and J. Popkin, 'A Measure of Technological Change and Returns to Scale', *The Review of Economics and Statistics*, vol. 44 (November 1962), pp. 402–11.

derived the result used a variety of approaches, employed different bodies of data, and covered different time periods. Although each has its deficiencies, these are not sufficient to negate the principal result, and hence it is probably not a spurious one.

It is not difficult to uncover reasons why the phenomenon of technological progress has become one of the focal areas of inquiry in economics. First, the predominant feeling that severe cyclical problems can be resolved—at least, at the theoretical level—has turned attention to policies that optimize the returns of available resources, and this has shunted technological change to the fore in these discussions. For the ruling technology sets the conditions for the optimum use of resources; and similarly, a change in technology alters the optimum use of resources. A second reason is that some industrial economies may begin to suffer an attrition in employment that is sometimes referred to as structural unemployment. It is certainly related to technological change, yet it remains one of the least understood and measured phenomena in contemporary economics. There may be other reasons for focusing attention on the role of technological progress, but these two justify the resources devoted to its analysis and its measurement.

The components of technological progress can be classified in a variety of ways. In terms of one framework, it includes the productivity benefits of increased education and skill attainment, of improved health, of design and product innovations attributable to research, of economies of scale, of improvements in the organization of markets such as the removal of restrictions on the mobility and economic effectiveness of resources, and of managerial efficiency. Clearly, these forces are meant to refer to the growth in output that is not accounted for by the contribution of labour inputs—measured by a straight count of undifferentiated man-hours or people employed—and of capital services—measured by the quantity of its inputs. The problem of measurement in this framework is the quantification of each of these forces so that their sum represents total technological advance. This is the path taken by Edward Denison in his remarkable book,† in which he clarifies the components of the Residual and tentatively quantifies their effect on economic growth. Yet, in spite of his *tour de force*—or perhaps, because of it

† *The Sources of Economic Growth in the United States and the Alternatives Before Us*, Supplementary Paper No. 13, Committee for Economic Development, 1962.

—this particular method of measuring the components of technological progress is in its infancy in terms of conclusive results.†

Technological change has another set of measurable properties that are classified as neutral and non-neutral. The former affects the labour and capital inputs equally, while the latter has a biased effect on the various factors of production; that is, it may be either labour-saving or labour-using. These components of technological progress can be analysed in terms of various characteristics such as (a) the degree of returns to scale associated with the ruling technology, (b) the degree to which technology is capital or labour intensive, (c) the ease with which the technology permits capital to be substituted for labour, and (d) its efficiency. These characteristics of technological progress are defined and discussed in detail below. Their importance derives from the fact that their interaction with the changes in factor endowments determine the growth of output and the distribution of income, among other things. For, as we show below, changes in the characteristics are necessary and sufficient conditions for the growth in output and other variables, given the growth in the factors of production. The present work, then, takes this approach to the analysis of technological advance. Specifically, it involves the theoretical specification and the measurement of the characteristics (a)–(d) of technological progress.

Why do we focus on these characteristics of progress rather than the first set noted above? The answer is that the results of such an investigation provide an insight into the mechanisms through which technological change affects the variables in which we are ultimately interested. In addition, we are provided with a framework with which to view changes in the components of the Residual such as education and research, etc. For example, suppose that we wish to determine the effect on the distribution of income of improvements in the design of capital items; to do this it may be necessary to determine the labour or capital saving consequences of the improvements. Without knowing how to define or specify non-neutral technological progress, it would be difficult to find the connection in which we are interested, much less measure it.

† See M. Abramowitz's review of Denison's book, 'Economic Growth in the United States', *The American Economic Review*, vol. 52 (September 1962), pp. 762–82.

The major purpose of the present study is to present various methods—some old, some new—which can be used to measure the neutral and non-neutral characteristics of a technology and their changes. In order to do this, it is necessary to define the characteristics in a production function framework and draw out some of their implications. In the production literature there is a vast amount of information on the roles of the conventional factors of production, capital and labour. But there is a paucity of material on the role of technological progress. W. E. G. Salter, in his excellent book,† took several important steps toward redressing the neoclassical under-emphasis on technology. I have attempted a different tack—or rather, have emphasized different aspects and measurement procedures in the process of reconstituting the role of technological progress. It is to be emphasized, though, that the slight excursion into theory is done for the purpose of facilitating the development and interpretation of measures of technological progress. In the present work, we are not concerned primarily with the benefits to theory provided by the measures of technological progress, but with the benefits to *measurement* provided by a theoretical framework.

The treatment of the theory and estimation of technological progress does not presume to be comprehensive. The problem of under-utilization of capacity and its effects on technological change is not discussed at all in the theoretical part, although a utilization adjustment is discussed and developed in the empirical sections. Nor is there any information which a programmer, linear or otherwise, or an engineer would find of much use. Finally, I have not gone into the problem of integrating the fundamental factors such as education, research and development, etc., into the neutral–non-neutral technological change framework. Except for a suggestive hypothesis in Chapter 10, there is no attempt to explain why neutral or non-neutral technological advance is what it is. This remains for the future. I would be more than gratified if the present work helps to clear some of the path for an assault on that formidable problem.

The book is divided into the customary three parts. Chapters 2–6 comprise the first part, containing the theoretical underpinnings for the measures of technological advance. The definitions of technological change are covered in Chapter 2 in verbal

† *Productivity and Technical Change* (Cambridge University Press, 1960).

and graphical terms. It is here that the concept of an abstract technology is introduced; the components of this concept are used extensively in what follows. In Chapters 3 and 4 two production functions are examined with a view as to the way in which they characterize technological change. Although one of the production functions, the Cobb–Douglas, is familiar, it is treated extensively because it provides a vehicle for some well-known measures of technological change. The production function in Chapter 4 is a relatively new one; it is called the constant elasticity of substitution production function. It is also given an elaborate treatment, since it produces some interesting and useful relations that help us understand some of the intricacies of technological advance. Chapter 5 is devoted to the problem of conceptualizing short-run, long-run and secular production processes so that they are amenable to testing by standard econometric techniques; this is cast in the same framework as the preceding chapter. Chapter 6, the last theoretical chapter, discusses the embodied–disembodied technological change distinction. Its purpose is to pinpoint the way in which embodied technological progress or obsolescence enters the construction of capital stock measures, among other things.

The second part of the book, Chapters 7–9, deals with various methods of measuring the characteristics of a technology. It begins with three methods that utilize ratios in order to quantify technological change; these are the productivity indexes, the Solow method (1957) and the Salter method. These are examined because they are well known and because they compete with methods that are treated subsequently. In Chapter 8, the Tinbergen method is outlined, followed by an attempt to generalize it to include additional characteristics of technological progress. Whereas the Cobb–Douglas function is the vehicle of measurement in this chapter, the constant elasticity of substitution production function provides the basis of measuring technological change in Chapter 9, the concluding chapter of Part II.

The third part consists of Chapters 10–12; there are three empirical applications of some of the measures. Using the Cobb–Douglas function, the effect on economic growth in the United States of neutral and non-neutral technological progress is quantified in Chapter 10. The effect on employment of these same factors is measured in Chapter 11 by means of a constant elasticity of substitution framework. In the last chapter, the change in the functional distribution of income in the United States is decomposed into changes in technology and other factors.

There are four appendixes, one giving the derivation of the constant elasticity of substitution production function, the second presenting two generalizations of the function and a method of fitting the generalized function, the third presents a general method of adding up the effects of discrete time changes in various forces, and the fourth contains the data used in Chapter 10.

PART 1

FRAMEWORKS FOR THE ANALYSIS OF TECHNOLOGICAL PROGRESS

2

TECHNOLOGICAL PROGRESS IN THE THEORY OF PRODUCTION

The main purpose of this chapter is to ensure that we agree on the nature of technological progress. It serves to introduce in verbal form a small part of the received theory in the field of production, but the emphasis is on technological change and its implications, not on changes in factor inputs. The proofs of these propositions are set out in a later chapter.

As is well known, there are two general kinds of technological progress, neutral and non-neutral change, and both of these are definable in terms of certain characteristics of a production function. Hence, we first introduce the concept of a production function. We can then discuss four technological properties of the production function concept; these four properties, taken together, are called an 'abstract technology'. Finally, neutral and non-neutral technological change can be easily defined in terms of changes in the abstract technology, and this concludes the chapter.

THE PRODUCTION FUNCTION

A production function expresses the relation between the maximum quantity of output and the inputs required to produce it, and the relation between the inputs themselves.

It enters economic analysis as a datum—given by technological or extra-economic considerations. The technology embedded in the production relation acts as a constraint on decision making. As such, the production function ideally embodies no economic magnitudes such as prices or interest rates; market variables which provide inducements for the diversion of resources, or which are expressions of equilibrium situations in the economic world should be excluded from the concept of a production function.† The reason for this is that the production

† The following sources elaborate on the concept of a production function: J. Schumpeter, *History of Economic Analysis* (Oxford University Press, 1954),

function should embody technological constraints that are *imposed* on economic decisions, whereas the economic decisions are not imposed on the way in which outputs relate to inputs, etc.†

The production function implies that a technical maximization problem has been solved. For a given output may be produced by a variety of combinations of labour and capital (we use the convenient two-factor analogy). But for any given combination of factors, several outputs may be obtainable depending on the efficiency of the organization.‡ Now, the production function is defined such that the maximum product is obtained for each combination of factors; in this sense it involves a technical maximization problem.

Who is responsible for constructing a firm production function as we have defined it? Surely not the engineers of the firm, since they are concerned not only with inputs and outputs but with the properties of the energy sources and other factors of production required to transform materials (e.g. the feed mechanism of certain equipment, horsepower requirements, tensile strength of structures, etc.). Indeed an engineering production function can be transformed into a production function as defined above so as to provide for it a physical–technical foundation.§ But it is the economist who makes the transformation from the physical–technical properties of production to the production function he requires in his analysis. And in the transformation some

pp. 1026 ff.; W. E. G. Salter, *Productivity and Technical Change*; H. B. Chenery, 'Process and Production Functions from Engineering Data', in *Studies in the Structure of the American Economy*, by W. W. Leontief *et al.* (Oxford University Press, 1953); S. Carlson, *A Study on the Pure Theory of Production* (Blackwell, 1939); J. R. Hicks, *Value and Capital* (Oxford University Press, 1957).

† It is extremely difficult to construct production functions without including some economic magnitudes. Engineers may articulate the relations between inputs and outputs in physical dimensions, yet they may have pre-selected the set of technical alternatives on the basis of relative factor costs. And, in so doing, economic magnitudes creep into the production relation (cf. Salter, *op. cit.* pp. 13–14). However, it *is* possible to construct a purely technological relationship, and the economist should not embed economic variables into it. In addition to this problem, there is the aggregation problem and the well-known difficulty raised by Joan Robinson concerning the aggregation of technically heterogeneous capital items into a 'capital' input. We return to this problem in Chapter 6.

‡ Carlson, *op. cit.* p. 14.

§ See H. Chenery, *op. cit.* For a survey of the literature in which production functions are derived from engineering data, see A. A. Walters, 'Production and Cost Functions: An Econometric Survey', *Econometrica*, vol. 31 (January–April 1963), pp. 11–14.

non-relevant information atrophies. The production function abstracts from those things in which an engineer is primarily interested.†

The objection is raised that the production function is a fiction. This is sometimes expressed by the statements that engineers do not work within a production function framework, and businessmen do not consider production functions as such within the set of constraints on their decisions. Since the production function is indirectly related to the physical–technical aspects of production, it is not directly measurable, and, since it is foreign to the world of common sense, it is a fiction fabricated by marginalist economists.

In one sense this argument is valid: the production function *is* fabricated by the economist and, as we have defined it, it *is* probably foreign to the engineering and business world. However, as Chenery and others have shown, it can be derived from purely engineering data.‡ Yet, even if their efforts were unsuccessful, the employment of production functions can be justified simply on the ground that it produces highly useful and verifiable hypotheses. One has only to point to the physical sciences for an example of a theory which postulates relations and quantities that cannot be immediately measurable, but which, nevertheless, produces valuable hypotheses. The abstractness of the production function concept is precisely its source of value; it enables economists to analyse a wide variety of problems, for example, the determination of relative income shares, the factors affecting economic growth, and the nature of technological unemployment.

The production function for the economist can be represented graphically by a set of curves, isoquants, each representing

† Moreover, it may abstract from certain things in which an economist is interested—at least with respect to its traditional formulation. For the fundamental factors affecting production—education, nutrition, research, etc.—usually are not treated explicitly in production functions. But see M. Brown and A. Conrad, 'Fundamental Economic Variables in a General System of Production' (Division of Balanced International Growth, Netherlands Economic Institute, 1962), and R. Nelson, 'Aggregate Production Functions and Medium Range Growth Projections', *American Economic Review* (September 1964).

‡ For a discussion of the relation between the production function approach and linear programming, which presumably is cast in the language of engineers, see R. Dorfman, P. Samuelson, and R. M. Solow, *Linear Programming and Economic Analysis* (McGraw-Hill, 1958), pp. 130 ff., and P. Samuelson, 'Parable and Realism in Capital Theory: The Surrogate Production Function', *The Review of Economic Studies*, vol. 39 (June 1962), pp. 193–206.

various combinations of inputs which produce a given output.†
Each isoquant is convex downwards, which expresses the law of
diminishing marginal rate of substitution between factors.‡ Of
course, *for any given technology*, no two isoquants can intersect.
An isoquant which represents a larger output is located farther
out from the origin than one representing a smaller output. With
these brief reminders of the neoclassical theory of production,
we can turn to the role of technology in production theory.

AN ABSTRACT TECHNOLOGY

The production function expresses the way in which outputs are
produced by inputs, and the way inputs co-operate with each
other in varying proportions to produce any given output. These
relations between outputs and inputs and between the inputs
themselves are determined by the technology that rules at any
given time. The technology is embedded in the production
function and can be expressed in terms of it. In fact there are
four characteristics of the production function which are
extremely useful for economic analysis.

We call these four characteristics of a production function,
taken together, an abstract technology. They are the efficiency
of the technology, the degree of economies of scale that are
technologically determined, the degree of capital intensity of a
technology, and the ease with which capital is substituted for
labour.

Each of the characteristics of the abstract technology is introduced in what follows. It will then be seen that it is relatively
easy to define a technological change in terms of a change in the
characteristics of the abstract technology.

---

† Symbolically, we have $X = f(N, C)$, where X is gross output, N and C are the
services of labour and capital, respectively, and f represents the functional relation
between the inputs and output. We say f is determined by the technology. The
equation for the isoquant is obtained directly from the production function by
stipulating a given output, say X_0, and writing $f_0(N, C) = 1$, where $f_0 = f/X_0$.

‡ We have the conditions: $\partial X/\partial N > 0$ and $\partial X/\partial C > 0$, i.e. each marginal
product is positive; $\partial^2 X/\partial N^2$ and $\partial^2 X/\partial C^2 < 0$, meaning that the marginal products
though positive throughout, should decrease; finally, $\partial^2 X/\partial N \partial C > 0$, which means
that the marginal product of labour, for example, should increase when capital
increases. These conditions are spelled out in the following chapter.

THE EFFICIENCY OF A TECHNOLOGY

This characteristic of an abstract technology enters only the relationship between inputs and output; it does not affect the relations of inputs to inputs. For given inputs, and given the other characteristics of an abstract technology, the efficiency characteristic determines the output that results. If it is large, then output is large, irrespective of the plant and equipment and the labour employed, etc. One can think of the efficiency characteristics as a scale transformation of inputs into output.

The efficiency of a technology can be seen in a two-factor graph of a family of isoquants. For each level of capital and labour inputs, the scale on the axes represents the efficiency of a technology. Suppose that there are two technologies with different efficiencies, everything, else the same. How can the more efficient technology be represented? There are two ways: in the less efficient technology, a certain output label is assigned to each isoquant (for given levels of inputs), while in the more efficient technology, a larger output label is assigned to each isoquant (for the same levels of inputs); a second way, which amounts to the same thing, is to simply rescale the axes. Since the important thing here is the change in—not the level of—the efficiency of a technology, these graphs can be discussed in a more meaningful way in the section on technological change.

TECHNOLOGICALLY DETERMINED
ECONOMIES OF SCALE

Economies of scale are defined as follows: for a given proportional increase in all inputs, if output is increased by a larger proportion, the firm enjoys increasing returns (or economies of scale); if output is increased by the same proportion, there are constant returns to scale; and if output is increased by a smaller proportion, decreasing returns result (or diseconomies of scale). Economies of scale can be dichotomized into those arising from 'the general development of industry; and secondly, those dependent on the resources of the individual houses of business engaged in it, on their organization and the efficiency of their management. We may call the former external economies, and the latter internal economies.'† Within the present work, we

† A. Marshall, *Principles of Economics* (London, Macmillan, 1922), p. 266.

are only able to deal with economies that are internal to the economic unit with which we are concerned. For instance, if we are focusing on the firm, we say that a proportional increase in the firm's inputs yields a given proportional increase in the firm's output, so that if the latter increase exceeds the former, these economies of scale are internal to the firm. But if we go to the industry level, and perform the same measurements on the industry's inputs and output, any economies of scale that may be observed are the combined internal and external economies to the firm, provided the external economies to the firm result only from the general development of the industry. A statistical problem associated with this point is discussed in Chapter 8.†

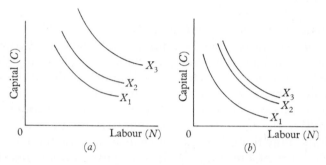

Fig. 1. A technologically determined change in returns to scale.

Technological progress can alter the way in which inputs are transmited into output in such a way that the production process formerly characterized, for example, by decreasing returns is now characterized, say, by constant returns, while the scale of operations of the firm remains unchanged. This characteristic of an abstract technology is easily presented graphically. Consider Fig. 1 a, which indicates decreasing returns to scale as output moves from X_1 to X_2 to X_3 ($X_3 > X_2 > X_1$). In Fig. 1 b, a technological change has occurred and a new configuration of isoquants indicates increasing returns to scale at the same

† D. H. Robertson stresses the role of internal economies in 'Increasing Returns and the Representative firm', *Economic Journal*, vol. 40 (March 1930), p. 87. Also see the remarkable article by G. Stigler, 'Division of Labor is Limited by the Extent of the Market', *Journal of Political Economy*, vol. 59 (June 1951), pp. 185–93. For a clarification of the role of economies of scale in the process of economic growth, see A. Young, 'Increasing Returns and Economic Progress', *Economic Journal*, vol. 38 (December 1928), pp. 527–42.

input levels as in Fig. 1 a.† Clearly, the alteration in technological returns to scale only provides the basis for obtaining a proportional increase in output for a less than proportional increase in the inputs; whether or not the firm benefits from the technological change depends on its scale of operations. It can be seen that this characteristic is very similar to the efficiency of a technology, since the transfer of production from the technology in Fig. 1 a to that in Fig. 1 b can be made by re-scaling the axes in Fig. 1 a. However, the re-scaling would be more complex than that required to represent a change in the efficiency of a technology.

THE CAPITAL INTENSITY
OF A TECHNOLOGY

The usual definition of capital intensity proceeds in terms of the quantity of capital relative to the quantity of labour used in the production process. For example, comparing two firms, the one which has the larger capital–labour ratio is more capital intensive than the other. This definition focuses on the labour and capital *variables*. But the larger capital–output ratio could have been produced by either a larger amount of capital being supplied to the firm relative to the amount of labour or it could have been due to the fact that the technology of that firm required a larger amount of capital relative to the amount of labour for given levels of factor supplies. Here we are concerned with the technological requirements of the production process, not the effects of relative factor supplies. The latter are represented by the scarcity prices of the factors of production. But for any given technology the capital intensity characteristic probably does not vary in response to the *current* changes in output or relative factor prices—it is part of the structure of the ruling technology.‡

† Between Figs. 1 a and b, all characteristics of the abstract technology have been held constant other than the one under discussion.
‡ There is a difficult identification problem here. We cannot say that long-term relative factor prices or even, perhaps, output changes, do not influence the capital intensity of a technology. For long-term relative factor prices influence the direction of research and development and probably the innovations that result. It is a familiar axiom in the theory of growth that the relatively capital-intensive technologies of industrialized economies were developed in response to the scarcity of capital. This is a problem in identifying a demand for technology relation. For the theoretical analysis of the problem, see J. R. Hicks, *The Theory of Wages* (New York, Macmillan, 1932); W. Fellner, 'Two Propositions in the

We can graph the capital intensity characteristic in two ways, both of which are instructive. Take the familiar isoquant diagram. The technologies denoted by the X' isoquants in Fig. 2 a and b are more capital intensive than those denoted by the X isoquants. In Fig. 2 a, the slope of X exceeds that of X'; i.e. the marginal rate of substitution between capital and labour

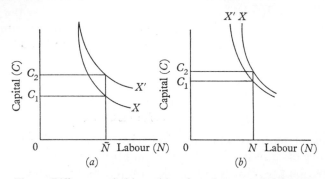

Fig. 2. Different capital intensities of an abstract technology, I.

in the X technology exceeds the marginal rate of substitution of capital for labour of the X' technology. Stated another way, the marginal product of capital under the X technology is smaller than the marginal product of capital under the X' technology for a given marginal product of labour. If a unit of labour is added to both production processes, a smaller amount of capital will have to be withdrawn from the X' process than from the X process. Hence, the X' technology is capital-using relative to the X technology. In Fig. 2 b, X' is still more capital intensive than X, but the reader can verify this.

A second method of graphing this characteristic is presented in Fig. 3, where both axes are measured in logarithms. The lines in Fig. 3 show the logarithmic relation between the ratio of labour to capital and the marginal rate of substitution of labour for capital. The intercepts on the ordinate are labelled $\log \kappa_1'$ and $\log \kappa_2'$. For a given value of (N/C), say s, the marginal rate of substitution is larger for the curve with the $\log \kappa_2'$ intercept than for that with the $\log \kappa_1'$ intercept. The technology represented

Theory of Induced Inventions', *The Economic Journal*, vol. 71 (June 1961), pp. 305–8; N. Rosenberg, 'Capital Goods, Technology and Economic Growth', *Oxford Economic Papers*, vol. 15 (November 1963), pp. 217–27.

by the former curve is more capital intensive than that represented by the latter curve. For the marginal product of capital relative to that of labour is larger for a $\log \kappa_2'$ capital intensity than for a $\log \kappa_1'$ capital intensity for any given labour–capital ratio. Therefore, if the marginal product of capital is higher

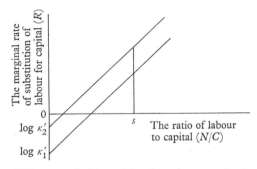

Fig. 3. Different capital intensities of an abstract technology, II.

under $\log \kappa_2'$ than under $\log \kappa_1'$ *cet. par.*, the production process would use more capital relative to labour. In this sense $\log \kappa_2'$ is more capital intensive than $\log \kappa_1'$, for any labour–capital ratio.

Degrees of capital intensity are reflected in the size of the labour–capital ratios for *given relative factor prices*. For example, two competitive firms in the same industry face identical supply curves of factors of production and thus relative factor supplies and prices are identical for both; if one firm has a smaller labour–capital ratio than the other, this is sufficient to indicate that, other things equal—namely, the elasticity of substitution of labour for capital in both firms must be identical—the technology of the first firm is more capital intensive than the technology of the second firm. But, as shown below, not only does the capital intensity of a technology affect the marginal rate of substitution, it affects output as well.

THE EASE WITH WHICH CAPITAL IS SUBSTITUTED FOR LABOUR

In Marshall's words:

Every agent of production, land, machinery, skilled labour, etc., tends to be applied in production as far as it profitably can be. If employers, and other business men, think that they can get a better result by using a little more of any one agent they will do so. They estimate the net product (that is the net increase of the money value of their total output after allowing for incidental expenses) that will be got by a little more outlay in this direction, or a little more outlay in that; and if they can gain by shifting a little of their outlay from one direction to another, they will do so.†

Moreover, 'It (the principle of substitution) is ...linked up with the broad tendency of a diminishing return to increased applications of capital and labour to land in old countries.'‡ The elasticity of substitution developed by John R. Hicks is a measure of this phenomenon; it tells us how rapidly diminishing returns set in to one factor of production when its price falls relative to another factor price.§ For two factors of production, labour (N) and capital (C), it is represented symbolically by

$$\sigma = \frac{(C/N)\,d(N/C)}{(f_N/f_C)\,d(f_C/f_N)},$$

where f_N is the marginal product of labour, and f_C is the marginal production of capital. The ratio of the marginal product of capital to the marginal product of labour is the marginal rate of substitution of labour for capital; by the marginal productivity theory, it is equal to the per unit rental of capital relative to the wage rate. Hence the elasticity of substitution as defined in the formula relates the proportional change in the relative factor inputs to a proportional change in the marginal rate of substitution between labour and capital (or the proportional change in the relative factor price ratio). Intuitively, it can be thought of as a measure of the ease of substitution of labour for capital; it can also be conceived as a measure of the 'similarity' of factors of production from a technological point of view.

The elasticity of substitution can take on any value between zero and infinity, always being positive. In Fig. 4a, it is zero and in Fig. 4b it is infinity. In the latter instance the factors are to all purposes identical. From the graphs it can be inferred that σ is related to the curvature of the isoquants; in fact, the larger is the curvature of the isoquants, the smaller is the elasticity of substitution. We note that σ is independent of the units of

† A. Marshall, *Principles of Economics*, p. 521.
‡ *Ibid.* p. 356.
§ J. R. Hicks, *The Theory of Wages*, pp. 119–35, 233–46; also, see Joan Robinson, *The Economics of Imperfect Competition* (Macmillan, 1933), pp. 256, 330.

measurement of the labour and capital inputs.† Nevertheless, we will measure all variables in index number terms with a common base period.

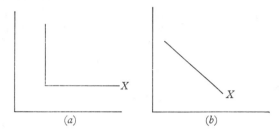

Fig. 4. Extreme values of the elasticity of substitution.

The elasticity of substitution may vary from one combination of factors to another.‡ *But in the present work we are concerned only with technologies that can be characterized by constant elasticities of substitution.*

Besides Fig. 4, there is another graphical representation of the elasticity of substitution which depicts, explicitly, the relation between the elasticity and the marginal rate of substitution. For, the reciprocal of the elasticity of substitution is the slope of the logarithmic relation between the marginal rate of substitution and relative factor inputs.§ Fig. 5 contains graphs of this relationship for the different values of the elasticity of substitution, and for two types of firms or economies, one where the growth of capital exceeds the growth in labour and the other where the growth rates are reversed. The intercept $\log \kappa'$ was discussed in the previous section, and we require it to be constant here. The rays with origin at $\log \kappa'$ and heading in the north-east direction refer to a firm in which labour is growing more rapidly than capital $(N > C)$; those heading in the south-west direction refer to a firm in which the growth of capital exceeds

† For the derivation of these properties, see R. G. D. Allen, *Mathematical Analysis for Economists* (London, Macmillan, 1950), p. 341.

‡ See J. R. Hicks, *op. cit.* p. 132.

§ As before, let σ be the elasticity of substitution, then

$$\log R = \log \frac{f_C}{f_N} = \log \kappa' + \frac{1}{\sigma} \log \frac{N}{C}.$$

This equation is derived in Appendix A and Chapter 4. The lines in Fig. 5 are based on it.

the growth of labour $(C > N)$. Since this graph is utilized below in the discussion of technological change, we only note two of its properties here. First, the slope of the relation is the elasticity of substitution between labour and capital. This means that as the rate of employment of labour increases relative to the rate of capital, the marginal product of capital rises relative to the

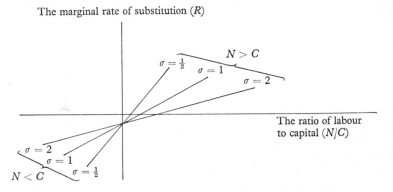

Fig. 5. Different elasticities of substitution.

marginal product of labour, and the rate at which it rises depends on σ. Secondly, if σ is large, say $\sigma = 2$, then a given change in the ratio of the marginal products is associated with a larger change in the labour–capital ratio than for a smaller σ.

With these definitions of the characteristics of an abstract technology, we can proceed directly to the discussion of techno-logical change.

A DEFINITION OF
TECHNOLOGICAL CHANGE

It is a simple matter to define a technological change in terms of changes in the characteristics of an abstract technology. But there are two general types of technological change, neutral and non-neutral, and it is helpful to think in terms of these categories. A neutral change neither saves nor uses labour; it is one which produces a variation in the production relation, itself, but does not affect the marginal rate of substitution of labour for capital. A non-neutral technological change alters the production func-tion and can be either labour-saving (capital-using) or capital-

saving (labour-using). If the production function is altered such
that the marginal product of capital rises relative to the marginal
product of labour for each combination of capital and labour,
there is said to occur a capital-using (labour-saving) technological change. A capital-saving change occurs when the marginal rate of substitution of labour for capital is lowered at every
combination of capital and labour.† In terms of the abstract
technology, variations in the efficiency of a technology and
economies of scale produce neutral technological changes. Non-
neutral technological changes are produced by variations in the
capital intensity of a technology
and in the ease of substitution
of capital for labour.

In Fig. 6, a neutral technological change has been graphed
on the familiar isoquant diagram.
The outputs X and X' have the
same value, they differ in that
X' is to be produced under a
new technology. Here is the case
where more output is obtained

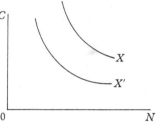

Fig. 6. A neutral technological
change.

with the same levels of inputs. The marginal rate of substitution
of labour for capital remains unchanged at each combination of
labour and capital. It is not difficult to see that this type of
technological progress simply alters the scale of the axes. Thus,
changes in the efficiency of a technology and in economies of
scale—two characteristics of an abstract technology—are
neutral technological changes.

Variations in the capital intensity and ease of substitution
characteristics can be either capital- or labour-saving. Before
specifically discussing changes in these two characteristics,

† These are the definitions developed by J. R. Hicks, *The Theory of Wages*,
pp. 121–7. A different approach is provided by R. Harrod, 'The Neutrality of
Improvements', *The Economic Journal*, vol. 71 (June 1961), pp. 300–4. W. E. G.
Salter (*Productivity and Technical Change*, pp. 32–4) has a discussion comparing the
two approaches. Also, see C. Kennedy, 'Harrod on "Neutrality"', *Economic
Journal*, vol. 72 (March 1962), pp. 249–350, who shows that Harrod's and Hicks's
definitions of *neutral* technological change refer to the same phenomenon at the
economy level, if $\sigma = 1$. This is also discussed by M. Blaug, 'A Survey of the
Theory Process-Innovations', *Economica*, vol. 30 (February 1963), pp. 13–32.
Various criteria of biased technological change are examined by A. Lowe,
'Structural Analysis of Real Capital Formation', in *Capital Formation and Economic
Growth*, National Bureau of Economic Research (Princeton, 1961), pp. 622 ff.

though, let us graph a non-neutral technological change in Fig. 7. The isoquant labelled X' represents a technology which saves labour relative to the isoquant labelled X; the interpretation is similar to that given for different capital intensities (see Fig. 2 above). The pivoting or twisting of an isoquant is characteristic of a non-neutral technological change. We note only that X' in Fig. 7 can differ from X for two reasons: the capital intensities and/or the elasticities of substitution of the two technologies can differ.

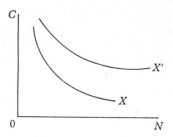

Fig. 7. A non-neutral technological change.

A SPECIFICATION OF THE DEFINITION OF NON-NEUTRAL TECHNOLOGICAL CHANGE

Changes in the capital intensity and ease of substitution characteristics produce non-neutral technological changes— i.e. they alter the marginal rate of substitution of labour for capital at each factor combination. There are two questions to ask: do specific variations in these characteristics produce labour- or capital-saving technological progress; and, what effect on output does a specific change in these characteristics produce? The answers are by no means easy to intuit, and we shall have to wait until Chapter 4 until a rigorous set of answers can be provided. However, we are able to go a considerable way by graphical methods and economic reasoning.

The first question can be stated, in part, as follows: is a rise in the capital intensity of a technology capital- or labour-saving? The answer is that it is labour-saving, since we know that an increase in capital intensity raises the marginal product of capital relative to that of labour. Therefore, a capital-using technological change is produced in all cases when the technology becomes more capital intensive.

What happens to the marginal rate of substitution of labour for capital when substitution between the factors becomes

THE THEORY OF PRODUCTION

easier? The reader who has studied Fig. 5 knows that the answer depends on whether capital is growing faster than labour or vice versa, where the relative growths are measured in terms of base period. Referring to Fig. 5, if one chooses an arbitrary value for N/C to the right of the ordinate, i.e. to the right of the point where the log of the labour–capital ratio is zero, then for that value the marginal rate of substitution falls as the elasticity of substitution is increased. For, in an economy in which labour rises relative to capital, a rise in the elasticity of substitution reduces the marginal product of capital relative to that of labour. Therefore, within an economy in which labour is the faster-growing factor, when substitution between capital and labour is eased, a labour-using technological change is the consequence. But in an economy in which capital is growing more rapidly than labour, a rise in the elasticity of substitution raises the marginal product of capital relative to that of labour, and we have a capital-using technological change.

The relationships between the relative rates of growth of the factors and changes in σ has an overt economic rationale. When capital is growing relative to labour, capital becomes the relatively cheap factor, and technological progress which eases the substitution of the relatively cheap capital for the relatively expensive labour must certainly be capital-using. Alternatively, if capital is relatively expensive, the easing of substitution possibilities points to a labour-using technological change.†

This simple result has an important application in the determination of the relative income shares of capital and labour.

What effect do these non-neutral changes have on output? For example, would an increase in capital intensity produce an increase in the rate of output as readily as would a decrease in capital intensity? The answer depends again on whether the growth in capital exceeds the growth in labour. An increase in capital intensity raises the rate of output if labour is growing less rapidly than capital and reduces the output rate if capital is the slow-growing factor. The reason is that if capital is relatively cheap, a new technology which calls for greater capital intensity generates a higher rate of output; on the other hand, if capital were relatively expensive, this new technology could not be satisfied except by a lower rate of output. In sum, a rise in capital intensity is always capital using, but increases the rate

† Salter arrives at the same result (*Productivity and Technical Change* p. 40).

of output only when capital is growing more rapidly than labour in terms of a base period measure, decreasing it when capital is lagging behind labour.

The variation in the capital intensity of a technology is only part of a non-neutral change, the other part consisting of a change in the elasticity of substitution. From above, we know that an increase in the ease of substitution is labour-saving when capital is growing relatively rapidly, and capital-saving when labour is the rapid grower. But what effect does a rise in the elasticity of substitution have on the rate of output? We assert that when it becomes easier to substitute capital for labour or labour for capital, the output rate always rises.

In order to rationalize the assertion that the rate of output always rises as the elasticity of substitution increases, consider the following. First, we know that the elasticity of substitution is the same when labour is substituted for capital as when capital is substituted for labour. And let us assume that one factor is growing relative to the other. If technological progress permits the substitution of the relatively cheap factor for the relatively expensive one with greater ease, the same rate of output can be maintained at lower unit costs; therefore, with a fixed budget outlay a higher rate of output can be obtained.

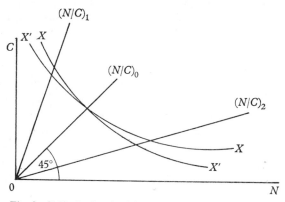

Fig. 8. Shifts in the elasticity of substitution and output.

A graph of this is shown in Fig. 8. Suppose we have two technologies reflected in X and X', where the elasticity of substitution associated with X' exceeds that associated with X. If capital grows at the same rate as labour, i.e. along the ray

$(N/C)_0$, both technologies yield the same rate of output. But if capital and labour grow along either of the rays, $(N/C)_1$ or $(N/C)_2$, then the X' technology yields a larger rate of output than the X technology. Hence, if capital and labour have been growing at different rates, a rise in the elasticity of substitution produces an increase in the rate of growth of output.

We have seen that there are types of non-neutral technological change that do not guarantee an increase in output, and have determined the specific effects of these changes. There are configurations of non-neutral technological changes that always produce an increase in output for particular types of economies; for example, a rise in the capital intensity and elasticity of substitution characteristics increase the rate of output by a labour-saving change *if capital* is the relatively rapid grower. Yet we may observe a rise in one characteristic and a fall in another; then, what happens to the output rate and the marginal rate of substitution? The answer, of course, depends on the relative strength of the changes, and this is an empirical problem. (But see Chapter 4 where some of the implications of these results are spelled out.)

Before summarizing the contents of this chapter, it is useful to say something about the significance of the results on non-neutral technology. The first thing, already mentioned, is a general point: now we know what kind of technological change promotes economic growth and the gross conditions under which it does so.

Secondly, we are more aware of the complexity of the process of technological change. If we hope to go further than simple observation, it behoves us to unravel these trends in analysis.

A third point is that we are now in a better position to understand technological movements, although the subject has become more complex. By isolating the abstract characteristics of a technology, and noting how their changes affect the rate of output, etc., we can come to grips more readily with the 'why' of the changes. However, a prior requirement to the understanding of the phenomenon is its measurement. In fact the measurement of technological change is the *raison d'être* for the small amount of theory presented in the present work.

Although non-neutral changes are examined in detail, we should not lose sight of the fact that any innovation comprises changes in all characteristics of an abstract technology, neutral as well as non-neutral. Moreover, even though an innovation may contain components pulling in opposite directions, in the long run we should expect it to be associated with an increase in the rate of output, given the factor endowments. But this is an empirical question.

The problems and methods of measuring technological progress constitute the subject-matter of Part II. In the remaining chapters of Part I, we shall attempt to render more precise the statements contained in this chapter (*inter alia*), and in so doing construct models which are amenable to testing.

SUMMARY

This chapter mainly contains a set of analytic definitions of technological change within the general framework of neo-classical production theory. In general there are two types of technological change, neutral and non-neutral change. Their definitions are based on the concept of production function.

(1) A *production function* expresses the relation between a maximum amount of output and the inputs required to produce it; in so doing it describes the manner in which inputs co-operate with each other in varying proportions to produce any given output.

(2) The production function embodies an *abstract technology*. Its generality derives from the fact that it abstracts from certain technical and economic magnitudes, and in so doing permits us to analyse a wide variety of economic problems and to determine the relation between types of technological change. There are four characteristics of an abstract technology.

(i) *The efficiency of a technology* determines the output that results for given inputs and given the other characteristics of an abstract technology. After defining the dimensions of the inputs, the efficiency characteristic is a scale transformation of inputs into output.

(ii) *Technologically determined economies of scale* are defined as the extent to which a proportionate change in inputs generates a proportionate change in output due to technology and not the scale of operations of the firm.

(iii) *The capital intensity of a technology* denotes a specific weight placed on capital. For a constant elasticity of substitution and unchanging relative factor prices, the larger is the capital intensity characteristic, the larger will the capital–labour input ratio be.

(iv) The *ease with which capital is substituted for labour or the elasticity of substitution* is the fourth characteristic of the abstract technology. It measures the proportional change in relative factor inputs in response to a proportional change in the marginal rate of substitution. In a familiar isoquant diagram, the elasticity of substitution measures the degree of curvature of the isoquants; the larger it is, the smaller is the curvature of the isoquants.

Non-neutral and neutral technological progress are defined in terms of these four characteristics. A *neutral change* alters the production function but does not affect the marginal rate of substitution. A *non-neutral* change does affect the marginal rate of substitution. If the marginal product of capital increases relative to that of labour, for given labour-capital combinations, then a *labour-saving* or *capital-using* change raises the marginal product of labour, relative to that of capital, *cet. par.*

Neutral technological changes include a change in the efficiency of a technology and/or a change in technologically determined economies of scale. A non-neutral change is associated with variations in capital intensity and the elasticity of substitution.

The definition of non-neutral technological change is specified to include the effect on output of variations in capital intensity and elasticity of substitution. The following relations are obtained.

An increase in capital intensity is always labour-saving. A decrease is capital-saving.

An increase in capital intensity increases output if labour is growing more slowly than capital. An increase would reduce output if capital is the slower-growing factor.

An increase in the elasticity of substitution is labour-saving when capital is growing more rapidly than labour. It is capital-saving when labour is the more rapidly growing factor of production.

An increase in the elasticity of substitution always raises the rate of increase of output. A decrease reduces the output rate.

An attempt is made to rationalize these patterns in economic terms. It is to be noted that there may be components of an innovation which are not associated with larger outputs or rates of outputs. Also, there are configurations of non-neutral changes which raise output only for certain growth configurations of the inputs. The significance of these results is briefly touched on.

In the following chapter, we examine the way in which a very well-known production function—named the Cobb–Douglas production function—represents changes in technology and output.

3

CHANGES IN OUTPUT
AND TECHNOLOGY IN A
COBB–DOUGLAS WORLD

Perhaps the most famous function indigenous to economics is the Cobb–Douglas production function. Its attraction derives not only from its simplicity—it is easy to comprehend and is economical to apply—but from the desirable neoclassical properties it possesses. The purpose of the present chapter is to examine these properties so that when the function is used to measure technological change, the measures so derived can be readily interpreted.

The procedure is to set forth a minimum set of neoclassical criteria that we would like any well-behaved production function to satisfy. The Cobb–Douglas function will then be examined in the light of these criteria to see how it meets neoclassical requirements. Finally, the technological characteristics of the function are described. In the following chapter the neoclassical and technological characteristics of a more general production function are examined.

NEOCLASSICAL CRITERIA

Consider a general function which specifies the dependence of output X on two factors of production, labour N and capital C: $X = f(N, C)$. Clearly, not only does such a function relate output to input, but the relation between the inputs is also presumed. But ignoring the relationship between the inputs for the moment, the first neoclassical criterion any production function should meet is that an increase in each input should have a positive effect on output. That is, (I) the marginal products should be positive. In symbols, $\partial X/\partial C > 0$ and $\partial X/\partial N > 0$. This implies that the constant product curves are downward sloping, or $dC = -g(dN)$, where g is a positive function of N and C. For if both factors contribute a positive amount to output, in order to keep output constant, when one factor is increased, the other

isoquant

factor can be reduced. Thus the slope of the constant product curve is negative. Certainly, this requires no further justification.

A second requirement for a production function is that (II) over a relevant range, each marginal product should decrease when labour and capital increase. Symbolically $\partial^2 X/\partial N^2 < 0$ and $\partial^2 X/\partial C^2 < 0$. This is one of the sufficient conditions for an equilibrium, which implies that the constant product curves are convex to the origin (see Chapter 4). Recall that convexity of the constant product curves means that, as labour increases, in order to keep output constant a larger amount of capital will be deducted. Another way of stating this is that the slope of the isoquants, represented by the marginal rate of substitution of labour for capital,

$$-\frac{dN}{dC} = \frac{\partial X/\partial C}{\partial X/\partial N},$$

increases as labour is substituted for capital. Now if (II) holds, the ratio of the marginal products $(\partial X/\partial C)/(\partial X/\partial N)$ will increase with a rise in labour, given the level of capital, or a fall in capital, given the employment of labour.

A third criterion can be stated as follows: (III) A production function should not specify *a priori* the degree of economies or diseconomies of scale. In mathematical terms, if we deal with homogeneous functions—and we will, for the most part—the function should be permitted to assume any degree of homogeneity that is dictated empirically. For non-constant returns to scale have such important implications for the economics of growth and the study of market organization that it is wise to allow the empirical situation to stipulate the degree of economies of scale.

If the marginal product of any factor increases, then the limit of the marginal product should be zero as the factor increases indefinitely. Thus $\lim_{C \to \infty} \partial X/\partial C = 0$. In turn, this implies that output should reach a finite limit if one factor is held constant while the other is allowed to increase indefinitely, i.e.

$$\lim_{C \to \infty} X = M_1 \quad \text{and} \quad \lim_{N \to \infty} X = M_2,$$

where M_1 and M_2 are positive constants. This implies that a production function should have asymptotes, i.e. should have a peak product obtainable from any given use of one factor while the other continues to increase indefinitely.[†] However, the reason for not including this property among our criteria is that it is very difficult to develop production functions which do not simultaneously violate one or several criteria stated above. For example, the function suggested by Allen that produces asymptotes is $X = 2HNC - AN^2 - BC^2$, where A, B and H are positive constants and are constrained by the following inequality: $H^2 > AB$. The difficulty with this function is that for any value of A, B and H subject to the constraint, a 1 per cent increase in labour and capital produces a 2 per cent increase in output. The function is homogeneous of degree 2, whatever the empirical values for A, B and H, and thus does not satisfy (III).[‡]

It should be noted that the properties we will discuss below refer to the two-factor Cobb–Douglas production function. However, they can easily be extended to the more general n factor function, but this is not pursued here.

THE NEOCLASSICAL PROPERTIES OF THE COBB–DOUGLAS PRODUCTION FUNCTION

In unrestricted form, the Cobb–Douglas function for two factors of production can be written as

$$X = AN^\alpha C^\beta, \qquad (3.1)$$

where A, α and β are constants to be determined empirically, X is output, N is a measure of labour services, and C is a measure of capital services.[§] The marginal products of labour and capital are respectively

$$\frac{\partial X}{\partial N} = \alpha \frac{X}{N}, \qquad (3.2)$$

[†] For a general discussion of the desirable properties of production functions see R. G. D. Allen, *Mathematical Analysis for Economists*, pp. 286 ff.

[‡] The function could be modified; for example, by taking its square root, it becomes homogeneous of the first degree. This does not help us though, since it still violates our criterion (III).

[§] It made its first appearance in Knut Wicksell's writings: see his *Finanztheorische Untersuchungen* (Jena, 1896), p. 53. In restricted form, $\alpha + \beta = 1$, it first appeared and was tested empirically in C. W. Cobb and P. H. Douglas, 'A Theory of Production', *American Economic Review*, Supplement (March 1928), pp. 139–65. Douglas and his colleagues used the unrestricted form of the function extensively in the following selected sources: P. H. Douglas and M. J. Handsaker, 'The Theory of Marginal Productivity Tested by Data for Manufacturing in Victoria', *Quarterly Journal of Economics*, vol. 52 (February 1937), pp. 1–36; P. H. Douglas and G. T. Gunn, 'Further Measures in Marginal Productivity', *Quarterly Journal of Economics*, vol. 54 (February 1939), pp. 399–428; P. H. Douglas and G. T. Gunn,

and

$$\frac{\partial X}{\partial C} = \beta \frac{X}{C}.$$ (3.3)

Both of these marginal products are homogeneous of degrees, $\alpha + \beta - 1$ or they should be.[†] Clearly, these expressions are positive, thus meeting criterion (I).

For reasonable values of the partial elasticities of production, the marginal products decrease as each factor changes, *cet. par.*; consider

$$\frac{\partial^2 X}{\partial N^2} = \frac{\partial(\partial X/\partial N)}{\partial N} = \frac{\alpha(\alpha - 1)}{N}\frac{X}{N}$$

and

$$\frac{\partial^2 X}{\partial C^2} = \frac{\partial(\partial X/\partial C)}{\partial C} = \frac{\beta(\beta - 1)}{C}\frac{X}{C}.$$

Since α and β each are normally less than unity, these expressions are negative; hence, the Cobb–Douglas function satisfies criterion (II).[‡]

In the marginal product of labour, (3.2), the parameter α multiplies the average product of labour, X/N. (Sometimes, output per unit of labour is called the 'labour productivity index', see Chapter 7.) If (3.2) is expressed in terms of α, we have

$$\alpha = \frac{N}{X}\frac{\partial X}{\partial N}$$ (3.4)

and this is the partial elasticity of production with respect to labour. It denotes the percentage change in output attributable

'The Production Function for Australian Manufacturing', *Quarterly Journal of Economics*, vol. 56 (February 1941), pp. 108–29; P. H. Douglas and G. T. Gunn, 'Production Function for American Manufacturing in 1914', *Journal of Political Economy*, vol. 50 (February 1942), pp. 595–602; P. H. Douglas and G. T. Gunn, 'A Production Function for American Manufacturing in 1919', *American Economic Review*, vol. 31, pp. 67–80; P. H. Douglas and P. Daly, 'Production Function for Canadian Manufacturers', *Journal of the American Statistical Association*, vol. 38 (1943), pp. 178–86; P. H. Douglas, P. Daly and E. Olsen, 'The Production Function for Manufacturing in the United States, 1904', *Journal of Political Economy*, vol. 51 (February 1943), pp. 61–5. In answer to his critics (see below), Douglas, together with M. Bronfenbrenner, published 'Cross Section Studies in the Cobb–Douglas Function', *Journal of Political Economy*, vol. 47 (December 1939), pp. 761–83. Finally, Douglas summed up his work in a classic survey article, 'Are there Laws of Production', *American Economic Review*, vol. 38 (March 1948), pp. 1–41. For a recent econometric survey, see A. Walters, 'Production and Cost Functions: An Econometric Survey', *Econometrica*, vol. 31.

Besides the studies executed by Professor Douglas and his colleagues there are numerous applications of the function to agricultural problems; for a bibliography and numerous applications, see E. C. Heady and J. L. Dillon, *Agricultural Production Functions* (Iowa State University Press, 1961).

† R. G. D. Allen, *Mathematical Analysis for Economists*, pp. 315–19.

‡ However, if α or β exceeds unity, then the marginal products slope upward. Such is the case when returns to scale are exceedingly large.

to a percentage change in labour input, keeping capital constant. Similarly, β is the partial elasticity of production with respect to capital inputs.

Since α and β represent individually the percentage change in output for percentage changes in labour and capital, the two coefficients taken together measure the total percentage change in output for a given percentage change in labour *and* capital. In short, $\alpha + \beta$ is the degree of homogeneity of the Cobb–Douglas production function. Suppose that labour and capital increased by 10 per cent; then

$$X = A(\text{1·10}N)^{\alpha}\,(\text{1·10}C)^{\beta} = A(\text{1·10})^{\alpha+\beta}\,N^{\alpha}C^{\beta}.$$

Thus output would increase by $(1.10)^{\alpha+\beta}$, and if $\alpha + \beta < 1$, output would increase by less than 10 per cent; if $\alpha + \beta > 1$, output increases by more than 10 per cent. In the Cobb–Douglas production function, returns to scale are characterized by the following:

$\alpha + \beta < 1$: diseconomies of scale,

$\alpha + \beta = 1$: constant returns to scale,

$\alpha + \beta > 1$: economies of scale.

Since the Cobb–Douglas function can characterize any degree of returns to scale, it clearly satisfies criterion (III).†

† For studies which utilize, and focus on, the function's ability to represent different degrees of economies of scale, see G. Tintner, *Econometrics* (New York, Wiley, 1953), pp. 132, 138, and 142; L. Klein, *A Textbook in Econometrics* (Row-Peterson, 1953), pp. 226 ff.; A. A. Walters, 'Economies of Scale in the Aggregate Production Function', *Discussion Paper, Series A, University of Birmingham*, no. 29 (April, 1962); V. H. Murti and V. K. Sastry, 'Production Functions for Indian Industry', *Econometrica*, vol. 25 (April 1957), pp. 205–21; M. Brown and J. Popkin, 'A Measure of Technological Change and Returns to Scale', *Review of Economics and Statistics*, vol. 44, pp. 402–11; G. Stigler, 'Economic Problems in Measuring Changes in Productivity', *Output, Input and Productivity Measurement, Studies in Income and Wealth*, vol. 25, National Bureau of Economic Research (Princeton, 1961), pp. 47–78; J. G. M. Hilhorst, 'Measurement of Production Function in Manufacturing Industry', *Statistical Studies*, The Netherlands Central Bureau of Statistics, no. 13 (October 1962), pp. 7–29; B. Wall, 'Cobb–Douglas Function for U.S. Manufacturing and Mining, 1920–1940', *Econometrica*, vol. 16 (April 1948), pp. 211–13; and R. Komiya, 'Technological Progress and the Production Function in the United States Steam Power Industry', *The Review of Economics and Statistics*, vol. 44 (May, 1962), pp. 156–66. The Komiya study not only employs the Cobb–Douglas function but also estimates a Leontief, fixed-coefficient production model. Also, see C. A. Smith, 'Survey of the Empirical Evidence on Economics of Scale', *Business Concentration and Price Policy*, National Bureau of Economic Research (Princeton 1955), pp. 213–30, and M. Friedman's 'Comment', *ibid.* pp. 230–8.

If the marginal products are positive, and are downward sloping, it follows that

$$\lim_{C \to \infty} \partial X / \partial C = 0; \qquad (a)$$

$$\lim_{C \to \infty} X = M, \qquad (b)$$

where M is a positive constant. Applying (a) and (b) to the Cobb–Douglas form we have

$$\lim_{C \to \infty} \partial X / \partial C = \lim_{C \to \infty} (A N^\alpha C^{\beta-1}) = 0 \quad \text{if} \quad \beta < 1, \qquad (a')$$

$$\lim_{C \to \infty} X = \lim_{C \to \infty} (A N^\alpha C^\beta) = \infty. \qquad (b')$$

It is evident that (a) is consistent with (a') but (b) is inconsistent with (b'). That is, if output is to rise indefinitely, the marginal product should approach a finite value (from above). Since it does not do so, the Cobb–Douglas function embodies, ostensibly, a contradiction. This is easily resolved as soon as we note that, in the Cobb–Douglas production function, output will become infinite to a higher order than the marginal product vanishes when capital grows indefinitely large while labour remains constant. In other words the incremental capital services contribute to output so as to permit it to diverge before the marginal product converges to zero as capital inputs grow very large.

Even though the Cobb–Douglas function does not embody a contradiction, we would still like it to converge to some finite limit as one factor of production grows indefinitely large. In fact, the function should converge and then fall as one factor is increased if we adhere to the strictures of F. H. Knight.[†] Clearly, the Cobb–Douglas production function does not possess this property.[‡] We will explore these asymptotic properties below

[†] *Risk, Uncertainty and Profit*, London School of Economics Reprints of Scarce Works (no. 16, 1933), p. 100.

[‡] It does possess two additional properties which are considered briefly here. For linear homogeneous production functions, one can write

$$X = N(\partial X / \partial N) + C(\partial X / \partial C).$$

This is Euler's theorem. It states that if factors are paid their marginal products then the total product is exhausted. In the Cobb–Douglas function, when $\alpha + \beta = 1$, we have $X = \alpha X + \beta X = X(\alpha + \beta) = X$, which satisfies Euler's theorem. There is a vast literature on the adding up problem in income distribution theory; see G. Stigler, *Production and Distribution Theories* (New York, Macmillan, 1941), chap. 12; E. Cannan, *A History of the Theories of Production and Distribution*, (Staples, 1898), chap. 8; J. R. Hicks, *The Theory of Wages*, Appendix; R. G. D. Allen, *Mathematical Analysis for Economists*, pp. 317–22, 434; Joan Robinson,

with reference to a production function that is more general than the present one, and show that the limits are ultimately associated with the elasticity of substitution.

THE ELASTICITY OF SUBSTITUTION IN THE COBB–DOUGLAS PRODUCTION FUNCTION

As stated in the previous chapter, the elasticity of substitution is defined in general as

$$\sigma = \frac{du/u}{dR/R}, \tag{3.5}$$

where

$$u = \frac{N}{C} \quad \text{and} \quad R = \frac{\partial X/\partial C}{\partial X/\partial N},$$

the marginal rate of substitution of labour for capital. The marginal rate of substitution as derived from the Cobb–Douglas production function is

$$R = \frac{\partial X/\partial C}{\partial X/\partial N} = \frac{\beta}{\alpha}\frac{N}{C} = \frac{\beta}{\alpha}u. \tag{3.6}$$

Suppose we consider the logarithmic transform of R,

$$\log R = \log (\beta/\alpha) + \log u. \tag{3.7}$$

Now, take the total differential of $\log R$ as follows

$$d\log R = \frac{\partial \log R}{\partial \log u}d\log u = d\log u \tag{3.8}$$

or

$$\frac{dR}{R} = \frac{du}{u}.$$

But

$$1 = \frac{du/u}{dR/R}. \tag{3.9}$$

Collected Economic Papers (Blackwell, 1951), pp. 1–19; and P. Samuelson, *Foundations of Economic Analysis*, (Harvard University Press, 1955), pp. 83–7.

The Cobb–Douglas production function yields another well-known result— marginal costs equal average costs and both are constant for all levels of output when the underlying production function is homogeneous of degree one. Thus, costs = $wN+qC$. Combining Euler's equation with the marginal productivity conditions of equilibrium $w/p = \partial X/\partial N$ and $q/p = \partial X/\partial C$, where p is product price, we have $pX = wN+qC$. If λ is a Lagrange multiplier (a constant), we obtain $(1/\lambda)\, \partial\, \text{costs}/\partial X = 1$; if marginal costs are constant, so must average costs be; thus costs$/X = p$. Product price, p, is equal to λ, and marginal and average costs are identical for the linear-homogeneous Cobb–Douglas production function.

The right side of this expression is the definition of the elasticity of substitution. Therefore, for the Cobb–Douglas production function, σ is unity for any values of N and C, and for any degree of returns to scale.†

The unitary elasticity of substitution is a famous property of the Cobb–Douglas form. It is famous because it guarantees that relative income shares of capital and labour are constant for any changes in the relative supplies of capital and labour, and thus provides a rationale for the 'relative' constancy of factor shares observed in developed economies.‡ Thus consider again the marginal rate of substitution of labour for capital,

$$\frac{\partial X/\partial C}{\partial X/\partial N} = \beta/\alpha \frac{N}{C} = \frac{\beta}{\alpha} u.$$

Under conditions of equilibrium, this is equal to the rental value per unit of capital q, relative to wage rate w; let $\rho = q/w$, and we have

$$\frac{q}{w} = \rho = \frac{\beta}{\alpha} \frac{N}{C}.$$

Rearranging terms, we have, for $\alpha + \beta = 1$,

$$\frac{qC}{wN} = \rho/u = \frac{\beta}{\alpha}, \qquad (3.10)$$

and the left-hand side represents the share of income accruing to capital relative to that going to labour. Note that relative income shares are equal to β/α, the ratio of *constant* elasticities of production that is determined by the technology that governs the Cobb–Douglas production function. If β is high relative to α, then the capital share is high relative to labour's share of income. If technology is unchanging, it follows that a proportionate change in relative factor prices produces a compensating proportionate change in relative factor inputs and relative shares remain constant and equal to β/α.§

---

† R. G. D. Allen proves that σ is unity for the Cobb–Douglas relation (*op. cit.*), but he assumes that $\alpha + \beta = 1$. The present proof does not require this assumption.

‡ Functional income shares are examined in Chapter 12. Suffice it to say here that there are few contemporary authors who subscribe to a rationale for the movement—or lack of movement—in income shares which requires the elasticity of substitution to be unity.

§ This simple analytical device provided the basis for most of the investigations into the functional distribution of income performed by P. Douglas and his colleagues. Professor Douglas's procedure, in brief, was to estimate α and β from the production function and then compare the estimated values with the shares of

Suppose that the elasticity of substitution was constant but not unity ($\sigma \neq 1$), then, rearranging (3.5) and integrating, we have

$$R = cu^{1/\sigma}, \tag{3.11}$$

where c is an arbitrary constant of integration.[†] Now, since $R = q/w$, $q/w = cu^{1/\sigma}$; multiplying both sides by $u^{-1}(= C/N)$ yields

$$\rho u^{-1} = cu^{(1/\sigma)-1} \quad (c = \text{constant}), \tag{3.12}$$

labour and capital in income; if the shares agreed with the respective estimated elasticities, Professor Douglas concluded that factors were receiving their marginal products. Although the literature contains extensive and effective criticism of Professor Douglas's statistical and methodological procedures, his was a seminal idea giving rise to some basic considerations in econometrics.

Most of the criticism of Professor Douglas's later work (from 1938 on) tended to emphasize the inadequacy of the data that was used in the production function estimation rather than the specification errors inherent in the procedure. Both the time series and cross-section studies came under heavy criticism. The principal time series critic was H. Mendershausen, 'On the Significance of P. Douglas's Production Function', *Econometrica*, vol. 7 (October 1938), pp. 143–53. A more recent criticism of the Mendershausen type is presented by E. H. Phelps Brown, 'The Meaning of the Fitted Cobb–Douglas Function', *Quarterly Journal of Economics*, vol. 71 (November 1957), pp. 546–60. It is maintained that the high multi-collinearity between labour and capital data prevented Douglas from obtaining structural estimates of the production function. I do not think this criticism destroys the usefulness of time series studies but this is taken up again in Part II. The cross-section studies were also criticized for not yielding estimates of the structural parameters—they measure short run disequilibria, monopoly imperfections, etc. If all firms are in equilibrium and no market imperfections exist, then cross-section estimates of the production elasticities measure real wages and real rentals. This is a convincing argument. (See M. W. Reder, 'An Alternative Interpretation of the Cobb–Douglas Function', *Econometrica*, vol. 11 (October 1943), pp. 259–64; G. Stigler, *Output, Input and Productivity Measurement*, and R. Solow, 'Comments', on pp. 64 ff.; C. S. Soper, 'Production Functions and Cross-Section Surveys', *Economic Record*, vol. 34 (1958), pp. 11–117. H. S. Konijn defends the use of the cross-section data in 'Estimation of an Average Production Function from Surveys', *Economic Record*, vol. 35 (1959), pp. 118–25. Finally, for an intensive analysis of the identification problem and a survey of the literature, see M. Nerlove, 'Notes on the Identification and Estimation of the Cobb–Douglas Production Function' (mimeographed, May 1959).

Aside from data difficulties, the Douglas model of production suffers from severe specification errors. In most of this time series studies, the assumption of no non-neutral technological change makes it difficult to accept the estimates. But, in general, the use of a production function which assumes that the elasticity of substitution is always on the knife edge of unity encourages the rejection of the results for anything but a very crude approximation to production function estimation.

[†] The steps are as follows:

$$\frac{dR}{R} = \frac{1}{\sigma}\frac{du}{u}; \quad \int \frac{dR}{R} = \frac{1}{\sigma} \int \frac{du}{u}; \quad \log R = \frac{1}{\sigma}\log u + \log c;$$

therefore $R = cu^{1/\sigma}$.

whereupon it is evident that if $\sigma = 1$ this expression reduces to the Cobb–Douglas result (3.10), but if $\sigma \neq 1$ a change in relative factor supplies alters relative income shares. For, given changes in relative factor supplies, the relative income share will rise or fall depending upon whether the elasticity of substitution exceeds or falls short of unity.† In sum, only for $\sigma = 1$ are relative income shares constant for an unchanging technology, and the Cobb–Douglas production function possesses this property.‡

TECHNOLOGICAL CHANGE IN A COBB–DOUGLAS WORLD

The foregoing discussion of the properties of the Cobb–Douglas production function assumed that technology is given and unchanging. That is, given the state of the arts, production will behave as discussed if one or both productive services are varied. Now, we ask how output is affected when technology changes if the underlying production function is of the Cobb–Douglas form. We know that technological change can be characterized in terms of changes in an abstract technology. This comprises changes in technological efficiency, in technologically determined returns to scale, in the capital intensity of a technology, and in the ease of substitution between the factors of production. Variations in three of the four characteristics of an abstract technology can be represented in the Cobb–Douglas form.

Technological changes find expression in variations in the

† This is a famous and important proposition of J. R. Hicks which we will explore in detail below.

‡ There are variants of the Cobb–Douglas form which yield variable elasticities of production and substitution; three examples are

$$X = C^{1-\alpha}N^\alpha e^{\beta N},$$

C. E. Ferguson and R. W. Pfouts, 'Aggregate Production Function and Relative Factor Shares', *International Economic Review*, vol. 3 (September 1962), p. 335;

$$X = AC^\alpha N^\beta \exp(\gamma \log N \log C),$$

P. K. Newman and R. C. Read, 'Production Functions with Restricted Input Shares', *International Economic Review*, vol. 2 (January 1961), p. 128;

$$X = AC^\alpha N^\beta e^{\gamma C} e^{\alpha N},$$

Heady and Dillon, *Agricultural Production Functions*, p. 93.

These functions satisfy the four properties for certain intervals; for example, the second variant has positive downward sloping marginal products for

$$0 < \alpha + \gamma \log N < 1 \quad \text{and} \quad 0 < \beta + \lambda \log K < 1$$

(Newman and Read, *op. cit.* p. 129).

parameters of the production function, in the Cobb–Douglas case, in variations in A, α and β. Each parameter has a particular significance so that their changes represent different types of technological progress. Thus, variations in the A parameter of equation (3.1) denotes neutral technological change, as do equal proportional algebraic changes in α and β. Non-neutral technological progress is depicted by a change in the ratio of α to β. But this requires a lengthier disquisition to which we now turn.

CHANGES IN THE EFFICIENCY OF A COBB–DOUGLAS PRODUCTION PROCESS

An increase in the efficiency of a technology augments output but does not alter the relationship between the inputs, nor does it change the degree of returns to scale. It is represented in the Cobb–Douglas form by a change in the parameter, A, in (3.1). Since $\partial X/\partial A = X/A$, a proportional change in A produces a proportional change in output, *cet. par.* Clearly, variations in A do not affect the marginal rate of substitution between labour and capital—for the Cobb–Douglas, this is $(\beta/\alpha)\,u$—since the A parameter does not enter into its determination. Therefore, an increase in the A parameter represents a neutral technological gain.

CHANGES IN TECHNOLOGICALLY DETERMINED RETURNS TO SCALE

The sum of the partial elasticities of production, α and β, indicate the degree of returns to scale in the Cobb–Douglas form. Though returns to scale can vary as a result of changes in the scale of operations, it is difficult to distinguish this type of variation from changes in returns to scale attributable to changes in technology in the Cobb–Douglas form.† Keeping this in mind, we say, somewhat arbitrarily, that changes in the sum of the elasticities of production are brought about by modifications in the technology.‡

† However, suppose that $\alpha+\beta > 1$; i.e. economies of scale are being enjoyed, then the degree to which they are being enjoyed in an absolute sense depends on the volume of inputs, not on changes in α and β.

‡ This is a defect that is due to the particular production function. Were we to consider a production function that specified changing elasticities of production, then this defect would vanish.

This transformation in the production function falls in the neutral category because the marginal rate of substitution remains unaltered. For, if the sum of the elasticities changes, such that the ratio of the elasticities remain unaltered, then the marginal rate of substitution is unaltered also.

NON-NEUTRAL TECHNOLOGICAL PROGRESS IN THE COBB–DOUGLAS FUNCTION

A non-neutral technological change is depicted by a variation in the ratio of the two elasticities of production, i.e. a change in α relative to β. Clearly, this alters the marginal rate of substitution of labour for capital for each capital–labour ratio.

Factor saving or factor using technological gains are indicated by the direction of change of the ratio, β/α. If β rises relative to α, then a capital-using technological change has occurred, since the marginal product of capital has risen relative to that of labour for each capital–labour combination.

The ratio of β to α determines the proportions of labour and capital used in the production process for given relative factor prices or supplies. Consider the marginal productivity conditions of equilibriums $q/w = (\beta/\alpha)\,u$. Now it is seen that for a given factor price ratio, ρ, the larger is β/α the smaller will be N/C; i.e. the more capital will be used relative to labour. Since the ratio of labour to capital denotes the capital intensity of a production process, the ratio of the elasticities of production *determine* the capital intensity of a production process. It is to be stressed that the capital intensity of a production process is determined by the technological conditions of production, and in a Cobb–Douglas world the production elasticities are the expression of these technological conditions.

It is difficult to determine *a priori* how non-neutral technological change affects output in the Cobb–Douglas case. However, it can be specified simply within the framework of a production function which subsumes the Cobb–Douglas function as a special case. This will be discussed in detail in the next chapter.

Variations in the elasticity of substitution between labour and capital, σ, would also result in a non-neutral technological change, but in a Cobb–Douglas function σ is always unity and thus unchanging. The production function to be discussed in the following chapter does not share this difficulty.

SUMMARY

This chapter spells out the principal properties of the Cobb–Douglas production function with respect to variations in output, labour, capital and technology. A minimal set of three criteria is introduced initially; these represent desirable properties that we would like any neoclassical production function to satisfy.

The first criterion requires that marginal products of factors of production be positive. Secondly, the marginal product should decrease, at least over some range of output. Thirdly, the function should not specify *a priori* the degree of returns to scale, but should permit the data to determine it. The unconstrained Cobb–Douglas production functions satisfies all three criteria.

Labour's marginal product is $\alpha(X/N)$, and capital's marginal product is $\beta(X/C)$, both of which are positive. The derivative of the marginal product of labour with respect to labour is $[\alpha(\alpha-1)]/N(X/N)$, which is negative for $\alpha < 1$; hence labour's marginal product falls as the quantity of labour employed increases; a similar statement holds for capital's marginal product. The degree of returns to scale is indicated by $\alpha + \beta$, the sum of the partial elasticities of production; thus the function does not specify returns to scale *a priori*.

The asymptotic properties of the function are examined. If one factor increases indefinitely while the other remains constant, output in the Cobb–Douglas function also grows indefinitely. However, the marginal product of the increasing factor vanishes. Ostensibly, this involves a contradiction, but it is resolved when it is recognized that increments to output are sufficiently large to permit output to diverge before the increments go to zero. In spite of this, it would still be desirable for a production function to possess the asymptotic properties suggested by F. H. Knight, i.e. to rise, reach a finite limit, and then fall as one factor increases indefinitely. In the next chapter, it is shown that these asymptotic properties depend in a crucial way on the size of the elasticity of substitution between labour and capital.

The elasticity of substitution in the Cobb–Douglas production function is shown to be equal to unity for all labour-capital combinations and for any degree of returns to scale. This unitary elasticity of substitution is a famous property of the Cobb–Douglas function—primarily because it provides a rationale for the constancy of relative income shares even when there are significant changes in relative factor supplies. If relative factor prices change by a certain proportion, relative factor inputs change by the same proportion, in the opposite direction of course, and relative income shares remain unchanged. It is assumed here that technology is unchanging.

In the final section we relax the assumption that technology is unchanging. The Cobb–Douglas function can represent changes in three of the four characteristics of an abstract technology. If the efficiency of a technology is varied, *cet. par.*, then a change in A will occur, where $X = AN^{\alpha}C^{\beta}$. Variations in A do not affect the marginal rate of substitution between labour and capital; hence, changes in the technological efficiency parameter, A, produce a neutral technological gain.

Assuming that changes in the degree of returns to scale are produced by modifications in the technology, then the Cobb–Douglas production function represents a change in a second characteristic of an abstract technology by a shift in the sum of α and β. This is also a neutral type of technological change.

Changes in the capital intensity of a technology are depicted by variations in the ratio of the two elasticities of production, i.e. a change in α relative to β. This is the only way in which non-neutral technological progress can be represented in the Cobb–Douglas production function. If β rises relative to α, then a capital-using technological change is said to occur. Conversely, a fall in β relative to α indicates that a less capital intensive technology has been introduced.

In the Cobb–Douglas function, the elasticity of substitution is unity for any given factor combination and for any given capital intensity (β/α). Therefore, this function is incapable of representing a change in the fourth characteristic of an abstract technology, i.e. a change in the ease of substitution of labour for capital.

4

CHANGES IN OUTPUT AND TECHNOLOGY IN A CONSTANT ELASTICITY OF SUBSTITUTION WORLD

The substitution between commodities or between factors of production is the primary point of emphasis of neoclassical economics, since its laws are based on the degree or ease of substitution of the relevant variables. A very useful measure of the ease of substitution between commodities or between factors of production is the elasticity of substitution, and in the field of production this measure embeds itself in the production function. In the previous chapter we have examined a production function which compels the elasticity of substitution between labour and capital to take on a value of unity, whether or not the empirical situation so dictates. For some empirical problems, this may be an adequate approximation. However, a less restrictive and much more fruitful approach would be to allow the elasticity to vary in accordance with the empirical requirements under consideration.

In the present chapter, a production function is presented which assumes that the basic measure of the degree of substitution is constant but is not restricted *a priori* to any value. It is called the 'constant elasticity of substitution (CES) production function'. Clearly, the Cobb–Douglas and Leontief production functions are special cases of the CES relation.

When the elasticity of substitution is specified as constant, it only is assumed that changes in relative factor inputs and prices do not alter the elasticity. The value of the elasticity is determined by the underlying technology, and changes in the underlying technology effect variations on the elasticity for every level of the factor inputs and prices. Hence, the constancy of the elasticity refers to its invariance with respect to changes in relative factor supplies and not to transformations of the underlying technology.

The characteristics of an abstract technology are identified by the CES production function. That is to say, it permits us to measure changes in the efficiency of a technology, in technologically determined returns to scale, in the capital intensity of a technology and in the ease of substitution of labour for capital. The CES production function was derived independently by two groups, one consisting of Kenneth J. Arrow, Hollis B. Chenery, Bagicha S. Minhas, and Robert M. Solow,† and the other of Murray Brown and John S. de Cani.‡ The two derivations are dissimilar; also the latter permits any degree of returns to scale. An elaboration of the Brown–de Cani derivation is presented in Appendix A. There is a small but rapidly growing— and shall I say, intense—literature which employs the CES production function or relations derived from it. Aside from the two papers by Arrow *et al.* and Brown–de Cani, selected references are listed below.§

† 'Capital-Labor Substitution and Economic Efficiency', *The Review of Economics and Statistics*, vol. 45 (August 1961), pp. 225–50.

‡ 'Technological Change and the Distribution of Income', *International Economic Review*, vol. 4 (September 1963), pp. 289–309.

§ M. Brown and J. de Cani, 'Technological Change in the United States 1950–1960', *Productivity-Measurement Review*, no. 29 (May 1962), pp. 26–39. M. Brown and J. de Cani, 'A Measurement of Technological Unemployment', *Report Number 6208, Econometric Institute*, Netherlands School of Economics (March 1962); M. Brown and J. de Cani, 'A Measurement of Technological Employment', *The Review of Economics and Statistics*, vol. 45 (November 1963); R. M. Solow, 'Capital, Labor and Income in Manufacturing', *Studies in Income and Wealth*, Princeton University Press for National Bureau of Economic Research (mimeographed), 1961; B. S. Minhas, 'The Homohypallagic Production Function, Factor Intensity Reversals, and the Heckscher–Ohlin Theorem', *Journal of Political Economy*, vol. 70 (April 1962), pp. 138–56; B. S. Minhas, *An International Comparison of Factor Costs and Factor Use* (North-Holland Publishing Company, 1963); J. G. M. Hilhorst, 'Measurement of Production Functions in Manufacturing Industry', *Statistical Studies*, The Netherlands Central Bureau of Statistics, no. 13 (October 1962), pp. 7–29; R. I. McKinnon, 'Wages, Capital Costs and Employment in Manufacturing: A Model Applied to 1947–1958 U.S. Data', *Econometrica*, vol. 30 (July 1962), pp. 501–21; R. A. Nelson, 'Aggregate Production Functions and Medium Range Growth Projections', *American Economic Review* (September 1964); P. Nelson, 'Production Functions, Establishment Size, and Labor Quality' (unpublished mimeographed), 1961; H. Uzawa, 'Production Functions with Constant Elasticities of Substitution', *Review of Economic Studies*, vol. 29 (October 1962), pp. 291–9; R. K. Diwan, 'An Empirical Estimate of the Constant Elasticity of Substitution Production Function', University of Birmingham (mimeographed), 1963; M. Kamien, 'A Comment on Alternative Derivations of the Two Input Production Function with Constant Elasticity of Substitution', Carnegie Institute of Technology (mimeographed), 1963; G. J. Stigler, *Capital and Rates of Return in Manufacturing Industries* (Princeton University Press, 1963), pp. 98–102; A. H. Conrad, 'Industrial Structure and the Distribution of Income: Some Basic Considerations Revised', *Econometric Institute*, Netherlands School of Economics (April 1962);

THE FORM OF THE CES PRODUCTION FUNCTION

It is not essential to know the mathematical derivation of the CES production function in order to understand its properties, since it will be seen that these properties are consistent with economic sense. We simply note here that the CES production rule can be derived in a straightforward manner from the definition of the elasticity of substitution (see Appendix A).

As before, let X represent output, C utilized capital services, and N the labour employed, where these variables are measured in index number terms with a common base period. The CES production function is then,

$$X = \gamma[\kappa C^{-\alpha} + (1 - \kappa) N^{-\alpha}]^{-v/\alpha}. \qquad (4.1)$$

The four parameters are α, κ, γ and v. They shall be discussed in detail below, since they represent the four characteristics of an abstract technology. Briefly, γ is a scale parameter denoting the efficiency of a technology; κ indicates the degree to which the technology is capital intensive and is defined in the interval $0 < \kappa < 1$; v represents the degree of homogeneity of the function or the degree of returns to scale; and

$$\sigma = \frac{1}{1 + \alpha},$$

where again σ is the elasticity of substitution of labour for capital.†

D. McFadden, 'Further Results on C.E.S. Production Functions', *Review of Economic Studies*, vol. 30 (June 1963), pp. 73–83; P. J. Dhrymes and M. Kurz, 'Technology and Scale in Electricity Generation', Technical Report no. 116, Institute for Mathematical Studies in the Social Sciences (Stanford University, 1962); R. E. Lucas, *Substitution Between Capital and Labor in U.S. Manufacturing, 1929–1958*, unpublished doctoral dissertation (University of Chicago, 1963); R. G. Bodkin, 'A Test of the Specification of the Aggregate Production Function', Cowles Foundation Discussion Paper 157; C. E. Ferguson, 'Cross-section Production Functions and the Elasticity of Substitution in American Manufacturing Industry', *The Review of Economics and Statistics*, vol. 45 (August 1963), pp. 436–8; V. R. Fuchs, 'Capital-Labor Substitution', *The Review of Economics and Statistics*, vol. 45 (November 1963), pp. 436–8.

† The name given to (4.1) is slightly misleading, since the Cobb–Douglas and Leontief production functions also embody constant elasticities of substitution. However, these functions restrict the value of σ: for the Cobb–Douglas, $\sigma = 1$, and for the Leontief, $\sigma = 0$. In the CES production function, σ can take on any

NEOCLASSICAL PROPERTIES
OF THE CES PRODUCTION FUNCTION

There are three criteria we would like the CES function to satisfy. These are: (I) the marginal products should be positive, (II) they should fall over relevant ranges of the inputs, and (III) the function should be able to characterize any degree of returns to scale.

As seen from the following, the CES production function satisfies (I). The marginal product of labour is

$$\frac{\partial X}{\partial N} = h_1 X^{1+(\alpha/v)} N^{-\alpha-1} \qquad (4.2)$$

where $h_1 = (1-\kappa) v\gamma^{\alpha-/v}$; if there are constant returns to scale $(v = 1)$, then

$$\frac{\partial X}{\partial N} = h_1' \left(\frac{X}{N}\right)^{1/\sigma}. \qquad (4.3)$$

In either case, labour's marginal product depends only on output and the employment of labour.

The marginal product of capital is

$$\partial X/\partial C = h_2 X^{1+(\alpha/v)} C^{-\alpha-1}, \qquad (4.4)$$

where $h_2 = \kappa v\gamma^{-\alpha/v}$; again if there are constant returns to scale, then

$$\frac{\partial X}{\partial C} = h_2' \left(\frac{X}{C}\right)^{1/\sigma}.\dagger \qquad (4.5)$$

It is obvious that the marginal products are positive whether or not constant returns to scale are present. Hence, the CES production function satisfies the first criterion.

value. It may be noted here that (1) can be written in a variety of ways, all of which are equivalent; viz.

$$X = \gamma[\kappa C^{\alpha'} + (1-\kappa) N^{\alpha'}]^{v/\alpha'}; \quad \alpha' = [1-(1/\sigma)];$$

or
$$X = \gamma\left[\frac{N^\alpha C^\alpha}{\kappa N^\alpha + (1-\kappa) C^\alpha}\right]^{v/\alpha}; \quad \alpha = -[1-(1/\sigma)]$$

or
$$X = [\kappa_1 C^{-\alpha} + \kappa_2 N^{-\alpha}]^{-v/\alpha}; \quad \alpha = -[1-(1/\sigma)],$$

etc. In the text, we will adopt the convention of writing the CES rule as it appears in (4.1).

† A comparison of the constant returns to scale marginal products of the CES with the Cobb–Douglas production function reveals that the only difference, formally, is the presence of an exponent $(1/\sigma)$ attached to the average product in expressions for the CES marginal product. Thus, if $\sigma = 1$, then the CES marginal product reduces to the Cobb–Douglas marginal product.

The second criterion requires that the marginal product be downward sloping, or that $\partial^2 X/\partial N^2 < 0$. For the CES production function under constant returns to scale ($\nu = 1$), we have

$$\frac{\partial^2 X}{\partial N^2} = (J/N)\left(\frac{\partial X}{\partial N} - \frac{X}{N}\right), \tag{4.6}$$

where

$$J = \left(\frac{1}{\gamma}\right)^\alpha \left(\frac{1-\kappa}{\sigma}\right)\left(\frac{X}{N}\right)^\alpha;$$

combining (4.3) and (4.6) yields

$$\frac{\partial^2 X}{\partial N^2} = \left(\frac{JX}{N^2}\right)\left[\frac{1}{[\kappa/(1-\kappa)](u)^\alpha + 1} - 1\right] \tag{4.7}$$

where $u = N/C$. If the first term in the square brackets is less than unity, then $\partial^2 X/\partial N^2 < 0$ and the marginal product is downward sloping. Now, $[\kappa/(1-\kappa)]u^\alpha$ is positive; hence, the first term in the square brackets is less than unity, and the second criterion is satisfied.†

When the possibility of economies or diseconomies to scale ($\nu \neq 1$) is admitted, then the marginal product of labour may still be downward sloping. Consider the second partial derivative with respect to labour when $\nu \neq 1$,

$$\frac{\partial^2 X}{\partial N^2} = \frac{1}{\sigma}h_1, X^{1+\alpha/\nu} N^{-\alpha-2}\left[\frac{\sigma(\nu+\alpha)}{[\kappa/(1-\kappa)]u^\alpha + 1} - 1\right]. \tag{4.8}$$

For $\nu = 1$, this reduces to the case we examined above in (4.7) For $\nu < 1$, (4.8) becomes more negative than when constant returns to scale exist. Of course (4.8) can be positive (and thus the marginal product slopes upward) for sufficiently large values of ν. But we would expect in any reasonable neoclassical model that strong economies of scale would prevent a decline in the marginal product of labour. Hence, the possibility that the CES production function does not satisfy the second criterion for this special case is not disturbing.‡

---

† We will show below that $[\kappa/(1-\kappa)](u)^\alpha$ is equal to the share of capital in the total product relative to the share of labour. Thus, from (4.7), the larger is labour's relative income share, the less will the marginal product of labour decline as labour is added to the production process.

‡ A similar situation was found above to exist for the Cobb–Douglas production function.

It should be clear by now that the CES production function satisfies the third criterion—namely, that it be able to represent any degree of returns to scale that an empirical situation would dictate. For the degree of homogeneity of the function is characterized by the parameter, ν, and this can assume any value whatsoever.

A criterion, which requires that the marginal product of each factor increase for increases in the other factor, is also satisfied by the CES production function. The proof is left for the reader.

The marginal rate of substitution of labour for capital can be derived in terms of the CES production function by taking the ratio of the marginal product of labour (4.2) and the marginal product of capital (4.4); i.e.

$$\frac{\partial X/\partial C}{\partial X/\partial N} = \frac{\kappa}{1-\kappa}\,(u)^{1/\sigma}, \qquad (4.9)$$

or $R = \kappa' u^{1/\sigma}$, where, again, $u = N/C$. This plays an important role in the following analysis. If the production process is highly labour intensive (κ small), the marginal product of labour is high relative to that of capital for each labour–capital ratio; thus, a unit reduction in the labour rate has to be compensated for by a larger increase in the rate of capital than if the process were less labour intensive. In this sense, κ is a measure of capital intensity of the technology.

Why is the elasticity of substitution involved in the expression for the marginal rate of substitution? If σ is high, then capital is easily substitutable for labour, and vice versa. The expression for R tells us that if we reduce the rate of capital inputs by one unit we have to increase the rate of labour inputs by more when factors are not easily substituted for each other than when they are, keeping other things constant. Perhaps the easiest way to rationalize this intuitively is to recall that the more easily substitutable are factors for each other, the more similar they are from an economic point of view. If σ is low, then the factors are dissimilar. This implies that when σ is low, diminishing returns to labour set in more rapidly for an increase in R than when σ is at a higher level.

There is a simple way to check whether σ in (4.9) is truly the elasticity of substitution. Take the logarithmic transform of R,

$$\log R = \log \kappa' + 1/\sigma \log u. \qquad (4.10)$$

The derivative of $\log R$ with respect to u is,

$$\frac{dR}{R} = \frac{1}{\sigma}\frac{du}{u}, \tag{4.11}$$

or, after rearranging,

$$\sigma = \frac{du/u}{dR/R}. \tag{4.12}$$

Since this is the definition of the elasticity of substitution, the parameter σ in (4.9) is correctly defined.

Before leaving the marginal rate of substitution, we note that by the marginal productivity conditions of equilibrium

$$R = q/w = \rho, \tag{4.13}$$

where q is the real rental of a unit of capital and w is the real wage rate. We have, combining (4.9) and (4.13), for $v = 1, \ldots$

$$\rho = \kappa' u^{1/\sigma} \tag{4.14}$$

or

$$\rho/u = \kappa' u^{(1/\sigma)-1} = \kappa' u^{\alpha}. \tag{4.15}$$

Thus $\kappa' u^{\alpha}$ is equal to the relative share of capital to labour (see Chapter 12). Clearly, as $\sigma \to 1$, the relative share of capital to labour approaches κ'. Hence, in a Cobb–Douglas world, κ' is represented by the ratio of the capital to labour production elasticities.†

The properties of the CES production function discussed so far have been consistent with neoclassical expectations, but nothing has been added to our knowledge by their consideration. However, an examination of the asymptotic properties of the function will contribute something new. That is to say, in determining whether the CES production function possesses 'asymptotes', we will clarify the reasons for the existence of these limits in all constant elasticity of substitution production functions.

Consider the CES production function when $\sigma > 1$

$$X = \gamma[\kappa C^{1-(1/\sigma)} + (1-k)\,N^{1-(1/\sigma)}]^{\sigma v/(\sigma-1)}. \tag{4.16}$$

Holding capital constant and expanding labour, we wish to determine whether output reaches a limit. Thus

$$\lim_{N\to\infty} X\Big|_{\sigma>1} = \lim_{N\to\infty} \gamma[\kappa C^{1-(1/\sigma)} + (1-\kappa)\,N^{1-(1/\sigma)}]^{\sigma v/(\sigma-1)}\Big|_{\sigma>1} = \infty. \tag{4.17}$$

† It may also be noted that when $u = N/C = 1$ (which would be the case in the base period if N and C are index numbers) income shares are equal to κ.

Leaving aside the interpretation of (4.17) for the moment, try the same thing on the CES production function when $\sigma < 1$, first writing it as

$$X = \frac{\gamma}{\left[\dfrac{\kappa}{C^{(1/\sigma)-1}} + \dfrac{1-\kappa}{N^{(1/\sigma)-1}}\right]^{\sigma v/(1-\sigma)}}, \qquad (4.18)$$

where all exponents are positive. Now

$$\lim_{N\to\infty} X\Big|_{\sigma<1} = \lim_{N\to\infty} \frac{\gamma}{\left[\dfrac{\kappa}{C^{(1/\sigma)-1}} + \dfrac{1-\kappa}{N^{(1/\sigma)-1}}\right]^{\sigma v/(1-\sigma)}}\Bigg|_{\sigma<1} \qquad (4.19)$$

$$= AC^v,$$

where $A = \gamma\kappa[-\sigma v/(1-\sigma)]$. Obviously, results similar to (4.17) and (4.19) are obtainable when C gets indefinitely large while N is held constant.

When $\sigma > 1$, it is seen from (4.17) that the CES function possesses no limit, and hence does not have a limit. However, when $\sigma < 1$, the function does reach a finite maximum as one factor increases while the other is held constant; hence limits do exist when the elasticity of substitution is less than unity. Thus the CES production function provides us with a new result.

The economic rationale for these results are seen as follows. When $\sigma > 1$, the factors of production resemble each other from a technological point of view, so that if one increases indefinitely, the other being held constant, the technology permits the expanding factor to be substituted relatively easily for the constant factor. Hence, both factors seem to be increasing indefinitely, and the product to which they contribute increases indefinitely. If $\sigma < 1$, the technology views the factors as being relatively dissimilar so that it is difficult to substitute the expanding for the constant factor. Even though one factor increases indefinitely, the growth of the product is restrained by the technologically scarce-constant factor†

† Are the asymptotic properties of the marginal products of the CES function consistent with (4.17) and (4.19)? For the case of constant returns to scale, it can be shown that

$$\lim_{N\to\infty} \frac{\partial X}{\partial N}\Big|_{\sigma>1} = \frac{1-\kappa}{\kappa}\gamma^{1/\sigma}(1-\kappa)^{1/(\sigma-1)},$$

$$\lim_{N\to\infty} \frac{\partial X}{\partial N}\Big|_{\sigma<1} = 0.$$

IMPERFECT COMPETITION
IN A CES WORLD

We have been assuming that the product and factor markets are organized competitively. The relaxation of this assumption leads to different equilibrium and stability conditions which can be derived as follows. Suppose that the demand for the product can be represented by (4.20)

$$X = B_1 p^{e_1}, \qquad (4.20)$$

where B_1 is a constant, e_1 is the (constant) price elasticity of demand, and p is the price of the product. The supply functions for the factors of production are also assumed to be of the same homogeneous form

$$N = B_2 w^{e_2}, \qquad (4.21)$$

$$C = B_3 q^{e_3}, \qquad (4.22)$$

where the B's are constants, the e's are elasticities of supply, and the variables have been defined above. We can rewrite these functions as follows:

$$p = b_1 X^{1/e_1},$$

$$w = b_2 N^{1/e_2},$$

$$q = b_3 C^{1/e_3},$$

where $b_1 = B_1^{-1/e_1}$, $b_2 = B_2^{-1/e_2}$, and $b_3 = B_3^{-1/e_3}$. Now, total revenue is

$$pX = b_1 X^{1+1/e_1},$$

the wage bill is

$$wN = b_2 N^{1+1/e_2},$$

and the capital rent is

$$qC = b_3 C^{1+1/e_3}.$$

The profit identity is simply the total revenue less costs (ignoring taxes)

$$\pi = pX - wN - qC.$$

The firm is assumed to maximize profits subject to the production function constraint, the production function in the present

Hence, output increases indefinitely, for indefinitely large labour inputs, when $\sigma > 1$; and labour's marginal product reaches a finite limit, as it should. When output approaches a finite limit as labour inputs increase indefinitely for $\sigma < 1$, labour's marginal product approaches zero, again as it should. Recall that in order to achieve this type of consistency in the Cobb–Douglas function, it was necessary to invoke the fact that output diverged of higher order than labour's marginal product converged.

instance being represented by the CES form. In short, it maximizes

$$\pi = b_1 X^{1+1/e_1} - b_2 N^{1+1/e_2} - b_3 C^{1+1/e_3}$$
$$- \lambda(X - \gamma[\kappa C^{-\alpha} + (1-\kappa) N^{-\alpha}]^{-v/\alpha}), \quad (4.23)$$

where λ is a Lagrangian multiplier. The first-order conditions of equilibrium are

$$\frac{\partial \pi}{\partial \lambda} = X - \gamma[\kappa C^{-\alpha} + (1-\kappa) N^{-\alpha}]^{-v/\alpha} = 0,$$

$$\frac{\partial \pi}{\partial X} = E_1 P - \lambda = 0,$$

$$\frac{\partial \pi}{\partial N} = -E_2 w + \lambda f_N = -E_2 w + \lambda(1-\kappa) v\gamma^{-\alpha/v} X^{1+\alpha/v} N^{-\alpha-1} = 0,$$

$$\frac{\partial \pi}{\partial C} = -E_3 q + \lambda f_C = -E_3 q + \lambda \kappa v\gamma^{-\alpha/v} X^{1+\alpha/v} C^{-\alpha-1} = 0,$$

where $E_1 = 1 + 1/e_1$, $E_2 = 1 + 1/e_2$, $E_3 = 1 + 1/e_3$, $f_N = \partial X/\partial N$, and $f_C = \partial X/\partial C$. Of course when competitive conditions prevail in all markets, $E_1 = E_2 = E_3 = 1$, since the elasticities of factor supply and product demand are infinite. As an illustration of the economic meaning of these conditions, consider $\partial \pi/\partial C$. From the second condition we obtain $\lambda = pE_1$, thus interpreting λ as the firm's marginal costs. We can then write $\partial \pi/\partial C$ as

$$\frac{qC}{pX} = \frac{E_1}{E_3} \frac{C}{X} f_C = \frac{E_1}{E_3} \kappa v\gamma^{-\alpha/v} X^{\alpha/v} C^{-\alpha}. \quad (4.24)$$

The share of capital in the total product is proportional to the elasticity of production with respect to capital, where the constant of proportionality is composed of the elasticity of product demand and the elasticity of capital supply. Note that capital's elasticity of production, $(C/X)f_C$, is variable in contrast to the constant elasticity of production that is present in the Cobb–Douglas world.† Also note that if competitive conditions pre-

---

† The first-order condition for the imperfectly competitive Cobb–Douglas world that corresponds to (4.24) is

$$\frac{qC}{pX} = \frac{E_1}{E_3} \beta,$$

where β is the constant elasticity of production with respect to capital.

vailed in all markets $(E_1 = E_3 = 1)$, the share of income accruing to capital is equal to its production elasticity; this would also be the case if the degree of monopoly is the same in both markets $(E_1 = E_3)$.

The second-order conditions of equilibrium—the stability conditions—require that $d^2\pi < 0$.† For the CES system, we must have

$$\frac{C}{X}f_C < \frac{E_3 + \alpha}{E_1 + (\alpha/v)},$$

$$\frac{N}{X}f_N < \frac{E_2 + \alpha}{E_1 + (\alpha/v)},$$

and

$$\frac{N}{X}f_N\left[\frac{E_1 + (\alpha/v)}{E_2 + \alpha}\right] + \frac{C}{X}f_C\left[\frac{E_1 + (\alpha/v)}{E_3 + \alpha}\right] < 1.$$

The last condition is interesting. It states that the weighted sum of the production elasticities must be less than unity in order for equilibrium to be stable in an imperfectly competitive CES world. But the weights are the interesting part of the condition. For not only do they contain the elasticities of product demand and factor supplies, as expected, but they also include the elasticity of substitution between labour and capital

$$(\alpha = -(1 - 1/\sigma)),$$

and the homogeneity parameter, v. Note that as $\sigma \to 1$, the limit of the last stability condition becomes

$$\frac{N}{X}f_N\frac{E_1}{E_2} + \frac{C}{X}f_C\frac{E_1}{E_3} < 1,$$

which is the same condition we would obtain if the Cobb–Douglas production function were substituted for the CES

---

† The conditions under which the quadratic form $d^2\pi$ is negative definite are that the principal minors of the bordered Hessian determinant,

$$\begin{vmatrix} 0 & \partial\pi/\partial N & \partial\pi/\partial C \\ \partial\pi/\partial N & \partial^2/\partial N^2 & \partial^2\pi/\partial N\partial C \\ \partial\pi/\partial C & \partial^2\pi/\partial N\partial C & \partial^2\pi/\partial C^2 \end{vmatrix},$$

alternate in sign; i.e. $\partial^2\pi/\partial N^2 < 0$, $\partial^2\pi/\partial C^2 < 0$,

$$(\partial^2\pi/\partial N^2)(\partial^2\pi/\partial C^2) > (\partial^2\pi/\partial N\partial C)^2.$$

See R. G. D. Allen, *Mathematical Economics* (London, Macmillan, 1956), p. 478.

function in deriving the stability conditions. But this is not surprising since we know that as $\sigma \to 1$, the CES function *becomes* the Cobb–Douglas function (see Appendix A).

TECHNOLOGICAL
CHANGE IN A CES WORLD

Our discussion of the CES world so far has assumed that the state of the arts is unchanging. But it is the representation of technological progress in the CES world which interests us here. For it embodies all four characteristics of an abstract technology, and in so doing provides us with the basis of insights into—and proofs of—technological relationships that would be impossible to obtain from less general production functions. It is the changes in the technological characteristics of the CES production function to which we now turn our attention.

NEUTRAL TECHNOLOGICAL PROGRESS

Variations in the efficiency of a technology and in technologically determined returns to scale are classified as neutral technological changes—i.e. neither labour- saving or -using. They are representable in the CES production function in a simple manner. For, proportionate increases in the parameter, γ, produce proportionate increases in output, holding all other things constant. Hence, an increase in γ represents an upward shift in the efficiency of a CES technology.

Another parameter change which does not affect the marginal rate of substitution of capital for labour is ν, which represents technological returns to scale. This parameter determines the degree of returns to scale but does not indicate how much of any change in output is attributable to the exploitation of economies of scale. The latter requires a knowledge of the volume of capital and labour actually employed. For example, a given technology may produce high returns to scale, but, if the firm chooses to operate with near zero inputs, clearly the benefits from utilizing a technology with those returns to scale are small in absolute terms.

We attribute a change in ν to technological advance. Obviously, our interpretation of the reason for a change in returns to scale is open to criticism, for economies or diseconomies of scale can also be due to variations in the scale of operations of the firm (see below).

In order to set the stage for an examination of non-neutral technological progress, we will first look at the way in which technological changes affect the marginal rate of substitution. This also provides us with a bonus in the form of an interesting proposition in the theory of technology which will prove useful in interpreting estimates of parameter changes in our measurement.

CHANGES IN THE MARGINAL RATE OF SUBSTITUTION DUE TO TECHNOLOGICAL PROGRESS

A non-neutral technological change has been defined above in the Hicksian manner as one which alters the marginal rate of substitution of labour for capital

$$R = \frac{\partial X/\partial K}{\partial X/\partial N}$$

for each combination of labour and capital. For example, if R falls for a given labour–capital ratio, then a labour-using or capital-saving technological change has occurred. For the CES production function

$$R = \kappa' u^{1/\sigma}.$$

Hence, non-neutral changes are associated only with variations in κ, the capital intensity parameter or σ, the elasticity of substitution. Suppose that a non-neutral technological change occurs such that only κ is increased; then

$$\frac{\partial R}{\partial \kappa} = \frac{R}{\kappa(\mathbf{1} - \kappa)},$$

and, as we would expect, capital's marginal product rises relative to labour's marginal product for each labour–capital ratio, and the change is capital-using. It is capital-using in the sense that, for any given R, a smaller labour–capital ratio is required when κ increases. Hence, to call a rise in capital intensity, labour-saving, is simply common sense.

The other source of non-neutral technological change is a

shift in the elasticity of substitution. Recalling that we measure inputs in index numbers with a common base period, then

$$\frac{\partial R}{\partial \sigma} = -\frac{R}{\sigma^2} \log u.$$

Whether a rise in σ leads to a rise or fall in R is easily determined. If labour is expanding more rapidly than capital, then u exceeds unity and $\log u$ is positive; on the other hand, if capital is the more rapidly growing factor, then $\log u$ is negative. Since R is always non-negative, we have

$$\frac{\partial R}{\partial \sigma} = \begin{cases} < 0 & \text{if} \quad u > 1, \\ > 0 & \text{if} \quad u < 1. \end{cases}$$

In other words, if labour grows more rapidly than capital a rise in the elasticity of substitution reduces R, i.e. raises labour's marginal product relative to capital's; conversely, if capital is the more rapidly growing factor, a rise in σ increases capital's marginal product relative to labour's.

The proposition can be rationalized as follows by noting that a rise in σ implies that it is relatively easier to substitute capital for labour at each labour–capital ratio; in other words, technology permits a larger amount of capital to be used for every reduction in the amount of labour used. Now, if capital is growing more rapidly than labour, capital will be substituted in the production process for labour at the margin. Therefore, in this instance, the rise in σ is capital using.

These results are highly useful in interpreting the non-neutral effect of changes in κ and σ. But now we ask how shifts in these magnitudes affect output.

THE IMPACT OF NON-NEUTRAL TECHNOLOGICAL PROGRESS ON CES PRODUCTION

It has been easy to determine how variations in the capital intensity and ease of substitution of a technology affect the bias of technological change—i.e. whether they are labour- or capital-saving. However, we must now attempt to understand how variations in these parameters affect output itself.

Consider the effect of a change in the elasticity of substitution on output. It can be shown that when it becomes easier to substitute capital for labour, output always rises for a given increase in the factors of production. The proof is cumbersome and is relegated to a footnote.† The economic rationale of the positive relation between the elasticity of substitution and the rate of output is given in Chapter 2.

One of the implications of the result is that in order for the elasticity of substitution to have an appreciable effect on the rate of growth of output, there must be a substantial divergence in the rates of growth of labour and capital. In general, though, since factors of production rarely grow at the same rates, a change in σ will have some influence on the rate of output.

A change in σ is one of two components of non-neutral technological progress, the other being a variation in the capital intensity parameter. It is easy to show that a rise in κ, the capital

† First, take the partial derivative of X with respect to σ

$$\frac{\partial X}{\partial \sigma} = \left\{\frac{\nu X}{\sigma^2[1-(1/\sigma)]^2}\right\} \left\{\frac{[1-(1/\sigma)](\kappa C^{-\alpha}\log C+(1-\kappa)N^{-\alpha}\log N)}{\kappa C^{-\alpha}+(1-\kappa)N^{-\alpha}}\right.$$
$$\left. - \log(\kappa C^{-\alpha}+(1-\kappa)N^{-\alpha})\right\}$$

At the outset, we note that when $C = N$, $\partial X/\partial \sigma = 0$. That is, when labour is growing at the same rate as capital, a change in σ has no effect on output. Now, if we assume that C becomes indefinitely large, *cet. par.*, then for $\sigma > 1$

$$\lim_{C\to\infty} \frac{\partial X}{\partial \sigma}\bigg|_{\sigma>1} = -\left\{\frac{\nu X}{\sigma^2[1-(1/\sigma)]^2}\right\}[\log \kappa],$$

and since $0 < \kappa$, $\log \kappa < 0$, and this limit is positive. If $\sigma < 1$, then

$$\lim_{C\to\infty} \frac{\partial X}{\partial \sigma} = -\left\{\frac{\nu X}{\sigma^2[1-(1/\sigma)^2]}\right\}[\log(1-\kappa)].$$

Again, $0 < (1-\kappa) < 1$, and $\log(1-\kappa) < 0$, hence this limit is positive. A similar set of limits for N also produces positive values for $\partial X/\partial \sigma$.

We must still show that $\partial X/\partial \sigma > 0$ for possible values of κ. A weak method of doing this is to take the limit of $\partial X/\partial \sigma$ as κ approaches unity, and as it approaches zero

$$\lim_{\kappa\to 1} \frac{\partial X}{\partial \sigma} = -\left\{\frac{\nu X}{\sigma^2[1-(1/\sigma)]^2}\right\}[\log \kappa],$$

which also is positive. As κ approaches zero we have

$$\lim_{\kappa\to 0} \frac{\partial X}{\partial \sigma} = -\left\{\frac{\nu X}{\sigma^2[1-(1/\sigma)]^2}\right\}[\log(1-\kappa)],$$

We have shown that all relevant limits are positive and can tentatively conclude that a rise in σ raises the output rate. However, this proof does not assure us that $\partial X/\partial \sigma > 0$ for all values of C, N and κ. See M. McCarthy, 'The CES Production Function and the Effect of the Elasticity of Substitution on Output' (unpublished mimeographed, 1963).

intensity parameter, increases output only if capital is growing more rapidly than labour; if labour is the faster grower, a rise in κ reduces output.†

The important thing to note is that here we have a component of technological change which does not increase output, *ipso facto*, for given levels of input. In fact, a capital intensification type of technological change generates a fall in production if capital is growing less rapidly than labour, *cet. par.*

The principal conclusion is that only under certain narrow circumstances can a non-neutral technological change have an unambiguous, positive effect on output. In an economy in which the growth of capital exceeds the growth of labour, we can definitely say that an increase in the capital intensity characteristic and an upward shift in the elasticity of substitution will increase the rate of growth of output. The same technological changes in an economy in which labour is the more rapidly growing factor will raise or lower the output rate—we do not know which until the parameter changes and the factor growth rates are quantified. Looked at in another way, a labour-or capital-saving technological change augments the rate of output only if the components of the technological changes are consistent with a specific resource growth configuration.

To illustrate these results, consider two economies, one in which capital is growing more rapidly than labour, and the second in which the relative growth rates of the factors are reversed. Suppose that both economies pursue an investment policy which embodies capital intensive techniques, i.e. the increase in κ is the same for both. If the elasticity of substitution remains unchanged in both economies during the implementation of this policy, there will be a reduction in the output rate of the second economy and an increase in the rate of output in the first. Therefore, if both types of economies choose investments which are

---

† Consider
$$\frac{\partial X}{\partial \kappa} = \nu \gamma^{-\alpha/\nu} \frac{X^{1+\alpha/\nu}}{C^\alpha} \left[\frac{1-(N/C)^{1-(1/\sigma)}}{1-(1/\sigma)} \right].$$

The contents of the square bracket are positive if $N/C < 1$ irrespective of the size of σ. For if $N/C < 1$, then $(N/C)^{1-(1/\sigma)} > 1$ when σ is less than unity; but then the numerator of the square bracketed term is negative; the denominator is negative, thus $\partial X/\partial \kappa > 0$. Even if $\sigma > 1$, $\partial X/\partial \kappa > 0$ if $N/C < 1$, for then the numerator is positive while the denominator is also positive. We have the following paradigm

$$\frac{\partial X}{\partial \kappa} = \begin{cases} > 0 & \text{if} \quad N/C < 1, \\ < 0 & \text{if} \quad N/C > 1. \end{cases}$$

more capital intensive than their existing technology by the same amount, the gap in income between them will widen even if the factors continue to grow at the same rates.†

This is a naive model for two reasons. First, a more capital intensive technology will probably be associated with a lower elasticity of substitution.‡ Then for both types of economies, a larger capital intensity parameter and a lower elasticity of substitution will yield a labour- or capital-saving technological change, and a larger or smaller output; it is not possible to say what the outcome will be unless the relative strengths of the two effects are quantified. Secondly, the model has held other things constant, among them being the neutral characteristics of the abstract technologies in the two economies. Certainly, these will not remain unchanged when non-neutral changes are being introduced; in fact, the comparison between the economies should consider all characteristics and their output effects. That is, a technological change should be viewed as a basket of neutral and non-neutral components, some of which may be exerting a positive and others a negative effect on output, but, certainly, in the long run the combined effects of all components on output must be positive.

LIMITATIONS OF THE CES PRODUCTION FUNCTION

Although the CES production function is more general than any alternative constant elasticity production functions, it possesses limitations that may be serious for some purposes.

The CES function combines in one parameter, v, two forces that affect it. In the first place, economies of scale can result from an expansion in the scale of operations for a given technology. Alternatively, given the scale of operations, a technological change can alter the rate of output. In empirical applications both forces may affect the homogeneity parameter,

† Arguments for the adoption of capital intensive investment policies in underdeveloped areas are contained in W. Galenson and H. Leibenstein, 'Investment Criteria, Productivity, and Economic Development', *Quarterly Journal of Economics*, vol. 69 (August 1955) pp. 343–70. These arguments are reinforced by H. Neisser, 'Comment on Galenson and Leibenstein', *Quarterly Journal of Economics*, vol. 70 (November 1956), pp. 644–6.

‡ See Brown and de Cani, 'Technological Changes in the United States, 1950–1960', *Productivity-Measurement Review*, no. 29.

ν, and it may not be possible to distinguish between them.† In the Cobb–Douglas function, the problem is even worse. For, not only does it confuse these two forces in the sum of the elasticities of production, but the elasticities have the additional burden of having to represent non-neutral technological changes. The CES function avoids this difficulty by separating the economies of scale measure from the other characteristics of the abstract technology. In any event, the interpretation of the economies of scale measure in empirical situations must be made with caution in any constant elasticity of substitution production function.

Another limitation of the CES function is that it is difficult to generalize it to n-factors of production. The generalizations developed by H. Uzawa, and discussed in Appendix C, are remarkable constructions, yet do not achieve complete generality while remaining in the constant elasticity of substitution framework. Parenthetically, Appendix C contains a methodology for fitting the generalized CES function.

A third limitation of the CES production function is associated with its principal virtue—the specification of elasticity of substitution which is invariant to changes in factor proportions. Recall that we have allowed the elasticity of substitution to change in response to particular variations in the underlying technology, not in response to changes in factor proportions. But this is an *a priori* specification; we really do not know whether the elasticity should vary when factor proportions change.‡ If the true structure prescribes a variable elasticity due to changes in factor proportions and we claim that the elasticity is changing for technological reasons, then we are ascribing to technological change more than is due to it. Unless a completely general function is specified—a polynomial of degree n—it seems that this difficulty must be accepted. Since it is impossible with the available data and statistical techniques to obtain estimates of completely general production functions, and since they do not necessarily satisfy all neoclassical criteria, we are forced for the immediate future to utilize the constant elasticity of substitution production function and live with the potential specification error.

---

† There are forms that permit these distinctions, for example, the logistic and the lognormal—but these forms require restrictions that do not satisfy our neoclassical criteria as well as possessing asymptotes which are difficult to measure.
‡ But see J. R. Hicks, *The Theory of Wages*, p. 132.

A fourth deficiency is that κ the capital intensity parameter is not dimensionless. This, together with its implications, are discussed in Chapter 9. Aside from these theoretical difficulties, there is an empirical problem: the CES production function is relatively difficult to fit to data. But this is the subject of Chapter 9.

SUMMARY

The general purpose of this chapter is to introduce the reader to the constant elasticity of substitution (CES) production function, which is applicable to general production situations characterized by a constant elasticity. Its two specific purposes are to examine the neoclassical properties of the CES function and to reveal the technology embedded in its structure.

The CES function satisfies the following neoclassical criteria: the marginal products of capital and labour are positive; they slope downward except when strong economies of scale are present; and the CES function is able to represent any degree of returns to scale that an empirical situation would dictate.

The marginal rate of substitution of labour for capital is shown to depend on the ratio of labour to capital inputs and on two parameters, the capital intensity parameter and the elasticity of substitution. Invoking the marginal productivity conditions of equilibrium, the relative shares of capital and labour income turn out to depend also on the ratio of labour to capital and on the capital intensity and elasticity of substitution parameters.

Specific asymptotic properties of the CES function depend on the elasticity of substitution. When it exceeds unity, the CES function possess no limit as one factor increases indefinitely while the other is constant. When the elasticity of substitution is less than unity, the function does reach a finite maximum as one factor increases while the other is held constant. Hence limits do exist when the elasticity of substitution is less than unity. The reason for this is that when the elasticity exceeds unity, both factors seem to be increasing indefinitely even while one is held constant, because the expanding factor is easily substituted for the constant factor; thus the product to which they contribute increases indefinitely.

Neutral technological progress is reflected in changes in the efficiency parameter and in the returns to scale parameter.

Increases in these parameters increase output while leaving the marginal rate of substitution unaffected.

Non-neutral technological changes are reflected in variations in the capital intensity and elasticity of substitution parameters. A rise in the capital intensity parameter produces a capital-using technological change; a rise in the elasticity of substitution produces a capital-using (saving) change if capital is growing more (less) rapidly than labour when the relative growth rates are measured in terms of a common base period. The economic rationale for these results is indicated.

The effect on output of non-neutral technological change is also indicated. It is shown that output is positively related to the elasticity of substitution; and it is positively related to the capital intensity parameter if capital is growing more rapidly than labour. If labour grows more rapidly than capital, then a rise in the capital intensity parameter reduces the rate of growth of output. This non-neutral component of technological change does not increase output, *ipso facto* for given levels of inputs. It increases output only if the components of non-neutral technological variations are consistent in a specific sense with the resource growth configuration. Some implications are briefly noted.

Finally, four general limitations of the CES production function are indicated. An empirical representation of economies of scale may be ambiguous because the function combines in one parameter scale economies attributable to variations in the scale of operations of the firm for a given technology and scale economies that may result from the implementation of a new technology for a given scale of operations. A second difficulty with the function is that it is difficult to generalize it for n factors of production. The third limitation noted is that it assumes that the elasticity of substitution between capital and labour is invariant with respect to relative factor inputs; this may be a source of specification error. Finally, the CES function is relatively difficult to fit to data, and one of its parameters is difficult to interpret unless certain precautions are taken.

The limitations of the CES production function or of any conceptual device should be evaluated in terms of alternatives in actual situations. When this is done, it is found that for several important economic problems, these limitations do not prevent its applicability.

5

LONG-RUN, SHORT-RUN, AND
SECULAR PRODUCTION PROCESSES

The purpose here is to try to build into our model of production, and thus into our measures of technological change, a time dimension. Up to now the models of production have represented equilibrium production processes. Firms rarely if ever operate with a set of equilibrium relations for there are numerous restrictions on the rapid achievement of an equilibrium situation.

Specifically, it has been assumed that the firm is able to substitute capital for labour with ease up to σ, the elasticity of substitution. There have been no limitations to hinder this substitution possibility other than the technological constraint, for σ is technologically determined. Clearly, the firm cannot substitute capital for labour with ease greater than the σ that is determined technologically. But the substitution elasticity at any given moment can be less than that which is technologically specified. For once capital is purchased, or built, and installed—once capital is in place—it may be very difficult to substitute capital for labour. Since the equipment is usually designed with requirements as to the number, skill levels and time of worker attendants, the opportunities for varying these requirements are small (some people claim it is almost zero). Therefore, the elasticity of substitution between labour and the structures and equipment which are already in place may be very small.

The alleged small size of the elasticity of substitution at a point in time has been invoked in arguments against the laws of neoclassical economics. If σ is close to zero, than the marginal productivity conditions of equilibrium do not apply. But as usual Hicks foresaw the problem and showed us the direction in which the answer lies:

An entrepreneur, by investing in fixed plant, gives hostages to fortune. So long as that plant is in existence, the possibility of economizing by changing the methods or the scale of production is small; but as the plant comes to be renewed, it will be to his interest

to make a radical change....Naturally, this is a slow process....
But there is a continual urge to such transformation.†

The discussion of short- and long-run production processes
centres around the elasticity of substitution concept. Accordingly,
we can begin with an examination of the marginal rate of substitution introduced in the previous chapter and which includes
σ as a parameter

$$\rho = \kappa' u^{1/\sigma}, \tag{5.1}$$

where $\rho = q/w$, the rental value of capital relative to the wage
rate, $u = N/C$, the inputs of labour relative to capital, and
$\kappa' = \kappa/(1-\kappa)$, where κ is the capital intensity parameter. We
call (5.1) and algebraic transformations of it, expansion path
functions, although strictly speaking they establish the conditions of expansion of the firm.‡ As noted before, only two
parameters enter the expansion path function, κ and σ; and
variations in these parameters reflect non-neutral technological
changes.§

If ρ is conceived as a datum, then the causal direction goes
from relative factor prices to relative factor inputs. This can be
made explicit by writing (5.1) as

$$u = \kappa'^{-\sigma}\rho^{\sigma}, \tag{5.2}$$

---

† *The Theory of Wages*, pp. 182–3. Also, see J. Schumpeter, *History of Economic Analysis*, p. 1003. J. Viner, 'Cost Curves and Supply Curves', *Zeitschrift für Nationalökonomie*, vol. III (1932), pp. 23–46, reprinted in *Readings in Economic Analysis*, edited by R. C. Clemence, vol. 2 (Addison-Wesley Press, 1950), pp. 8–35. This short-run–long-run distinction was recently embedded in two different models: L. Johannsen, 'Substitution Versus Fixed Production Coefficients in the Theory of Economic Growth: A Synthesis', *Econometrica*, vol. 27 (April 1959), pp. 157–76; Salter, *Productivity and Technical Change*, pp. 17 ff.

‡ See S. Carlson, *A Study on the Pure Theory of Production*, pp. 31–40.

§ Equation (5.1) assumes that the degree of imperfect competition in the labour and product markets is the same. It also assumes that distinct factor markets exist. This has been called to question by T. Scitovsky, 'A Survey of Some Theories of Income Distribution', unpublished (mimeographed, 1961). We should note here that the expansion path function as written in (5.1) conceives of the relative factor price ratio as a datum to be used as a signal to the firm to vary relative factor inputs within the limits of the relevant technology. When more than two factors of production are under consideration, relative factor input decisions can only be handled by a more general model. In order to generalize the model to n factors, the elasticities of factor supplies must be introduced along with the partial elasticities of substitution. See J. R. Hicks, 'Distribution and Economic Progress: A Revised Version', *Review of Economic Studies*, vol. 4 (October 1936), pp. 1–8, 10–12. The problem has been recently revived and looked at anew by A. Conrad, 'Industrial Structure and the Distribution of Income: Some Basic Considerations Reviewed', *Econometric Institute* (April 1962).

which states explicitly that the firms decisions on relative factor inputs is a function of the value of relative factor prices. We use a variant of (5.2) in the empirical work below.

It is important to note that the expansion path function (5.2) is an equilibrium relation. This concept is used in its static sense to mean that the firm or economic unit whose decisions on relative factor inputs are described by (5.2) achieves its desired labour–capital ratio, instantaneously, for any given variation in ρ. In another sense, equation (5.2) assumes that it is possible to vary u, for a given change in ρ, to achieve the level of u consistent with κ' and σ with the only constraint on the variation of u being the technology as expressed in κ' and σ. This is a fiction for anything but a very long-run analysis. For periods of time which are typically considered, there are many obstacles to the achievement of equilibrium of an institutional, technical and psychological nature.† In the next section we discuss a major limitation to the instantaneous achievement of the desired u ratio, and methods to represent this limitation in our production model.

LONG- AND SHORT-RUN PRODUCTION

We begin with two definitions. Let the *short run* be a period of time within which the elasticity of substitution is determined by the capital in place. In the *long run* the ease of substitution is determined by the fund of feasible technical knowledge.

As implied above the rationale for this time distinction is that once a piece of equipment has been produced, on the basis of a best practice technique,‡ it is relatively difficult to vary the amount of labour used in co-operation with the machine. For the machine or structure has been designed to produce an optimum output in co-operation with a certain amount of labour. True, minor variations of labour applied to the machine may possibly be compensated by variations in the machine time utilized while approximating the optimum output. Yet, the degree of substitutability is circumscribed; in the short run, the combination of labour and capital is characterized by a high

† See M. Nerlove, 'Distributed Lags and Demand Analysis for Agricultural and Other Commodities', *Agricultural Handbook*, no. *141*, U.S. Department of Agriculture (June 1958).

‡ See Anne P. Grosse, 'The Technological Structure of the Cotton Industry', in *Studies in the Structure of the American Economy*, by W. W. Leontief et al. and W. E. G. Salter, *Productivity and Technical Change*.

degree of complementarity. However, whether fixed production coefficients (elasticity of substitution equal to zero) are symptomatic of the short run is an empirical question.

Imagine a certain capital item in place and suppose that relative factor prices have remained constant during its gestation period to the present. And, suppose now that relative factor prices change such that the price of labour services falls relative to capital services. The question is: to what extent can the capital be reduced (aside from depreciation) and to what extent can more labour be applied to the equipment, keeping output constant, in response to the change in relative factor prices? To some extent, variations in the combination are possible (for example, more careful planning of 'down' time, or the addition of assistants to feed material to the machines if they are not automatically fed already, etc.). But, clearly the variations are limited.

Suppose that after the initial change in relative factor prices, there are no further changes. The firm wishes to adjust the capital stock–labour ratio to reach the new expansion path for any variation in output. We know that the expansion path cannot be reached immediately because of the rigidity of the fixed capital. However, if the expansion path could be reached instantaneously for any change in relative factor prices, then we say the firm operates under long-run production conditions. Under these conditions the ease of substitution is limited not by the resistance of the capital stock to change, but by the whole range of feasible technical alternatives facing the firm. For if the firm could operate under long-run conditions, the combinations of factors it would choose would involve labour and the whole range of different capital stocks—different by virtue of representing alternative techniques.

Although the factor-input ratio is relatively insensitive to the factor-price ratio, because of the capital in place, this same capital embodies consideration of relative factor prices at the time the capital was installed.† And, at the time of its installation, the set of constraints that restricted variations in the capital–labour combinations could not have been the installed capital, since it was not installed yet. The set of constraints must have been the whole range of feasible technical alternatives. It is easy to conclude that the ease of substitution

† J. Schumpeter, *History of Economic Analysis*, p. 1030, footnote 5.

between labour and the whole range of technical alternatives is greater than the ease of substitution between labour and any given alternative which is finally chosen. In short, the long-run elasticity of substitution—that which refers to the ease of substitution between labour and the whole range of feasible technical alternatives—is larger than the short-run elasticity of substitution—that which refers to the ease of substitution between labour and the capital in place.†

At any moment there is a range of technical alternatives which are feasible. These are either at the end of their planning stage or are feasible from a production point of view. Mrs Robinson's concept of a spectrum of techniques is descriptive of this phenomenon.‡ This spectrum comprises what can be called the technology of the moment.

A long-run function embodies the technology of the moment. It describes the relation between given inputs and the maximum output, the only constraint being the technology of the moment. The short-run function describes these relations, but under an additional constraint, the capital in place. In relaxing the capital in place constraint, the short-run production function merges into the long run.

The difference between the two elasticities depends on two things: the restraint exercised by the existing technology on the long-run elasticity and the degree of rigidity of the capital to vary in response to current changes in relative factor prices. Clearly, if the existing technology permits capital to be substituted with relative ease, but the existing stock of capital changes very little, if at all, to market stimuli, then the difference between the two elasticities is large. There is little we can say about the size of the long-run elasticity—it is what the technology determines it to be. But the reasons for the rigidity of the capital stock can be made manifest. They include the average economic life of the capital items, the rate of investment, and the range of variation of the application of labour to the existing capital stock. As an approximation, one can say that changes in

---

† This distinction is similar to the Marshallian short- and long-run distinction. In the Marshallian world, the constraints that limit the short-run variation of all factors of production disappear in the long-run. In terms of the present dichotomy, the elasticity of substitution increases as the capital in place constraint is relaxed. Thus the distinction between short- and long-run elasticities imply the Marshallian distinction.

‡ Joan Robinson, *The Accumulation of Capital* (Homewood, 1956), chap. 10.

depreciation and the rate of investment cannot effect substantial variations in the capital–labour ratio in the short run, say, one or two years. We are then left with a technological reason for the rigidity of the capital stock. Hence, the major part of the difference between the two elasticities is attributable to the characteristics of the technology.

An immediate question arises as to what we want to measure, the short- or long-run production function. The answer is that both are necessary. There are two reasons for this, one being related to the measurement problems, and the second to problems of prediction. Suppose that we are only concerned with the short-run function and that our measurement procedure is oriented accordingly. It is still necessary to account explicitly for the long-run function, since it is difficult to account for the short-run forces without holding the long-run forces constant. Hence the measurement of short- and long-run functions is necessary. As for prediction of the relevant quantities, even though our interests may lie in the short-run movements, knowledge of the long-run function provides the basis for the prediction of changes in the relevant magnitudes when they are in disequilibrium situations.†

A MODEL OF SHORT- AND LONG-RUN PRODUCTION PROCESSES

There remains the task of building the analytical, short–long run, time dimension into the model of the firm outlined above. A leading requirement is that the resulting construction be amenable to empirical tests. There are two methods of which I am aware which meet this requirement, one developed by Salter and the other by Brown and De Cani.‡ The latter is presented here not only for the obvious reasons, but because it permits the measurement of long-run, short-run, and even inter-mediate-run production functions by standard econometric techniques.§

† See J. Viner, 'Cost Curves and Supply Curves', *Zeitschrift für Nationalökonomie* vol. III (1932), p. 14 of the Clemence reference.

‡ The Johannsen model is much more explicit and elegant than the one I present below. However, to my knowledge it has not been modified so as to be amenable to empirical tests.

§ For a different view, see W. E. G. Salter, *Productivity and Technical Change*, p. 7.

We begin from the assumption that the past history of the capital–labour price ratio, as well as the current factor-price ratio, is relevant to the determination of the current labour–capital input ratio. We can denote the ratios at time points as follows: ρ_0 is the capital price–labour wage ratio at time t, ρ_{-1} is the value of the ratio one period prior to t; similarly u_0 is the current labour–capital ratio, etc. We assume that u_0 is influenced not only by ρ_0 but by $\rho_{-1}, \rho_{-2}, \rho_{-3}, \dots$. Now variations in the current factor-price ratio may be very influential in eliciting variations in the current relative labour-input ratio. This means that it is not difficult to substitute labour for capital in the current period in response to changes in current relative factor prices. On the other hand, if changes in u_0 are somewhat insensitive to variations in ρ_0, then it is difficult to substitute labour for capital in the current period in response to changes in relative factor prices. It follows that the more the past history of the factor-price ratio affects the current factor-input ratio, the more resistant to change will be the installed capital–labour ratio to current changes in the relative factor-price ratio.

Let us approximate the historical stream of the factor-price ratio, whose variations influence the current factor-input ratio, by a distributed lag of the following type

$$\rho = \rho_0 \rho_{-1}^{\lambda} \rho_{-2}^{\lambda^2} \dots \rho_{-n}^{\lambda^n}, \tag{5.3}$$

where ρ is what we call the 'decision based' factor-price ratio—it is the factor-price ratio that determines the proportions of labour and capital in the production process. We restrict the constant, λ, to the interval $0 \leqslant \lambda \leqslant 1$. Equation (5.3) claims that the effect of the factor-price ratios decreases geometrically the further back they are in the past. Now, if $\lambda = 0$, then $\rho = \rho_0$, and the decision based factor-price ratio depends only on the current factor-price ratio. This is a multiplicative version of the well-known distributed lag introduced by L. M. Koyck.†

† *Distributed Lags and Investment Analysis* (North-Holland Publishing Co., 1954). In order to use the Koyck distribution in multiplicative form, it is necessary that ρ meet certain conditions. Of course, we must have $\rho > 0$ for all t. Then, if $\rho < 1$ and increases through time, $\lim\limits_{t\to\infty} \rho = 0$, and the infinite product diverges to zero; if $\rho > 1$ and decreases through time then $\lim\limits_{t\to\infty} \rho = \infty$ and the infinite product is divergent. Therefore, we can only use the Koyck distribution in multiplicative form if (a) initially $\rho < 1$ and decreases through time, and (b) initially

From an economic point of view, the λ coefficient is interpreted as the degree of rigidity of substitution of the installed equipment in response to a change in the current factor-price ratio. Thus, if $\lambda = 0$, then the decision-based factor-price ratio, ρ, is solely determined by the current factor-price ratio, ρ_0; in effect the installed equipment offers little resistance to a change in factor proportions solely in response to changes in the current factor-price ratio. Clearly, the degree of resistance is represented by the size of λ; let us call λ the 'rigidity parameter'. Ignoring all psychological and institutional limitations on the variation of the factor-input ratio, the rigidity parameter is technologically determined. That is, it is determined by the nature of the installed capital in terms of its willingness to be substituted for labour for a given output. Some types of equipment—probably the less automatic types—have this ability to some extent. Also, the less durable types can be more easily substituted for labour at given outputs than the more durable types.

This distributed lag (5.3) can be combined with the expansion path function (5.2) and we obtain

$$u_0 = \kappa'^{-\sigma}(\rho_0 \rho_{-1}^{\lambda} \rho_{-2}^{\lambda^2} \cdots \rho_{-n}^{\lambda^n})^{\sigma}. \tag{5.4}$$

This states that the current factor ratio depends on the relative capital intensity parameter, the elasticity of substitution, the rigidity parameter, and on the current and historical factor-price ratios. If (5.4) is lagged one period and raised to the λth power, we have

$$u_{-1}^{\lambda} = \kappa'^{-\sigma\lambda}(\rho_{-1}^{\lambda} \rho_{-2}^{\lambda^2} \cdots \rho_{-(n+1)}^{\lambda^{n+2}})^{\sigma}. \tag{5.5}$$

Dividing (5.5) into (5.4) produces

$$u_0 = \kappa'^{-\sigma(1-\lambda)} \rho_0^{\sigma} u_{-1}^{\lambda}. \tag{5.6}$$

Equation (5.6) is the short-run form of the expansion path function. To simplify the exponents, (5.6) can be rewritten as

$$\rho_0 = \kappa'^{(1-\lambda)} \left(u^{1/\sigma}\right) \left(u_{-1}^{-\lambda/\sigma}\right),$$

$\rho > 1$ and increases through time. Actually, all we need is that ρ be bounded; this takes care of (a) and (b).

If the crucial assumption—i.e. the impact of the ratios decreases geometrically—does not hold empirically, there are alternative, and more general distributed lags which can be tried before rejecting this particular method of treating the time-dimension problem.

so that the short-run relative capital intensity parameter is $\kappa'^{(1-\lambda)}$, and the short-run α is $\alpha = 1 - 1/\sigma$. Hence the short-run CES production function which accompanies (5.6) is

$$X = \gamma'[\kappa^{(1-\lambda)}C^{-\alpha} + (1-\kappa)^{(1-\lambda)} N^{-\alpha}]^{-\nu/\alpha}. \qquad (5.7)$$

The long-run expansion path function and production function depend on the degree of rigidity of the installed equipment to current changes in ρ, i.e. they depend on λ. If $\lambda = 0$, (5.6) becomes

$$u_0 = \kappa'^{-\sigma}\rho_0^{\sigma}, \qquad (5.8)$$

which is the expansion path function (5.2) with which we began (since $\rho = \rho_0$). But if $\lambda \neq 0$, we still would like to know what the long-run functions will be. In this case, we assume that in the long run, steady-state conditions will prevail, such that $u_0 = u_{-1}$ which yields from (5.6)

$$u_0 = \kappa'^{-\sigma}\rho_0^{\sigma/(1-\lambda)}. \qquad (5.9)$$

Now κ' is the long-run capital intensity coefficient and $\sigma/(1-\lambda)$ is the long-run elasticity of substitution. The long-run production function that accompanies the long-run expansion path function (5.9) is

$$X^* = \gamma[\kappa C^{-\alpha*} + (1-\kappa) N^{-\alpha*}]^{-\nu/\alpha*}, \qquad (5.10)$$

where X^* is long-run output, i.e. the output toward which the system would tend given the constraint of the existing fund of technical knowledge and the inputs N and C.† The output X^* is derived with no restrictions on substitutions from the existing capital. Also, we interpret σ from

$$\alpha^* = -\left(1 - \frac{1-\lambda}{\sigma}\right).$$

In sum, the interpretation of the long- and short-run output can be made as follows. The short-run output is produced by a combination of factors of production which are relatively invariant for given changes in the current factor-price ratio. The long-run output is produced by a combination of factors which can vary with an ease up to the technologically determined elasticity of substitution. The rigidity parameter λ determines the extent

† There is no reason to expect the γ and ν parameters to differ between the long- and the short-run production functions, since the difference between the two functions derives from the difference in the relations between the factors of production, and γ and ν do not enter these relations.

to which the long-run production relationship differs from the short-run. It implies that the more rigid is the current factor-input ratio to variations in the current factor-price ratio, the larger is the discrepancy between the short- and long-run production relations. This follows from what was said in the introduction to the present chapter.

One property of the model is that the short-run σ can never be larger than the long-run σ. However, it is not assumed that the short-run σ is zero. It could take on any value, empirically, although we expect it to be small.

We have said nothing so far about the short- and long-run capital intensity parameters. The short-run parameter is $\kappa'^{(1-\lambda)}$ and the long-run parameter is κ'. Since $(1 - \lambda) < 1$, the short-run capital intensity parameter is larger than the long-run κ. Is this consistent with our interpretation of κ? Recall that a large κ means that for a given σ, a given labour–capital ratio and given output, the marginal product of capital is large relative to that of labour. Since relatively more capital is to be used in the long run, its long-run marginal product is smaller than the short-run marginal product. Such a movement along the isoquant is precisely what one would expect.

This movement, denoted by a difference between the long-run and short-run σ's and κ's, does *not* signify a technological change. The technology is the same in both time periods. What we are concerned with here is the path which production takes to reach the optimum use of the prevailing technology. The difference between X and X^* represents the cost of having on hand a capital stock that resists change in response to change in factor prices, i.e. it represents the cost of a certain kind of economic inflexibility.

Now, let us see what happens when technology does change.

PRODUCTION IN THE SECULAR PERIOD

We have defined the long- and short-period production processes such that a longer time period (analytically, of course) is achieved by eliminating the obstacle to the substitution of capital for labour in the short run. We have assumed that no technological change takes place in either period. If there is a technological change, though, then the fund of technological knowledge which operates as a constraint on substitution possibilities in the long run must change. This changes the long-run production function, of course; the difference between the long-run function and the short-run function is altered.

Now, a secular production period is defined as one in which the long-run production function can vary, i.e. as one in which the nature of the equipment which embodies the old technology and the applicable fund of technological knowledge may vary in a significant† way. In the secular period, all restraints are suppressed.

Let us assume that the short- and long-run production functions have remained unchanged for a certain period of time, say t years. Within these t years, there may have been changes in economies or diseconomies enjoyed by the firm as it varied its scale of output. But this does not constitute technological change.

A technological change occurs when the long-run *structural* relationship between inputs and output changes in a significant way, for example, when the parameters of the CES production function, γ, κ, σ, ν and λ, that rule in the t years are no longer valid in year $t+1$. We say that this technological change has ushered in a new 'technological epoch', which is defined as a period of time within which the short- and long-run production functions are *stable*. (The criteria for stability are discussed below.)

The number of technological epochs is equal to the number of the significant changes in the fund of technological knowledge— knowledge that is sufficiently crystallized to be used in designing capital items. There can be no pre-judgement as to the length of the epochs. However, we might guess that the more significant the change in technological knowledge the longer the epoch.

This discrete or epochal change in the characteristics of an abstract technology is an aspect of the watershed analysis that was pioneered by Joseph Schumpeter.‡ In contrast, gradual changes in the characteristics of an abstract technology can occur—these are the type of changes suggested by Abbott Payton Usher.§ It is possible to measure both types, but this is developed in Chapters 8 and 9.

---

† The word 'significant' is used in the statistical sense; criteria for determining significance are outlined below.

‡ *Business Cycles* (McGraw-Hill, 1939).

§ *History of Mechanical Inventions* (McGraw-Hill, 1954).

THE TRANSITION PERIOD

Does an epochal change occur in one year, three years, etc.? How long is the transition period from one epoch to another? If we are measuring the production process of the firm, this is not too much of a problem, for each firm can usually be identified with a particular technique. The problem arises when we wish to measure production processes for an aggregate larger than a firm, say an industry. Thus, one firm in the industry may implement a new technology at t; another firm at $t+1$, and so on; during the time the major firms have introduced the new technology, say, at $t+8$, another technology is introduced and one firm begins to implement it at $t+4$, another at $t+5$, etc. The point is that the gradual introduction of technology blurs the epochs as they have been defined. Of course, we can guess that a significant change will be detected by our tests, but, when an aggregate is being considered, the structural change may be more Usherian than Schumpeterian.†

Transition periods between epochs in different industries vary. In an interesting study on the diffusion of technical change for twelve innovations, Edwin Mansfield‡ finds that (*inter alia*) 'the rate of imitation varies widely. Although it sometimes took decades for firms to install a new technique, in other cases they followed the innovator very quickly. For example, it took about 15 years for half the major pig-iron producers to use the by-product coke-oven, but only about 3 years, for half of the major coal producers to use the continuous mining machine.'§ From this pattern it follows that the epochs for an aggregate such as an industry are more sharply defined when the rate of imitation is high than when it is low, for then the structural breaks are more distinct.

† It may be objected that there is a counterpart problem for the firm: at t, a bank of equipment is changed over to a new technology, at $r+1$ another bank is changed over, etc.; thus even in the firm there is a gradual change depending on the rate of depreciation, the cost of the new investment and degree of technological interrelatedness. See M. Frankel, 'Obsolescence and Technological Change', *American Economic Review*, vol. 45 (June 1955), p. 296.

‡ Technical Change and the Rate of Imitation', *Econometrica*, vol. 29 (October 1961), pp. 741–66. Another recent paper on the diffusion problem is by Z. Griliches, 'Hybrid Corn: An Exploration in the Economics of Technological Change', *Econometrica*, vol. 25 (October 1957), pp. 501–22. The problem is looked at from another point of view by Salter, *Productivity and Technical Change*, chap. 4.

§ E. Mansfield, 'Technical Change and the Rate of Imitation,' *Econometrica*, vol. 29 (October 1961), p. 744.

The rate of imitation, in turn, depends on the rate of investment, since many innovations are carried into place by means of investment. For when the opportunity to change the existing capital stock arises, either through replacing the depreciated equipment or adding to the existing stock, the firm probably purchases or constructs capital which embodies the most productive techniques.† If the innovation requires investment for its implementation, if the technological change is of the embodied type, then the higher the rate of investment relative to the capital stock, the more distinct will be the technological epochs.

If the innovation does not require much investment to implement it, then the transition period between epochs may be smaller than if the innovation were more of the embodied type. However, in this case, the innovation would probably be too insignificant to generate an epochal change. But the question of the relation of investment to innovation requires a lengthier disquisition to which the following chapter is devoted.

SUMMARY

Three time periods have been defined. The *short run* is a period within which the ease of substitution between capital and labour is circumscribed by the rigidity of the installed capital in response to variations in relative factor prices. In the *long run*, the constraint exercised by the installed capital vanishes and is replaced by the fund of technical knowledge. This fund of technical knowledge contains the alternative capital–labour combinations under which production is feasible and thus determines the elasticity of substitution when the technological character of the capital in place can be varied without restraint. The *secular period* of production, in turn, relaxes the constraint given by the fund of technical knowledge; in the secular period, technology changes. If the technology is invariant for a given period, a technological epoch is defined. Thus, there are two or more epochs in the secular period. This is a Schumpeterian type of technical change. An Usherian technological change is

---

† When a firm invests, it does not mean that the new capital items always embody a significantly different technology from the technology embodied in the existing stock. If technological complementarities among existing capital items are present, then replacement capital, at least, would have to be similar to that which it is replacing. Of course, when whole plants are replaced or built, it is safe to assume that they represent best practice techniques.

represented in the secular period by gradual rather than discrete changes in an abstract technology.

The difference between the long- and short-run elasticities of substitution in any given epoch depend on the lifetime of the capital stock, the rate of investment, and the particular technology underlying the equipment. Since it makes a considerable difference whether the production process is of the long- or short-run type, any special policy question or research objective requires a clear understanding of which type of production process is relevant.

The long- and short-run time dimension is built into the theory of the firm by postulating that a distributed lag in relative factor prices determines relative factor inputs. In the equilibrium model, only current factor prices—not the historical stream of factor prices—determine relative factor inputs. This assumes that a change in relative factor inputs is accomplished instantaneously in response to changes in relative factor prices. In the short-run model, the past stream of relative factor prices, as well as the current value, influence relative factor inputs. A simple Koyck distributed lag is used, but there is no reason in principle why more complicated lag systems cannot be embedded in a production model. The model gives the expected result that output is greater in the long run, when only technology constrains the movement in relative factor inputs, than in the short run, when the capital in place constrains the movement in relative factor inputs.

The length of the transition period between technological epochs is seen to depend on whether or not the innovation requires investment in fixed assets to implement it. This brings into our discussion the question of embodied technological change to which we now turn.

6

EMBODIED TECHNOLOGICAL PROGRESS

Recently, Professor R. Solow and W. E. G. Salter introduced a typology of technological changes which emphasizes the method, *inter alia*, by which these changes are actually introduced into the production process. Certain technological changes are designated as *embodied*; in Professor Solow's words:

> Improvements in technology affect output only to the extent that they are carried into practice either by net capital formation or by the replacement of old-fashioned equipment by the latest models, with a consequent shift in the distribution of equipment by date of birth.†

Salter's statement can also be quoted:

> A...feature of the model is the role of gross investment as the vehicle of technical change. When there is no technical change, investment is required only to make good the depletion of the existing capital stock through physical deterioration, and to add to this stock. But when technical change is taking place, gross investment has another extremely important role: that of providing the necessary specialized capital equipment required for new techniques, irrespective of whether or not they are more or less mechanized than their predecessors. Without gross investment improving technology that requires new capital equipment simply represents a potential for higher productivity; to realize this potential requires gross investment. An economy with a low rate of gross investment is restricted in the rate at which new techniques can be brought into use; an economy with a high rate of gross investment can quickly bring new methods into use, and thus realize the benefits of improving technology.‡

An alternative method of introducing technological improvements is called *disembodied* by Solow; this results in an alteration of the production function but does not require gross investment to carry it into place. That is, the productivity of both old and

---

† R. Solow, 'Investment and Technical Progress', in K. J. Arrow, S. Karlin and P. Suppes, editors, *Mathematical Methods in the Social Sciences, 1959* (Stanford, 1960), p. 91.
‡ W. E. G. Salter, *Productivity and Technical Change*, p. 63.

new investment goods rises. Managerial and/or organizational changes are usually cited as examples of disembodied technological progress.

It has been claimed that certain old-style models do not explicitly recognize the embodiment of technological progress.† Furthermore, it is suggested that initially an increase in investment in the old-style model generates a smaller rate of growth of output than the same increase in investment in the embodied type model. That is, the effects of investment changes are biased downward in the old model. These assertions seem to have been accepted into the body of economics, but I believe they are incorrect. The present chapter indicates the correct role that the disembodied-embodied distinction plays in the construction of capital stock measures and economic growth.

I first outline Solow's original model and then proceed to discuss the old and new views of investment.

SOLOW'S EMBODIED TECHNOLOGICAL CHANGE MODEL

The Solow embodied technological change model focuses on $C_v(t)$, the number of capital items produced at time v and still operative in the current period. Each vintage investment co-operates with a quantity of labour, $N_v(t)$, to produce a given output at time t, which is denoted by $X_v(t)$. By integrating over all vintages we obtain total output at any given time,

$$X(t) = \int_{-\infty}^{t} X_v(t) \, dv. \qquad (6.1)$$

For each vintage capital good, there is a production function; if the Cobb–Douglas form is specified, we have

$$X_v(t) = F(v, t) \, N_v(t)^\alpha \, C_v(t)^{1-\alpha}, \qquad (6.2)$$

where α is the elasticity of production with respect to the labour

† Solow, *op. cit.* p. 90. It has been shown that in the long run the embodied and disembodied models yield the same rate of growth when the elasticity of substitution between labour and capital is unity. However, when that elasticity differs from unity, differential rates of growth may result. See R. C. O. Mathews, 'The New View of Investment: Comment', *Quarterly Journal of Economics*, vol. 78 (February 1964), pp. 164–71, and the reply by E. S. Phelps and M. E. Yaari in the same issue. This is not the problem in the present chapter though. Our objective is to indicate that the old style model when properly constituted yields the same theoretical results as Solow's model.

employed on vintage v capital goods, and $F(v, t)$ denotes the efficiency of the process which utilizes vintage v capital goods. Solow, and others who work with this model, specify an exponential efficiency term,

$$F(v, t) = B e^{\lambda v + gt}, \tag{6.3}$$

where B, λ and g are constants; λ is the rate of productivity advance of the vintage capital and g is the rate of productivity advance due solely to the passage of time.[†] Hence, g is the rate of disembodied technological progress.

The supply of labour is given by

$$N(t) = \int_{-\infty}^{t} N_v(t) \, dv, \tag{6.4}$$

which implies that it is utilized in association with capital of all vintages. Moreover, it is assumed that capital goods decay at a constant rate due to physical wear and tear; this is equivalent to applying a declining balance depreciation formula (the annual depreciation charge is obtained by applying a constant percentage to the undepreciated part of the investment); we have

$$C_v(t) = I(v) e^{\gamma(v-t)}, \tag{6.5}$$

where $I(v)$ is investment in vintage v capital goods and γ is the rate of depreciation due to *physical* deterioration.

The labour supply must be allocated over the vintage capital goods; by invoking marginal productivity theory an optimal allocation is obtained when the marginal product of labour in all uses, i.e. in co-operation with all vintages of capital goods, is equalized. From (6.2) and (6.3) we take the marginal product of labour that co-operates with vintage v capital goods

$$m(t) = \frac{\partial X_v(t)}{\partial N_v(t)} = \alpha B \exp\left[\lambda v + gt + \delta(v - t)\right] I(v)^{1-\alpha} N(t)^{\alpha-1}. \tag{6.6}$$

Since the marginal product of labour is the same for all vintages of capital, (6.5) and (6.6) can be combined and an expression for $N_v(t)$ can be obtained

$$N_v(t) = m(t)^{-1/(1-\alpha)} (\alpha B)^{1/(1-\alpha)} I(v) \exp\left[\frac{\lambda v + gt}{1 - \alpha} + \delta(v - t)\right]$$

$$= h(t) I(v)\left[\exp zv + \left(\frac{g}{1 - \alpha} - \delta\right) t\right], \tag{6.7}$$

† Solow, *op. cit.* p. 91; B. Massell, 'Investment, Innovation and Growth', *Econometrica*, vol. 30 (April 1962), pp. 239–52; and E. Phelps, 'The New View of Investment: A Neoclassical Analysis', *Quarterly Journal of Economics*, vol. 86 (November 1962), pp. 548–67.

where
$$z = \frac{\lambda}{1-\alpha} + \delta.$$

Now, substitute (6.7), (6.5) and (6.3) into (6.2),

$$X_\nu(t) = B \exp\left[\frac{gt}{1-\alpha} - \delta t\right] h^\alpha(t)\, e^{z\nu}\, I(\nu). \tag{6.8}$$

Integrate (6.7) and (6.8) and combine the integrals, and we have the Solow embodied technological change model

$$X(t) = B\, e^{gt} N(t)^\alpha J(t)^{1-\alpha} \tag{6.9}$$

where
$$J(t) = \int_{-\infty}^{t} I(\nu)\, e^{z\nu}\, d\nu. \tag{6.10}$$

The variable $J(t)$ is a measure of the productivity adjusted capital stock.†

In the model, each vintage capital good is weighted by a productivity improvement factor, $e^{z\nu}$. This means that a given investment good is more productive by an amount e^z than the investment goods produced in the prior period. But consider the marginal rate of substitution of new investment goods, say $I(T)$, for vintage investment goods, $I(\nu)$,

$$\frac{\partial X(t)/\partial I(\nu)}{\partial X(t)/\partial I(T)} = -\frac{dI(T)}{dI(\nu)}.‡$$

From (6.9), we have
$$-\frac{dI(T)}{dI(\nu)} = e^{z(\nu-T)}.$$

In words, $e^{z(\nu-T)}$ is the increase in the investment goods, $I(T)$, required to compensate for a given reduction in vintage investment, $I(\nu)$, in order for the change in output to be zero. The more recent is the investment, i.e. the larger is T, the smaller is the increase in the Tth investment goods that is required to compensate for a given reduction in a vintage capital to maintain the productivity of the capital stock. In the Solow formulation, T is chosen as time zero with no loss of generality. Hence, the term that weights the vintage investment goods $e^{z\nu}$ is simply

† This derivation of the embodied technological change model follows Solow's faithfully (*op. cit.* pp. 91–3) except for a trivial modification. In the present derivation, a trend term was included in (6.3) to represent disembodied technological change.

‡ See M. McCarthy, *Technical Progress: A Theoretical and Empirical Analysis of its Effects on Aggregate Output and of its Sources* (Southern Methodist University, 1964), chap. 5. This contains an excellent discussion of the productivity improvement weights, *inter alia*.

the marginal rate of substitution of the vintage zero investment good for the vintage t investment good.

The weights are formed from the marginal rate of substitution of the Tth investment good for the vth investment good, and are independent of all other inputs; hence, they satisfy the Leontief–Solow condition for the aggregation into a capital stock measure of technically heterogeneous capital items.[†] Notice that we took the marginal rate of substitution from the final form (6.9) rather than (6·2). This assumes that the market has performed its job of allocating labour in an optimal manner. Hence, the procedure of aggregating technically heterogeneous capital goods rests on the assumption that labour is allocated optimally. We return to this below.

It is to be noted that embodied technological change is neutral or non-neutral depending on the size of the elasticity of substitution between labour and capital. If the elasticity is less than unity then, by the Hicksian proposition, a rise in the capital stock lowers the income share of capital and is capital-saving. Since the productivity improvement factor operates like an increase in capital then, for any given capital–labour ratio, the share of capital is reduced and the embodied technological change is capital-saving. If the elasticity of substitution exceeds unity, the embodied technological change is labour-saving and, if it is equal to unity, as it is in the Cobb–Douglas production function, there will be a neutral technological change as a result of the productivity improvement weights.[‡]

We can now turn to a comparison between the old-style model and the embodied model.

THE OLD AND NEW VIEW
OF CAPITAL STOCK

In nearly all cases, those who work with the old model approximate the services of capital by means of a net capital stock

† See R. Solow, 'The Production Function and the Theory of Capital', *The Review of Economic Studies*, vol. 23 (1955–56), pp. 101–8. Also, T. Haavelmo, *A Study in The Theory of Investment* (University of Chicago Press, 1960), p. 96 states that if all vintage investments vary as a function of a given parameter, then aggregation is possible. This is precisely the weighting scheme developed by Solow. See below.

‡ See R. M. Solow, 'Capital, Labor and Income in Manufacturing', Conference on Research in Income and Wealth, National Bureau of Economic Research (April 1961) (mimeographed), pp. 4–5.

BT

measure.† In order to compare the old and new views of capital, it is necessary to set out some of the elements of the construction of net capital stock.

A measure of the net capital stock is based on a time series of gross investment; it includes all previous investments which have not exhausted their useful lives. Moreover, each surviving investment good is added into the stock net of its loss of value. The rate of attrition of the value of capital items is called the depreciation rate. This is intended to approximate the rate of reduction in economic usefulness of productive facilities as a result of their use in production, their age and their obsolescence. In depreciation theory, obsolescence of existing facilities arises from the introduction of new and technically superior methods of production or products, and/or from changes in demand, the latter giving rise to capital gains or losses. The reason that obsolescence enters depreciation calculations is that the quality and quantity of existing facilities declines in relation to the services of new and technically superior capital goods even though the quantity and quality of the services of the existing facilities do not decline absolutely.‡ Hence the appearance on the market of technically superior capital items implies an increase in the cost of operating existing equipment, and it is this increase in opportunity cost that is represented in the obsolescence component of depreciation charges.

We can look at this in another way. Consider the marginal rate of substitution of vintage capital goods and new capital goods. As new and technically superior capital goods enter the market, the marginal product of vintage capital declines relative to the marginal product of new capital. If the market correctly assesses the relative marginal products, the value of the vintage capital will decline relative to the value of new capital; the vintage capital suffers obsolescence. How much will the relative market value of the vintage asset decline? If there is a competi-

---

† But this is quite controversial. See E. Dennison, *The Sources of Economic Growth* (Committee on Economic Development, 1962), pp. 97–8, who argues in favour of using a measure of capital stock gross of depreciation. However, we shall ignore this facet of the controversy and only deal with the relation between the net capital stock measure and the Solow productivity adjusted capital concept.

‡ S. Kuznets, *Capital in the American Economy*, National Bureau of Economic Research (Princeton University Press, 1961), pp. 59–60; G. Terborgh, *Realistic Depreciation Policy*, Machinery and Allied Products Institute, 1954, p. 33; and V. Smith, *Investment and Production* (Harvard University Press, 1961), chap. 5.

tive market for capital,† then the decline in the market value of vintage capital relative to the new capital must equal the decline in the marginal product of the vintage capital relative to the marginal product of the new investment good. We will make use of this point below.

There are numerous methods of writing off depreciable assets—the straight line, the declining balance, the sum-of-the-year's digits, and the annuity formulas are the more frequently used methods. We can illustrate the construction of a net capital stock magnitude by means of the declining balance formula

$$C_\nu(t) = I(\nu)\,e^{w(\nu - t)}, \qquad (6.11)$$

where w is the rate at which the investment of vintage ν, $I(\nu)$ is written off; clearly w includes the rate of attrition of fixed assets due to physical wear and tear as well as obsolescence.‡ For example, in terms of discrete time units, suppose that the average service life of capital is 10 years, the investment in a given year is \$100, and w is 20 per cent; then at the end of the first year the remaining investment is \$80, at the end of the second year it is \$64, and so forth. If we integrate (6.11) over all surviving vintages at each t, we obtain declining balance net capital stock

$$C(t) = \int_{-\infty}^{t} I(\nu)\,e^{w(\nu - t)}\,d\nu.\S \qquad (6.12)$$

We know that w is composed of the rate of depreciation attributable to obsolescence and the rate attributable to physical wear and tear (declining balance depreciation assumes that both components of depreciation proceed at a constant rate). Since, in competition, the value of vintage capital declines relative to the value of new capital in the same measure as the marginal product of vintage capital declines relative to the marginal product of new capital, the obsolescence component in declining

† Capital goods markets are notoriously imperfect, but we ignore this for the present purposes.

‡ In the embodied model, Solow has $C_\nu(t) = I(\nu)\,e^{\delta(\nu - t)}$ (op. cit. p. 92); i.e. the vintage investment is written off only because of physical wear and tear. This is correct for the embodied model because the attrition due to productivity improvements is treated elsewhere. But it is not valid as a designation of depreciated assets in the net stock model.

§ See the excellent exposition by R. Goldsmith and H. Kaitz of the construction of capital stock measures under alternative depreciation formulas, in R. Goldsmith, *The National Wealth of the United States*, National Bureau of Economic Research (Princeton University Press, 1962), chap. 3.

balance depreciation is clearly equal to Solow's productivity improvement factor and deterioration rate

$$z = \left(\frac{\lambda}{1-\alpha} + \delta\right)$$

in

$$J(t) = \int_{-\infty}^{t} I(v)\, e^{zv}\, dv.$$

Let us compare the net capital stock model and the embodied model within a Cobb–Douglas production world. Suppose that labour inputs and investment were constant over time, and there was no physical deterioration of fixed assets; in other words, only obsolescence or embodied technological change is occurring. The embodied model is

$$X(t) = A_1\, N(t)^{\alpha_1} J(t)^{1-\alpha_1} = A_1\, N(t)^{\alpha_1} \left[\int_{-\infty}^{t} I(v)\, e^{zv}\, dv\right]^{1-\alpha_1},$$

$$(6.13)$$

and a preliminary old net capital stock model is

$$X(t) = A_2\, N(t)^{\alpha_2} C(t)^{1-\alpha_2} = A_2\, N(t)^{\alpha_2} \left[\int_{-\infty}^{t} I(v)\, e^{w(v-t)}\, dv\right]^{1-\alpha_2}$$

$$(6.14)$$

From the embodied model, (6.13), one finds that

$$X(t) = \bar{A}_1\, e^{z't}, \tag{6.15}$$

where $z' = \lambda$, and A_1 is constant; but from the preliminary old model (6.14), we obtain

$$X(t) = \bar{A}_2 = \text{constant.} \tag{6.16}$$

Clearly, something is in error, since $X(t)$ in (6.13) and (6.14) refer to the same magnitude—namely measured output—and this cannot be double valued. Of course, our models contain the error. But the embodied model is not mis-specified, since output must grow under our assumptions and it must grow at λ rate as indicated in (6.15). The error must be in the preliminary old model because it is not depicting accurately the growth of output. If we include a trend term in the old net capital stock model, it will depict this accurately, and in order for both models to depict the true rate of growth of output, output in the old model must grow at λ rate. Thus the correct comparison should be between the embodied model (6.13) and

$$X(t) = A_2\, e^{\lambda t} N(t)^{\alpha_2} C(t)^{1-\alpha_2}, \tag{6.17}$$

not between (6.13) and (6.14). Now, under the special assumptions noted above, the time path of output in (6.17) is

$$X(t) = \bar{A}_2 e^{z't}, \tag{6.18}$$

which gives, of course, the same time path as the embodied model.†

We can continue the comparison of the two models under these assumptions: gross investment remains constant, I_0, up until t; at this point it increases to $(1+h) I_0$ and continues at that level indefinitely; also, employment is constant throughout. Now, the ratio of output at $t+r$ to output at t for the old net stock model (6.17) is

$$\frac{X(t+r)}{X(t)} = (1+h)^{1-\alpha_2} (e^{wr} - 1)^{1-\alpha_2},$$

and the same ratio for the embodied technological change model (6.13) is

$$\frac{X(t+r)}{X(t)} = (1+h)^{1-\alpha_1} (e^{zr} - 1)^{1-\alpha_1}.$$

Clearly, both models yield the same rate of growth of output as a result of an increase in investment if $w = z$ and $\alpha_1 = \alpha_2$.‡

It is Solow himself who has proved that (6.17) is the correct old-style model; at the end of his remarkable proof he states the following result: 'Thus if asset valuations faithfully reflected perfect foresight, the "homogeneous capital" model would be accurate, provided the capital stock were measured not by a count of machines but by the *real market value* of the stock of capital.'§ Of course, the rate of decline of the real market value of investment includes the obsolescence rate.‖ In short, the net

---

† In Professor Kuznets's words: 'Zero net capital formation does not...mean failure to increase the productive capacity of the capital stock. It only means limiting the increase to the sum represented by the product of the annual rate of secular obsolescence and the already existing capital stock', *Capital in the American Economy*, p. 60.

‡ A different result is obtained by Professor Solow in comparing the embodied model with a disembodied model in which investment is depreciated only at δ rate —i.e. it is written off only because it deteriorates physically ('Capital, Labor, and Income in Manufacturing', pp. 98–9).

§ *Op. cit.* p. 100. My italics.

‖ How do the old style analysts handle the assumption of perfect foresight when they construct net capital stock magnitudes? In one explicit treatment, it is assumed that the changes in the '...service value (of fixed assets)...due to obsolescence...is spread indeterminatedly over time, hence...its incidence is random. When we are dealing with occurrences spaced in random fashion over

stock model and Solow's embodied model are two different ways of conceptualizing the same economic phenomenon—but in principle both yield the same results. We noted above that if competition were perfect, and the future decline in the market value of capital proceeded at a constant rate, then the rate at which the productivity of old capital deteriorates relative to new capital—the rate is z—would be reflected in the rate of decline of the relative valuations of old and new capital— denoted by w. In principle, both z and w refer to the same phenomenon—one reflects its physical properties, the other its economic properties. In practice, though, there can be a wide divergence; it can be due to imperfections in competition, or even if competition were perfect it may be impossible to obtain accurate, independent measures of w and z. But, if w is equal to z, then, again in principle, $\alpha_1 = \alpha_2$, and the two models would yield the same growth rates. However, in empirical applications, the estimates of α_1 and α_2 would tend to be unequal, and *this is the only substantive difference* between the two models.† Unfortunately, we are faced here with a statistical specification problem about which little can be said *a priori*.‡

Note that the quality changes in fixed assets are explicitly treated in both models—in the old model, by means of the obsolescence factor in the depreciation rate, and in the new model, by means of the productivity improvement factor. In both models the vintage investment are weighted before entering the respective capital stock variables. The two weighting schemes

time, the best assumption we can make is that they will occur at a uniform rate. It is reasonable to suppose, therefore, that insofar as the decline in current service values with age is attributable to the effect of obsolescence, the decline proceeds, on the average, in this fashion.' G. Terborgh, *Realistic Depreciation Policy*, p. 34. Also, see V. Smith, *Investment and Production*, pp. 143–5.

Although the rate chosen is determined empirically, this is a difficult estimation problem and one that has provoked a great deal of controversy (see below).

† The two estimates of labour's elasticity of production could differ empirically because of the intercorrelation, *inter alia*, between the time trend and the capital stock variables.

‡ We can relax the assumptions under which the comparisons are made without having to change the principal conclusion that both models must yield the same growth rate when investment is varied. For example, we can allow employment and gross investment to grow exponentially, or postulate that gross investment is a constant proportion of output. The principal conclusion remains because what is put in one model must be included in the other model if both models presume to measure the same thing. Hence the result remains unaltered had we compared the Solow capital stock model with a net capital stock model based on any depreciation formula, provided that an obsolescence factor was included in it.

differ in the way they value the productivity improvements. The Solow stock includes all surviving vintage investments, with each vintage investment good weighted by the ratio of its relative marginal product to the relative marginal product of a 'numeraire' vintage investment. In (6.13) the numeraire investment is selected at time zero. This produces a capital stock measure that is valued in constant productivity terms. Hence, as time progresses, the weight on $I(\nu)$ remains constant for given ν. In contrast, the net capital stock model includes all surviving investment goods with each vintage weighted by $e^{w(\nu-t)}$. As time progresses the weight on $I(\nu)$ in the depreciation model falls for given ν. This produces a capital stock in which the vintage investment goods are valued in current productivity terms.†

In spite of the fact that each capital stock concept assigns different weights to vintage investments, both capital stocks weight the vintage investments internally in the same way. To see this, consider the marginal products in the old net stock model of the νth and the Tth investment:

$$\frac{\partial X(t)}{\partial I(\nu)} = (1 - \alpha_2) \frac{X(t)}{C(t)} e^{w(\nu-t)};$$

and

$$\frac{\partial X(t)}{\partial I(T)} = (1 - \alpha_2) \frac{X(t)}{C(t)} e^{w(T-t)}.$$

The marginal rate of substitution of $I(T)$ for $I(\nu)$ is

$$\frac{\partial X(t)/\partial I(\nu)}{\partial X(t)/\partial I(T)} = e^{w(\nu-T)}.$$

This is the increase in the Tth investment goods required to compensate for a reduction in the νth investment goods in order for the change in output to be zero.

The marginal rate of substitution of $I(T)$ for $I(\nu)$ in the Solow model is

$$\frac{\partial X(t)/\partial I(\nu)}{\partial X(t)/\partial I(T)} = e^{z(\nu-T)},$$

and since at this level of abstraction, we can have $z = w$, then it follows that the depreciation method of constructing a measure

† For a similar view, see B. G. Hickman, 'A New Method of Capacity Estimation', paper presented at the Meetings of the American Statistical Association (September 1963).

of the capital stock weights the vintage investments internally in the same way as the Solow productivity adjusted capital stock measure. In other words, in both capital stock concepts, the weights are internally identical and are equal to the ratio of the marginal product of the vth investment good to the marginal product of the Tth investment good.

One important consequence of the weighting scheme in both types of models is that they provide a basis for aggregating technologically heterogeneous capital goods. For the marginal rate of substitution depends only on time—it is independent of all other inputs. This satisfies the Leontief–Solow condition for the aggregation of inputs. Hence, by using weights which are formed from the marginal rate of substitution, not only does the Solow model, but the old-style model as well, avoid one of Mrs Robinson's objections. Of course, the last statement is valid only to the extent that the assumption underlying the marginal rate of substitution is valid. This is an empirical problem; certainly more attention should be devoted to such a crucial issue, but at least, both models are conceptually honest in dealing explicitly with the problem.†

We have seen that both models yield the same growth rates in output, and that neither one assigns a larger or smaller role to investment, unless the estimate of Solow's total improvement factor z differs from the estimate of the total depreciation rate w, and/or unless the estimates of the labour elasticity in the two models differ. It is in the estimation of the various magnitudes, then, where the two models can yield different results. The question naturally arises: can we obtain a better estimate of technological improvements in capital goods, separately from other kinds of productivity improvements, by utilizing the embodied model or by following the old approach.

Briefly, the old approach attempts to estimate the depreciation rate, ω, by various empirical and judgemental devices. Accountants, economists, statisticians and others examine service lives historically, using data reported for tax purposes (*inter alia*), scrutinize second-hand markets, interrogate producers and users of capital goods, etc. A depreciation rate, consisting in the main of an obsolescence factor and a deterioration factor, is approximated from the available data. This is then combined with a

† Additional aggregation problems relating to fixed capital assets are discussed in Haavelmo, *A Study in the Theory of Investment*, chap. 18.

gross investment series and a capital stock measure is produced, usually by the perpetual inventory method.† This requires the cumulation of the annual, capital expenditures for a period of years that is equal to the assumed life, but deducting each year's depreciation accrual. The old-style analysts then use the net capital stock measure in their model to obtain structural estimates of the production elasticities, among other things. The traditional method of constructing a net capital stock measure has not been particularly successful judging by the controversy in the area and the tongue-in-cheek attitude of the people who utilize the measures.

The alternative is the Solow stock model, but this also has not proved tractable to date to attempts at estimating the focal parameter λ in z. Solow's original attempt to estimate λ required that the labour elasticity of production be postulated, *a priori*, not estimated along with the λ parameter. This is also the procedure followed by Richard Nelson in his stimulating paper.‡ In a later work Solow attempts to estimate λ and the labour elasticity simultaneously by an iterative technique.§ That is, a λ_0 is postulated, a productivity adjusted capital stock is constructed, and an estimate of α is obtained by least-squares regression applied to (6.13). A new capital stock is then constructed with a different improvement factor λ_1, and a new regression is obtained. This proceeds until the residual variance is sufficiently low and the results appear to be reasonable. There are several problems with the iterative procedure, some of which have been noted by Berglas.‖

There is an alternative method of estimating λ, suggested by

† If balance sheet capital figures are used, the depreciation rate is still approximated by the methods indicated in the text.

‡ 'Aggregate Production Functions and Medium Range Growth Projections', *American Economic Review* (September 1964).

§ 'Technical Progress, Capital Formation and Economic Growth', *American Economic Review*, vol. 52 (May 1962).

‖ E. Berglas, 'Investment and Technological Change', University of Chicago (mimeographed), 1963. He follows up Solow's iterative procedure using Solow's data, for the most part, and finds that the λ that yields the minimum residual variance is equal to 140 per cent. He concludes that Solow's model is unreasonable. Berglas's conclusion is unacceptable because the estimates he finally obtains for the elasticity of production with respect to labour are unreasonably low. In order to use the iterative procedure to test Solow's model, the labour elasticity has to be constrained to some reasonable range. Alternatively, the Solow production function should be embedded in a complete model, which includes the marginal productivity conditions of equilibrium; and the iterative technique should then be applied to the simultaneous estimates of the complete model.

Richard Nelson,† that appears to be promising. It involves approximating the Solow stock measure by a function of gross stocks and the change in the average age of gross stocks; specifically

$$J(t) = B(1 + \lambda)^t C_G[1 + \lambda(\bar{a}_{t-1} - \bar{a}_t)],$$

where C_G is the gross capital stock at time t, B is a constant and $\bar{a}_t$ is the average age of gross capital at time t. By including the approximate J in a regression model, λ may be estimated along with the other parameters in the model.‡ This would be an enormous step forward because then the obsolescence factor would be estimated within the model. It would supplant—or at least complement—the controversial methods used by statisticians, etc., who give us the depreciation rate.

CONCLUSIONS

Suppose there are two economies: one in which technological change is embodied and proceeds at a given rate, and the other in which technological change is disembodied and proceeds at the same rate. The question arises, in which economy does investment play a greater role in generating economic growth? Solow and Phelps have taught us that in the short-run embodied technological change economy, one that is characterized by a unitary elasticity of substitution, a percentage increase in investment will exert a larger effect on output than the same percentage change in investment in the short-run disembodied technological change economy. They have indicated many more interesting and important differences between the two economies. *But their comparisons refer to two different economies, not two different models or two different views of the same economy.*

In addition to the Solow–Phelps points of focus, there is an important dimension of the embodied-disembodied distinction that seems to have been neglected. Both types of technological progress refer to secular changes in production process, i.e. they alter the production function for given values of real capital and labour. These changes can be of a non-neutral as well as a neutral type, but we have played down the former in these

† *Op. cit.* pp. 11 ff. A variant is employed in the paper by F. Raines, 'An Econometric Study of Labor Productivity in Manufacturing and the Total Private Nonfarm Economy', presented at American Statistical Association Meetings (September 1963).

‡ See Raines, *op. cit.* for some interesting, but preliminary results.

remarks. Yet, each type of technological change can generate a new technological epoch. How rapidly does a new epoch succeed an old one? It would seem that the transition between epochs depends, in part, on the degree to which the new technology requires investment goods for its implementation.† In other words, the embodied-disembodied distinction derives its importance by contributing to the explanation of the calendar time required for a transition from the production process that utilizes the old technology to one using the new technology.

The major conclusion is that the net stock model which includes an obsolescence factor yields the same growth rate as the embodied model for changes in investment and technology. The old and the new concepts of capital are simply two different ways of conceptualizing the same phenomenon. Specifically, the Abramowitz Residual, obtained by using a net capital stock measure of capital services, is an unbiased measure of the contribution to growth of forces other than unadjusted labour and capital inputs. Hence, it is not necessary to jettison the major result that has emerged on the basis of old-style net stock models concerning the striking importance to the growth of output and other variables of technological advance.‡

Whether the analyst wishes to use the old or new concepts of capital depends, at this point, on his tastes, his purposes, and the availability of data. There are no theoretical deterrents to *either* model. If he desires to quantify the embodied and disembodied components of technological progress, it is possible to obtain estimates from the net capital stock model as well as Solow's embodied model. He will find the embodied component of progress embedded in the estimate of the trend term in his

† For support of this, see E. Mansfield, 'Technical Change and the Rate of Imitation', *Econometrica*, vol. 29 (October 1961), pp. 741–66.

‡ See M. Abramowitz, 'Resource and Outout Trends in the United States Since 1870', *Papers and Proceedings of the American Economic Association*, vol. 46 (May 1956), pp. 5–23; R. Solow, 'Technical Change and the Aggregate Production Function', *The Review of Economics and Statistics*, vol. 39 (August 1957), pp. 312–20, J. Kendrick, *Productivity Trends in the United States*, National Bureau of Economic Research (Princeton University Press, 1961); B. Massell, 'Capital Formation and Technical Change in United States Manufacturing', *The Review of Economics and Statistics*, vol. 42 (May 1960), pp. 182–8; M. Brown and J. Popkin, 'A Measure of Technological Change and Returns to Scale', *The Review of Economics and Statistics*, vol. 44 (November 1962), pp. 402–11; M. Brown and J. S. de Cani, 'Technological Change and The Distribution of Income', *International Economic Review*, vol. 4 (September 1963), pp. 289–309.

regression of the net stock production function. Of course, the disembodied part is there also (holding constant non-neutral technological change); but it is possible to decompose the estimate of the trend into the two types of progress. For once the analyst chooses the obsolescence rate in his depreciation estimates, he has made a prior commitment to an embodied technological progress rate no matter what his estimate of the trend turns out to be. But this is only one procedure that could be used to obtain a measure of the two types of progress. An alternative is to estimate the Solow embodied model with a trend term representing disembodied progress. It is difficult to say which model will yield superior estimates of the embodied or obsolescence component of technological progress. We will have to wait for the evidence to accumulate, for the arguments in favour of either method are inconclusive.

In short, the distinction between embodied and disembodied progress is a real one from a theoretical point of view; furthermore, it is important from a policy point of view. But the distinction between the old-style net stock model and the Solow productivity adjusted capital stock model is not a real one; yet, it may turn out to be important from an econometric point of view.

PART II

FRAMEWORKS FOR THE MEASUREMENT OF TECHNOLOGICAL PROGRESS

7

PRODUCTIVITY INDEXES, THE SOLOW METHOD AND THE SALTER METHOD: THREE MEASURES OF TECHNOLOGICAL PROGRESS

The three measures discussed in this chapter have in common the use of a ratio analysis to uncover the movements of technological progress or productivity, although it is stretching the point to include here the sophisticated measures that Salter developed. The productivity ratios which relate output to factor inputs are taken up first. There are two types, labour or capital productivity indexes—output per unit of labour input or output per unit of capital input—and the multi-factor or total factor productivity index—output per unit of combined labour and capital inputs. We will examine both types briefly, first to determine what they represent, and to assess the reasons for their variations. We also discuss the derivation of the Abramowitz Residual from the total factor productivity index.

The Solow measure, which we examine next, separates out from the labour productivity index the effect of changing inputs and all other forces. In so doing it clarifies the underlying economics of the Abramowitz Residual.

Finally, we consider the Salter measures, which attempt to decompose the Residual into its components. Salter's work is well known—and deservedly so—not so much for the measures of technological progress he developed, but for the wealth of insight and analysis into production economics and technical change which surrounds them. We note that our comments touch upon a small part of the area circumscribed by all three measures.

PRODUCTIVITY RATIOS AND THE MEASUREMENT OF TECHNOLOGICAL PROGRESS

The two types of productivity ratios can be represented by

$$AP_N = X/N, \qquad (7.1)$$

which is the average product of labour or the labour productivity index; by

$$AP_C = X/C, \qquad (7.2)$$

which is the average product of capital, or capital productivity index, and by

$$AP_M = \frac{N}{\alpha N + \rho C}, \qquad (7.3)$$

which is the average product of labour and capital combined, where α and ρ are weights.† The AP_M ratio is called the multi-factor or total productivity index.‡ In a static sense, these ratios are interpreted as a measure of the output per unit of resources foregone in its production. This is an unassailable interpretation. It is in the dynamic sense that ambiguity arises in the meaning of the productivity ratios. For changes in these ratios between any two periods are taken as a comparison '. . . of the actual real output of (period) II with what the output of the factors would have been in II had the productive efficiency of (period) I prevailed.'§

What are the sources of change in these productivity indexes? If output is generated by the CES production function, they can be stated explicitly by writing

$$AP_N = \frac{X}{N} = \frac{\gamma[\kappa C^{-\alpha} + (1 - \kappa) N^{-\alpha}]^{-\nu/\alpha}}{N}. \qquad (7.4)$$

---

† The weights are the prices of the services of the respective factors or the shares of the income of the factors. See below.

‡ In general, the statistical requirements for constructing the productivity indexes can be stated as follows. (i) The output, input, and productivity indexes should be consistent with each other—i.e. the data for the input index should have the same coverage as the data for the output index. (ii) The estimates of each quantity should represent an internal average of the component relatives. (iii) A final requirement is that each index be derivable from the other as a product or quotient. See I. Siegel, 'On the Design of Consistent Output and Input Indexes for Productivity Measurement', *Output, Input and Productivity Measurement*, Studies in Income and Wealth, vol. 25, NBER (Princeton, 1961). p. 26.

§ J. Kendrick, *Productivity Trends in the United States*, p. 11.

Taking the total differential of AP_N we have

$$d(AP_N) = \frac{\partial AP_N}{\partial \gamma} d\gamma + \frac{\partial AP_N}{\partial v} dv + \frac{\partial AP_N}{\partial \kappa} d\kappa + \frac{\partial AP_N}{\partial \alpha} d\alpha + \frac{\partial AP_N}{\partial C} dC$$
$$+ \frac{\partial AP_N}{\partial N} dN. \quad (7.5)$$

This expression decomposes changes in the labour productivity index into (*a*) neutral technological changes

$$\frac{\partial AP_N}{\partial \gamma} d\gamma + \frac{\partial AP_N}{\partial v} dv;$$

(*b*) changes in inputs and economies resulting from changes in the scale of operations

$$\frac{\partial AP_N}{\partial N} dN + \frac{\partial AP_N}{\partial C} dC;$$

and (*c*) non-neutral technological changes

$$\frac{\partial AP_N}{\partial \alpha} d\alpha + \frac{\partial AP_N}{\partial \kappa} d\kappa.\dagger$$

From (7.5) it is observed that a change in AP_N could be due to changes in any one or several of the forces listed on the right-hand side of (7.5). It is well known that just the observation of the movement in the labour productivity index does not permit us to say which force or set of forces generated that movement; it may have been due to a change in capital inputs or to a neutral technological change. What then does a movement in AP_N denote? It does not have to denote a technological change, since $dAP_N \neq 0$ could have arisen by means of a change in capital inputs. A movement in AP_N simply denotes the change in the amount of labour foregone in the production of an additional unit of output, and that is all. Whether a change in the average product of labour is called a productivity change or not is simply a matter of terminology, but it should not be identified as a change in efficiency as we are using the term.‡

† Equation (5) omits some important sources of change in labour productivity, such as the utilization of resources and the change in market structures. See G. Stigler, 'Economic Problems in Measuring Changes in Productivity', *Output, Input and Productivity Measurement.*

‡ It is generally recognized that it is the movement in the marginal products rather than average products that are important in determining such magnitudes as factor remuneration, relative factor incomes, etc. Although the average and

THE MULTIFACTOR
PRODUCTIVITY RATIO

Here, output is expressed as a percentage of a weighted sum of labour and capital.† The weights are usually the prices of the factors in certain selected periods.‡ In certain applications, the

marginal product cannot be too far apart over large intervals, we would like a less imprecise indication of their divergence. We can see how closely the average product approximates the marginal product of labour by writing the marginal product of labour from the CES production function as

$$f_N = \frac{\partial X}{\partial N} = \left(\frac{v}{\frac{\kappa}{1-\kappa}\left(\frac{N}{C}\right)^{\alpha} + 1} \right) \left(\frac{X}{N} \right).$$

Then, taking the ratio of the average to marginal products, we have

$$\frac{AP_N}{f_N} = \frac{\frac{\kappa}{1-\kappa}\left(\frac{N}{C}\right)^{\alpha} + 1}{v}.$$

The divergence between the productivity index, AP_N, and what we would really like to measure f_N depends on the ratio (N/C), the elasticity of substitution of capital for labour (σ), the size of returns to scale (v), and the capital intensity parameter, κ. Focusing on the case for $\sigma < 1$, we can state the following.

Average product understates marginal product, (a) the smaller is the labour–capital ratio, (b) the larger is the degree of economies of scale, (c) the smaller is the capital intensity coefficient, and (d) the larger is the elasticity of substitution if capital is growing more rapidly than labour. To see the last point, we note that

$$\frac{p}{w} AP_N = \frac{pX}{wN},$$

where p is the product price and w is the wage rate; hence, this is the reciprocal of labour's share in income or product. Now

$$\frac{\partial(pX/WN)}{\partial \sigma} = \frac{1}{v\sigma^2}\left(\frac{\kappa}{1-\kappa}\right)\left(\frac{N}{C}\right)^{[(1/\sigma)-1]}\left(\log \frac{N}{C}\right).$$

If $N < C$, then $\log \dfrac{N}{C} < 0$ and $\dfrac{pX/wN}{\sigma} < 0$.

We will come back to this point in Chapter 12.

Of course, if technology remains invariant over the period for which we are using AP_N to approximate the changes in labour productivity, then the only reason for the divergence between AP_N and f_N, within this framework, is due to movements in N/C, and only if $\sigma = 1$ will AP_N be proportional to f_N, the constant of proportionality being equal to $1/v$; in this case, AP_N is a 'good' approximation to f_N, since the bias is constant. But if a unitary σ holds for any given time it is unlikely that it will hold during periods in which technology is changing in a non-neutral fashion.

† The multifactor index cannot include all factors that influence output, for if it did, all changes in the ratio would be zero.

‡ Kendrick's study is the prototype of multi-factor productivity studies; it uses factor price weights (*Productivity Trends in the United States*, pp. 8 ff.).

price weights are changed several times so as to conform to a moving set of weights. Let us examine the weighting problem first. From marginal productivity theory, we know that $q = m_1 f_C$, where q is the real rental per unit of capital, and m_1 is a monopoly factor depending on the elasticity of supply of capital and the elasticity of demand for the product. For the wage rate we have $w = m_2 f_N$, where m_2 depends on the elasticity of supply of labour and the elasticity of demand for the product. Let us assume that m_1 and m_2 vary only in response to changes in monopoly power in the various markets. We then have

$$AP_M = \frac{X}{wN + qC} \sim \frac{X}{m_1 f_N N + m_2 f_C C}. \tag{7.6}$$

Suppose now that output is produced under Cobb–Douglas conditions and neutral technological change is occurring in the form of an exponential increase in the technological efficiency parameter:

$$X = A_0 e^{\lambda t} N^\alpha C^\beta, \tag{7.7}$$

and

$$f_N = \alpha(X/N), \tag{7.8}$$

$$f_C = \beta(X/C). \tag{7.9}$$

Combining (7.6)–(7.9) yields

$$AP_M \approx \frac{X}{m_1 \alpha X + m_2 \rho X} = \frac{1}{m_1 \alpha + m_2 \beta}. \tag{7.10}$$

We come to the startling conclusion that if moving weights are employed and if *only neutral technological change is occurring, then AP_M is approximately constant.* Since it omits an important part of technological progress, this version of the total productivity index is biased downward.† In other words, movements in a changing weight version of AP_M reflect changes in monopoly forces, economies of scale, non-neutral technological changes, and, in a CES world, changes in the factors of production.

A type of total factor productivity index is used in calculating the Abramowitz Residual.‡ Given the percentage change in output over a period of time, dX/X, the percentage changes in

† It can be shown that any homogeneous production function would give us this result. The reader may wish to execute the algebra using the CES production function.

‡ M. Abramowitz, 'Resource and Output Trends in the United States since 1870', *Papers and Proceedings of the American Economic Association*, vol. 46.

labour, dN/N, and capital, dC/C, we wish to determine how much of dX/X is attributable to something other—a something called the Residual—than dN/N and dC/C. Lettering a^1 represent labour's share of income in a base period and b^1 capital's share of income in a base period. We have

$$\frac{dX}{X} - a^1 \frac{dN}{N} - b^1 \frac{dC}{C} = \text{residual.} \qquad (7.11)$$

Accordingly, the computation of the Residual proceeds easily since data for all terms on the left-hand side of (7.11) are available.

The left-hand side of (7.11) is a kind of total factor productivity index. Thus integrate (7.11), to obtain

$$\frac{X}{N^{a^1} C^{b^1}} = \int (\text{Residual}) \, dt. \qquad (7.12)$$

Here, the left-hand side is a total factor index of a form recognizable as derived from the Cobb–Douglas production function.†
Hence, the Abramowitz Residual is obtained on the basis of a production process which assumes a unitary elasticity of substitution.

Perhaps the total productivity ratio, output as a percentage of a weighted sum of labour and capital, can be used as a

† See E. Domar, 'On Total Productivity and All That', *Journal of Political Economy*, vol. 70 (December 1962), pp. 597–608. Domar recommends the use of this form of the total factor index. Kendrick's form uses a linear combination of labour and capital with factor prices as weights. What Kendrick did was to use the Euler Theorem on homogeneous functions,

$$X = m_1 f_N N + m_2 f_C C = wN + qC,$$

modified to include imperfect competition (the modification is implicit). Actually, the Kendrick form is more general than the constant weight Domar form because the latter specializes the underlying production function to one homogeneous function, the Cobb–Douglas, whereas Kendrick's use of the Euler transformation assumes that the production function can be of any form so long as it is homogeneous. If the Domar weights are allowed to vary, one obtains (for $v = 1$)

$$\frac{dX}{X} = C_1^1 \left(\frac{X}{N}\right)^{[(1/\sigma)-1]} \frac{dN}{N} + C_2^1 \left(\frac{X}{C}\right)^{[(1/\sigma)-1]} \frac{dC}{C}$$

$$= \frac{wN}{pX} \frac{dN}{N} + \frac{qC}{pX} \frac{dC}{C},$$

which is as general as the Kendrick formulation for constant elasticity of substitution production processes. It is to be emphasized that Kendrick does not use a production function directly; he uses the Euler transformation and, hence, he does not specify a particular production function. His is a very general formulation, requiring only that the underlying production function be homogeneous.

reasonably close approximation to a measure of technological change. Let us take the total differential of the total factor productivity index using the CES production function, and observe which terms of the total differential refer to technological change. Then, we will compare the total productivity ratio with those terms to determine the bias, if any, resulting from use of the total productivity ratio. The total productivity ratio is

$$AP_M = \frac{X}{aK + bN} = \frac{\gamma[\kappa C^{-\alpha} + (1-\kappa) N^{-\alpha}]^{-v/\alpha}}{aC + bN}, \quad (7.13)$$

where $a+b$ are constants. Now, take the total differential of (7.13)

$$dAP_M = \frac{\partial AP_M}{\partial \gamma} d\gamma + \frac{\partial AP_M}{\partial v} dv + \frac{\partial AP_M}{\partial \alpha} d\alpha + \frac{\partial AP_M}{\partial \kappa} d\kappa$$

$$+ \frac{\partial AP_M}{\partial N} dN + \frac{\partial AP_M}{\partial C} dC, \quad (7.14)$$

where the first four terms on the right-hand side refer to the change in the total factor productivity ratio which is attributable to technological change, and the last two terms refer to the change attributable to changes in inputs. Clearly, if the last two terms are non-zero, taken together, then the total factor productivity ratio is a biased estimate of the technological change, without considering the problems inherent in the weights, a and b at all. Writing out the last two terms of (7.14):

$$\frac{\partial AP_M}{\partial N} = X \left[\frac{v(1-\kappa)(aC/N+b)}{\kappa(N/C)^\alpha + (1-\kappa)} - b \right] [aC + bN]^{-2} \quad (7.15)$$

and $$\frac{\partial AP_M}{\partial C} = X \left[\frac{v\kappa(a+bN/C)}{\kappa + (1-\kappa)(C/N)^{-\alpha}} - a \right] [aC + bN]^{-2}. \quad (7.16)$$

In general, an unusual combination of values of coefficients would have to exist to make (7.15) and (7.16) vanish and thus ensure that the total productivity measure does approximate technological change.† At the most, the total factor index tells us the changes in the output per unit of combined resources foregone.

It is possible to determine under fairly restrictive assumptions how much bias is involved in using the total factor index as an

† If one specified a linear production function, then the chances of $\partial AP_M/\partial N$ and $\partial AP_M/\partial C$ vanishing are greater.

approximation to a measure of technological change.† However, there are more fruitful approaches to this measurement problem to which we can now turn.

THE SOLOW MEASURE OF TECHNICAL CHANGE IN THE AGGREGATE PRODUCTION FUNCTION‡

This measure introduces a new dimension in the measurement of technological change by specifying a simultaneous equation system. Not only does it utilize a production function, but the marginal productivity conditions, the conditions underlying the expansion path, are incorporated also.§ Yet, as Solow states, the measure itself is a catch-all, for it combines all factors influencing output other than labour and capital without providing a means of distinguishing the impact of the various factors.

The assumptions underlying the measure are that the economy is operating in the range of constant returns to scale and that technological change is of the neutral type.‖ If technological progress is only of the neutral type, then the production function is

$$X = A(t)f(C, N), \qquad (7.2.1)$$

where the multiplicative factor $A(t)$ measures the accumulated effect of shifts in the production function over time. Taking the total differential of (1) with respect to time and dividing by X yields

$$\frac{\dot{X}}{X} = \frac{\dot{A}}{A} + A\frac{\partial f}{\partial C}\frac{\dot{C}}{X} + A\frac{\partial f}{\partial N}\frac{\dot{N}}{X}, \qquad (7.2.2)$$

† See G. Stigler, 'Economic Problems in Measuring Changes in Productivity', *Output, Input and Productivity Measurement*, pp. 48–50.

‡ R. Solow, 'Technical Change and the Aggregate Production Function', *Review of Economics and Statistics*, vol. 39.

§ This was suggested by J. Marschak and W. H. Andrews in 'Random Simultaneous Equations and the Theory of Production', *Econometrica*, vol. 12 (July–Oct. 1944), pp. 143–205. However, no empirical findings were presented in that article. An empirical application which focuses on production function estimates and not on technological change, and which uses a method of estimating production function parameters upon which the Solow measure is also based is found in L. Klein, *A Textbook of Econometrics*. The statistical properties of this particular method of estimating parameters of a production function are examined by P. Dhrymes, 'On Devising Unbiased Estimators for the Parameters of the Cobb–Douglas Production Function', *Econometrica*, vol. 30 (April 1962), pp. 297–304.

‖ There are the usual assumptions as to the homogeneity of the labour force, the measurability of the capital stock, etc., which are required in the production function applications.

where the dots are time derivatives, for example, $\dot{X} = dX/dt$. The next step is easily understood when we state $\partial X/\partial C = q/p$, i.e. the marginal product of capital is equal to the real rental of capital, and, for labour,

$$\partial X/\partial N = w/p;$$

therefore, $\qquad (\partial X/\partial C)\,C/X = W_C,$

which is the relative share of capital, and

$$(\partial X/\partial N)\,N/X = W_N,$$

which is the relative share of labour. Now substituting these into (8.2), one obtains

$$\frac{\dot{X}}{X} = \frac{\dot{A}}{A} + W_C\frac{\dot{C}}{C} + W_N\frac{\dot{N}}{N},$$

or $\qquad \dfrac{\Delta X}{X} = \dfrac{\Delta A}{A} + W_C\dfrac{\Delta C}{C} + W_N\dfrac{\Delta N}{N},$ $\qquad$ (7.2.3)

where the Δ's are discrete approximations to the time derivatives. Equation (7.2.3) is the basic equation for which it is possible to obtain time series for every term in it except $\Delta A/A$ which is the expression for technological change. Note that (7.2.3) is the Abramowitz total factor productivity index. Thus, for each year $\Delta A/A$ can be derived as a residual once all the other terms in (7.2.3) are evaluated. But Solow simplifies the expression still further: letting

$$\frac{X}{N} = x, \quad \frac{C}{N} = \kappa \quad \text{and} \quad W_M = 1 - W_C,$$

he derives $\qquad \dfrac{\dot{x}}{x} = \dfrac{\dot{A}}{A} + W_C\dfrac{\dot{\kappa}}{\kappa}.$ $\qquad$ (7.2.4)

In order to find $\dot{A}/A$, one only needs series for output per man-hour, capital per man-hour and the share of capital.

The question which Professor Solow now asks is: how much of the increase in output per man-hour is due to technological change and how much to the increase in capital. Dividing $X/N(t)$ by $A(t)$, he finds the output per man-hour that would have obtained had there been no shift in the production function of the type measured; the quotient represents the increase in output per man-hour that is attributable to the increase in capital. The main empirical result is that for the American economy, for the

40-year period beginning in 1919, technical change accounted approximately for nine-tenths of the total change in labour productivity, the remainder being accounted for by the growth in capital.†

There are several difficulties with the Solow measure. Aside from assuming constant returns to scale in order to derive a measure of $A(t)$, what would happen if non-neutral technological change did exist in the data? There is no way of treating this phenomenon unless one assumes it away. Solow's test for non-neutral technological change is to scatter the proportional changes in the function that he has just measured against the capital–labour ratio. If there is no relationship, then he concludes that technological progress is of a neutral variety 'on average'. However, the capital–labour ratio can change in such a way as to allow the proportional changes in the function to be zero, and still there might be non-neutral technological change.‡ The Solow and Massell empirical results quantify the 'implications of an untested assumption that technological change is neutral'.§

Another difficulty with the approach is that operating on such a high level of aggregation there is a confounding of changes in the composition of output, and changes in the production function. It is only the latter that should be measured. However, if the economy utilized more intensively sectors which boast comparative advantages, the overall productivity measure would increase even though each individual sector's production function may have remained unchanged. But this is a difficulty which all aggregates bear in common.

The Solow measure also contains an arbitrary element. Herbert Levine points out that one would obtain one measure if the relative contribution of technical change were calculated

---

† A similar result was found by B. F. Massell for the manufacturing sector using the Solow measure: cf. Massell's 'Capital Formation and Technical Change in United States Manufacturing', *The Review of Economics and Statistics*, vol. 39. The Solow method was also applied to the farm sector of the United States by Lester Lave, and the Solow–Massell conclusions were found to hold there, also; see L. Lave, 'Empirical Estimates of Technological Change in United States Agriculture, 1850–1958', *Journal of Farm Economics*, vol. 44 (November, 1962), pp. 941–52.

‡ This was pointed out by Professor Solow, himself, in his 'Reply' to W. P. Hogan, 'Technical Progress and Production Function', *The Review of Economics and Statistics*, vol. 40 (4), (November 1958), p. 413; and S. G. Winter, Jr., 'Testing for Neutrality of Technological Change', Cowles Foundation Discussion Paper, no. 61 (November 1958); also see R. W. Resek, 'Neutrality of Technological Progress', *The Review of Economics and Statistics*, vol. 45 (February 1963), pp. 55–63.

§ Winter, *op. cit.* p. 4.

first leaving the remainder to capital and another measure, not necessarily the same, if the procedure were reversed.† To some extent this criticism is met by assuming an exponential rate of growth of technical progress and labour productivity.‡ But even if the Solow and Abramowitz measures were to be resuscitated, the problem of breaking open the Residual would remain. The next set of measures, developed by W. E. G. Salter, attempts to do just that.

THE SALTER MEASURE
OF TECHNOLOGICAL CHANGE

The Residual comprises various forces affecting output and labour productivity aside from the inputs, themselves. The decomposition of the Residual into its component influences on output, etc., cannot be accomplished by the methods discussed up to the present point. W. E. G. Salter has developed a measure which attempts to break the Residual open.§ Although there have been attempts to measure an isolated component of the Residual, such as returns to scale, I think Salter's measures are the first to do so in a comprehensive and systematic way.

The specific problem faced by these measures is to decompose movements over time of the best practice techniques in individual industries. The best practice technique is that which 'yields minimum costs in terms of the production function and relative factor prices of each date'.‖ According to Salter, there are three main influences on changes in best practice techniques.

The first is what we have called neutral technological change, represented by T_r (the subscript r denotes proportionate rates of change). The neutral influence bears equally on both factors of production and is measured by

$$T_r = \frac{w(dN/dt) + q(dC/dt)}{wN + qC}, \qquad (7.3.1)$$

where w is the wage rate, q is the price of capital services, and t is a unit of time. This is a measure of the extent to which unit production costs change while holding factor prices constant.

† 'A Small Problem in the Analyses of Growth', *The Review of Economics and Statistics*, vol. 42 (May 1960), pp. 225–8.

‡ Cf. B. F. Massell, 'Another Small Problem in the Analyses of Growth', *The Review of Economics and Statistics*, vol. 44 (August 1962), pp. 330–2.

§ *Productivity and Technical Change.*

‖ *Ibid.* p. 23.

A second source of change in the best practice technique is called the bias effect and attempts to quantify changes in the ratio of capital and labour which are attributable only to technical progress. Salter measures this by

$$D_r = \frac{d(C/N)}{dt} \frac{N}{C}. \qquad (7.3.2)$$

If D_r is positive, we are to infer that the bias is labour-saving— i.e. there are additional savings of labour and fewer of capital. Thus, '... the rate of growth of labour productivity exceeds the rate of technical advance, and the rate of growth of capital productivity is retarded'.† A capital saving bias $(D_r < 0)$ retards the growth of output per unit of labour and increases the ratio of output to capital.

The third source of change of best practice techniques is termed the substitution effect. With a constant elasticity of substitution (and an unchanging technology), substitution of capital for labour, for example, increases the rate of growth of labour relative to that of capital. Of course, this kind of substitution is generated by changes in the rate of growth of relative factor prices

$$\frac{dq/w}{q/w} = \frac{d\rho}{\rho}.$$

Finally, an increase in the elasticity of substitution (σ), due to a non-neutral technical change, increases the rate of growth of labour productivity, for example, while decreasing that of capital productivity if the supply of capital is increasing relative to the supply of labour.‡ As noted above, the reason is that as the elasticity of substitution increases, it becomes easier to substitute capital for labour, since capital is increasing faster than labour in supply; costs are reduced by substituting up to the limit set by

† *Ibid.* p. 39.
‡ The elasticity of substitution is given by

$$\sigma = \frac{d(C/N)}{C/N} \frac{\rho}{d\rho}.$$

Salter assumes an equilibrium situation and competitive factor markets. Now

$$\rho = \frac{w}{q} = \frac{\partial X/\partial N}{\partial X/\partial I},$$

where I is investment. Salter, treats the price of real investment as the capital costs per annum of a unit of capital, since he assumes there is no cost to the utilization of existing assets (*op. cit.* pp. 20–1, 31).

the new σ, thus increasing the marginal products (and average product) of labour relative to the marginal (average) product of capital.

Now, let N_r and C_r be the proportionate rates of change of unit labour and capital requirements respectively; i.e.

$$N_r = \frac{dN}{N}, \quad C_r = \frac{dC}{C}.$$

Salter then adds up the separate effects, after weighting them in terms of N_r and C_r. He derives

$$N_r = T_r - \Pi D_r + \sigma \Pi (q/w)_r, \tag{7.3.3}$$

$$C_r = T_r + (1 - \Pi) D_r + \sigma (1 - \Pi) (q/w)_r, \tag{7.3.4}$$

where Π is the share of capital costs in total costs.

Although there is a remarkable amount of empirical material in the book, the principal result in terms of our interests are as follows:

the variation between industries in the extent of increases in labour productivity can be explained primarily by the uneven impact of three influences: (i) improvements in technical knowledge, (ii) potential economies of scale and the extent of their realization, and (iii) factor substitution. . . .

The analysis has suggested that, to explain the data, primary emphasis must be placed on technical progress and economies of scale.†

These are well thought out measures but they embody a serious difficulty which limits their applicability. Each of the measures on the right-hand side of (7.3.3) and (7.3.4) are supposed to represent one phenomenon independently of the others; yet all types of technological change and variations in factor supplies and prices are on-going processes. It is difficult to see how Salter has held each of these constant while measuring the others. That is, each of the terms on the right-hand side of (7.3.3) and (7.3.4) involve labour, capital and factor prices, but changing factor supplies and technological progress underlay all the movements. Thus, for example, D_r can take on a non-zero value even if no change in the bias aspect of technology has occurred, provided

† *Op. cit.* pp. 143–4. The data from which these conclusions were derived were drawn from inter-industry surveys for the United Kingdom for selected years of the period 1924–50 and the United States for selected years of the period 1923–50.

that relative factor prices do change. The same type of problem is noticeable in the empirical work, for the method of first order correlations is employed in certain crucial places.[†] This statistical method is particularly unreliable in multivariate analysis such as Salter conducts.

SUMMARY

There are two types of productivity indexes: single factor indexes —output per unit of labour or capital inputs—and multifactor or total factor indexes—output per unit of combined labour and capital inputs. The static interpretation of these ratios as measures of output per unit of resources foregone in its production is unassailable. However, one must interpret their variations as measures of changes in the efficiency of the productive process with caution. For not only are the ratios affected by alterations in the four characteristics of an abstract technology, they also move in response to changes in the factor inputs, themselves. They do not indicate changes in the efficiency of production processes in the way the term is used in the present work.

In constructing total factor productivity indexes, the denominators are usually a linear combination of labour and capital with the factor prices as weights. The weighting system is important for, if moving weights are employed, the measure of total factor productivity is biased downwards.

The Abramowitz Residual is derived from a variant of the total factor productivity index, one that implies a Cobb–Douglas production function. Hence, the Residual is obtained on the restrictive assumption that the elasticity of substitution between capital and labour is unity and unchanging.

The section on productivity ratios concludes with some brief comments on the sources of change of the total factor productivity index. It is shown that, as expected, only an extremely special type of production process and factor growth configuration would permit the index to approximate a measure of technological change as we have defined it.

In the second section the Solow measure of technological progress is briefly outlined. It employs a variant of the total factor productivity index; in fact, it is the Abramowitz–Domar method of isolating the Residual. However, at the time of its

† *Ibid.* p. 126, but especially p. 131.

appearance it elucidated the underlying production and equilibrium assumptions which, in itself, was a significant contribution. Solow found that for the American economy, from 1919 to 1954, technical change accounted for nine-tenths of the total change in labour productivity, the remainder being accounted for by the growth in capital. We noted certain difficulties with the Solow measure—namely, the inadequate treatment of non-neutral technological change, and a kind of index number arbitrariness.

The third section examines the Salter measures which attempt to decompose the Residual into its components. Salter focuses on the proportionate change in each factor of production. These proportionate changes can result from neutral technological progress, non-neutral technological progress, and the substitution between labour and capital; a measure of each component is developed. His empirical results suggest that changes in labour productivity in the United Kingdom and the United States for the period *ca*. 1924 to 1950 were primarily attributable to technical progress and economies of scale. In translating an analytically correct set of definitions of the forces affecting labour productivity into measures of these forces, certain difficulties are noted which limit the applicability of the measures.

The three measures discussed here have in common the usage of ratios to measure productivity. The Solow measure isolated the Residual by using a kind of total productivity ratio. The Salter measures attempt to decompose the Residual into its components, also by means of ratios—very complex ones, to be sure. The methods differ, however, not only in that the productivity indexes do not, in general, measure technological change, but in another important respect. As a rule, productivity studies use available capital stock, whereas an analysis of technological change would approximate the services of fixed assets by a utilized stock measure, however unsatisfactory it may be. Clearly the two types of analyses are directed towards different problems, but, be that as it may, there is a question of the interpretation of productivity measures which contain utilized labour services and available capital services. This is not meant to imply that productivity studies have a monopoly on ambiguity; considerable burdens weigh upon technological change analyses also, as we have already shown.

8

THE EXPLICIT USE OF
THE COBB–DOUGLAS PRODUCTION
FUNCTION TO MEASURE
TECHNOLOGICAL PROGRESS

In the previous chapter three methods of quantifying technological progress were outlined and evaluated. These measures estimated some of the parameters of a production function, but they did so in an indirect way. The two measures to be discussed in the present chapter require direct estimates of the production function. By a direct measure I mean the application of statistical techniques to data on output, labour and capital inputs so as to drive an estimate of the explicit physical–technical relationship between these variables. Clearly, a direct measure of a production function in this sense requires that a particular form of the function be specified prior to its confrontation with data.

One of the first economists to measure technological progress by estimating directly a particular production function was Jan Tinbergen. The form he used was the Cobb–Douglas production function; and he restricted the measure to neutral technological change. I shall first set out the Tinbergen measure and then show how it is generalized to account for non-neutral as well as neutral technological progress. The generalization also permits returns to scale to be quantified. In so doing, it goes a considerable distance toward decomposing the Abramowitz Residual.

PROFESSOR TINBERGEN'S METHOD†

The particular form used by Professor Tinbergen is the Cobb–Douglas production function:

$$X = AN^{\alpha}C^{\beta}, \qquad (8.1)$$

† 'On the Theory of Trend Movement', first published in German in *Weltwirtschaftliches Archiv*, vol. 55 (1942, I), pp. 511–49, and reprinted in J. Tinbergen, *Selected Papers*, edited by L. H. Klaassen, L. M. Koyck and H. J. Witteveen (North-Holland Publishing Co. 1959), pp. 182–221. I refer to the latter source.

where A is a scale parameter. A change in A represents a neutral technological change since it does not affect the marginal rate of substitution of capital for labour. Recall that the function is homogeneous of degree $\alpha + \beta$, where α and β are the elasticities of production with respect to labour and capital, respectively.

In his studies of the efficiency of the economy, Paul Douglas either found or specified constant returns to scale. He assumed that technology was invariant in the periods he considered, and therefore the increase in labour productivity was due exclusively to the replacement of labour by capital, *cet. par.*

Professor Tinbergen introduced an additional source of change in labour (and capital) productivity, which he calls a rise in efficiency. He asserted that the production function can change, 'in other words obtain a higher volume of production with the same volume of labour and capital.'[†] This efficiency component is specified by an exponential $e^{\gamma t}$, so that the production function is

$$X = A_0 N^\alpha C^\beta e^{\gamma t}, \qquad (8.2)$$

which can be converted to logarithms and fitted to time-series data to obtain an estimate of the productivity advance coefficient γ, and the elasticities of production with respect to labour and capital α and β. Actually, Professor Tinbergen specified the α and β coefficients, *a priori*, on the basis of Douglas's findings ($\alpha = \frac{3}{4}, \beta = \frac{1}{4}$), but this is an unnecessary restriction.

Recently, there have been more elaborate attempts to estimate neutral technological change in the fashion of Professor Tinbergen.[‡] For example, Niitamo tries to measure the trend term in the scale parameter by the number of persons graduating from secondary schools. This is an attempt to determine the sources of the improvement in technology. In that sense the trend term $e^{\gamma t}$ is an expression for returns of education, research,

† *Op. cit.* p. 193.
‡ O. Aukrust, 'Investment and Economic Growth', *Productivity Measurement Review* (no. 16, 1959), pp. 35–53; O. Niitamo, 'Development of Productivity in Finnish Industry, 1925–1952', *Productivity Measurement Review* (no. 15, 1958), pp. 30–41; A. A. Walters, 'Economies of Scale in the Aggregate Production Function', *Discussion Paper, Series A, University of Birmingham*, no. 29; G. Tintner, *Econometrics*; B. Wall, 'Cobb-Douglas Function for U.S. Manufacturing and Mining, 1920–1940', *Econometrica*, vol. 16 (April 1948); R. Solow, 'Technical Change and the Aggregate Production Function', *The Review of Economics and Statistics*, vol. 39; Z. Griliches, 'An Aggregate Agricultural Production Function and the Measurement of Technical Change', *University of Chicago Office of Agricultural Research, Paper no. 6206* (August 1962).

improvements in labour skills, morale, etc. This is a dubious procedure, though, since it assumes that these forces only have a neutral effect on technology.

In retrospect, Professor Tinbergen's introduction of a trend term appears so obvious that one wonders why it was not done before. The obviousness of the innovation should not detract from its importance: it provides an operational means of quantifying neutral changes in the production process.

There are numerous deficiencies in this model even when we do not specify constant returns to scale *a priori*. In the first place, the Cobb–Douglas function specifies a unitary elasticity of substitution. Secondly, it does not permit economies of scale to vary as a function of changes in the scale of operations of the economy. Thirdly, when the model is used on aggregate data, as it so often is, it does not permit a distinction between technological change and the movements in labour from a less productive to a more productive sector.† Fourthly, it assumes that all productivity change is of the neutral type. There are problems of a statistical nature that plague the Tinbergen type model—namely, the high correlation between labour and capital, the identification of the parameter estimates, the derivation of consistent parameter estimates, and so on. But these are common to a greater or lesser degree to all direct estimates of production functions.

† The Cobb–Douglas function can be aggregated in a straightforward manner if the various variables are aggregated into micro variables by means of geometric means. Unfortunately, the analyst seldom is able to obtain the geometric means of the micro variables—arithmetic means are customarily provided—so that this constitutes a further source of specification error. However, Walters (*op. cit.* p. 10) shows that the relative biases of the parameter estimates will be equal if the relative variances of the variables are equal, which is some consolation to the empirical worker. But in addition there are the statistical problems of aggregation that have been spelled out by H. Theil, *Linear Aggregation of Economic Relations* (Amsterdam, North-Holland Press, 1954); also, see Z. Griliches, 'Specification Bias in Estimates of Production Functions', *Journal of Farm Economics*, vol. 39 (November, 1957). A noteworthy analysis of aggregation problems with specific attention to the measurement of the Residual is provided by E. Domar, 'On Measurement of Technological Change', *Economic Journal*, vol. 71 (December 1961), pp. 717–21.

The principal lesson one learns from these admonitions concerning aggregation bias is that estimates of firm production functions, and perhaps industry production functions, may be the only feasible ones.

A GENERAL MEASURE OF TECHNOLOGICAL PROGRESS AND RETURNS TO SCALE USING THE COBB–DOUGLAS PRODUCTION FUNCTION

The method proposed by Professor Tinbergen to measure technological progress does so in a straightforward manner by adding up the changes in a single parameter of the production function; these changes are susceptible to quantification by expressing all technological change in exponential form, but only neutral technological progress is represented in the Tinbergen method. Yet it is possible to generalize the method so that changes in all parameters in the production function are quantifiable. If this can be done, then non-neutral as well as neutral technological progress is capable of being measured. Not only that, but the generalization permits to a certain extent the measurement of economies of scale separately from the effects of technological change. Thus, this goes a considerable distance toward breaking open the Abramowitz Residual.†

We begin by noting that for any production function the total change in output is produced by changes in the factors of production and in the parameters that define the function itself. Let the parameters be denoted by a_i $(i = 1, 2, 3, ..., w)$. Then we can form the following identity

$$\Delta X = X(N_r, C_r, a_{i,r}) - X(N_{r-1}, C_{r-1}, a_{i,r-1}). \qquad (8.3)$$

This identity is satisfied when we know the production function and the values of the inputs for two epochs r and $r-1$. It forms the basis for the measurement of the effect of the separate forces contributing to the temporal change in output. We will show directly how it can be expanded to provide measures of the separate forces acting on ΔX. But first we must uncover epochal values for the production function.

---

† The method appeared originally in M. Brown and J. Popkin, 'A Measure of Technological Change and Returns to Scale', *The Review of Economics and Statistics*, vol. 44. It is presented here in a modified form.

STATISTICAL METHODOLOGY FOR
ISOLATING TECHNOLOGICAL EPOCHS

The meaning of a technological epoch and their changes have been discussed above in Chapter 5. Here, I shall set out the operational procedures of isolating epochs in time series data. The Cobb–Douglas function is specified but the procedure is general. It consists essentially of applying stability analysis to estimates of production functions from times series, in order to discover periods of time within which the production function is stable. To state this another way, consider two regressions, both specified by the Cobb–Douglas function; one is derived from n observations and the other derived from $n+m$ observations. Is the first regression homogeneous with the second?† If it is, then we can say, at this level, that no structural change occurred in the period from which n and m observations were drawn. In order for this conclusion to hold in a strict sense, the regression on m observations must meet the criterion of stability itself. I shall outline two procedures to isolate epochs, where the second embodies fewer difficulties than the first.

(1) Consider a regression on n observations. Is this homogeneous with the regression derived from $n+m$ observations? If it is not, then a structural break has occurred, and we cannot reject the hypothesis that the period $n+m$ constitutes a technological epoch. The next epoch may be isolated by the same procedure.

Consider the Cobb–Douglas function fitted to data on output, capital inputs and labour inputs for the period 1890–99. Another

---

† The analysis of variance and the tolerance interval test may be used to test whether the additional observations are consistent with the structure which is generated by the original observations. The Brown–Popkin measure (*op. cit.*) uses the tolerance interval test. See the excellent article by G. Chow, 'Tests of Equality Between Sets of Coefficients in Two Linear Regressions', *Econometrica*, Vol. 28 (July 1960), pp. 591–605. Chow shows that the tolerance interval test and the analysis of variance are special cases of a general theory of linear hypotheses. Since the analysis of variance is much easier to use, it is to be recommended. The reader interested in the first use of stability analysis in economics may wish to consult the important critique by C. Christ of L. Klein's first econometric model; C. Christ, 'A Test of an Econometric Model for the United States, 1921–47', *Conference on Business Cycles* (New York, National Bureau of Economic Research, 1951).

Parenthetically, I might mention that testing for a structural break is quite simple if a computer is available; one simply uses the same regression form on contiguous sets of observations while noting the parameter estimates, sampling errors, residuals, etc., for each regression.

regression is run on data for 1890–1901 to yield a second set of estimates. At this point, an F test can be performed on the residuals of the two regressions in order to test the hypothesis that the two regressions were generated by the same structure. If the hypothesis is acceptable at a suitable significance level, two more observations are added and a new regression is run, and a second F test is performed. We proceed in this way until a structural break is uncovered.

The principle deficiency with this procedure is that there is a substantial chance that we are not rejecting the hypothesis that no structural change occurred when we should be doing so— i.e. the power of the test is low. Consequently, the method may gloss over an actual structural break with the further consequence that the epochal estimates are not valid. It is possible to remedy this, still using an F test to help us discriminate between regressions.

(2) It is helpful to use the following notations to outline the second and more powerful method of isolating epochs. Let n be the number of observations used to estimate the first regression; m is the number of additional observations; p is the number of parameters (in the Cobb–Douglas case, there are four parameters to be estimated, A, a, b and c); H is the sum of squares of the residuals from the regression estimated by the $n+m$ observations; J is the sum of squares of the residuals from the regression estimated by the first n observations; and K is the sum of squares of the residuals from the regression estimated by the second m observations.

In the preceding method the number of additional observations m was less than the number of parameters p. The present method permits m to exceed p. Thus, we first run a regression using the first n observations (say, from 1890 to 1899) and compute J_1. Then run a second regression on m observations (for $m = 5$, from 1900 to 1904) to give us H_1. With these values, compute

$$F(p, n+m-2p) = \frac{H_1 - J_1 - K_1}{J_1 + K_1} \frac{n+m-2p}{p}, \qquad (8.4)$$

and suppose this is less than the theoretical F with p and $n+m-2p$ degrees of freedom at the 5 per cent level of significance; thus the second set of observations derive from the same structure as the first set of observations.† Since the obser-

† Chow, *op. cit.* pp. 602–4.

vations from 1890 to 1904 are generated by the same structure, try a regression on m additional years, say, 1905–09 to give K_2. A regression on the observations from 1890 to 1905 is required to provide H_2. Now compute

$$F(p_1, n+2m-3p) = \frac{H_2 - J_1 - K_1 - K_2}{J_1 + K_1 + K_2} \frac{n+2m-3p}{p}, \quad (8.5)$$

comparing this with the theoretical F with p and $n+2m+3p$ degrees of freedom indicates whether the observations from 1905 to 1909 are homogeneous with those from 1890 to 1904. We can proceed in this way until a structural break is uncovered, then starting at that point repeat the procedure until another structural break is found, etc.[†]

Suppose that a structural break is found, for example the observations from 1890 to 1918 generate a structure different from those of 1919 to 1923. Hence the hypothesis that somewhere in the period, 1919 to 1923, a technology was introduced which differed from the technology ruling during 1890 to 1918 cannot be rejected. But we still do not know in what year or years between 1919 and 1923 the technological change may have occurred. This is a transition period problem which was discussed above (Chapter 5). It is the period of time required to change from one technology to another.

If the transition period were very short, say one year, it would be desirable to have a method which enables us to choose that year out of the period 1919–23. Of course, m is too small to use the procedure outlined immediately above. What can be done though is to compute a regression for the period, 1890–1917 and a corresponding sum of squares of residuals, call it J^1. Compute another regression from observations from 1918 to 1922 with a corresponding K^1. An H^1 is also required from a regression on observations from 1890 to 1922. An F test can reveal whether observations from 1890 to 1917 are homogeneous with those of 1918 to 1922. If these two sets do not come from the same structure, it follows that the technological change probably occurred somewhere toward the beginning of the period, 1919–23. On the other hand, if two sets of observations come from the same structure, the technological change occurred toward the

† This is a nested design on variance analysis. See H. Scheffé, *The Analysis of Variance* (J. Wiley, 1959), pp. 178 ff., especially pp. 185–6.

end of the period 1919–23. One can try various combinations of years to narrow down the structural break.†

Suppose, however, that the transition period is very long, say longer than m ($=p$) years; this does not mean that the present procedure cannot isolate the epochs, if they exist. But a long transition period makes it difficult to determine the cut-off points for the epochs.

It may be objected that the epochal, or watershed, concept loses meaning when transition periods are very long. For then there are gradual technological shifts and cut-off points which may be impossible to isolate in the present stage of the technique. Although this phenomenon makes it difficult to employ the Cobb–Douglas function to measure technological change, it can be handled by the more general CES production function (see below). In any case no excuses are necessary. If epochs exist, but are indistinguishable in any given situation, our techniques are deficient.

There is a further difficulty common to both of the methods suggested for isolating epochs. This involves the arbitrariness of the end-points of the analysis. One usually tries to have as many observations as possible, pushing the series back as far as one can, and terminating it in the most recent year. When we apply either method to the beginning of the series—running a regression, for example, on observations from 1890 to 1899—we assume that technology was stable within that period from which the initial observations were drawn (in the example, from 1890 to 1899). The initial period can be shortened so that $m = p + 1$, but the problem still remains to a smaller extent and, as far as I can see, cannot be resolved further. Less pessimism is required for the most recent terminal period. For then one can simply employ the method suggested above for narrowing down the transition period when the transition period between epochs is less than m.

Suppose that using one or the other of the methods R epochs are isolated. There will then be R sets of parameter estimates,

† For certain purposes, one may wish to have a 'smooth time series of parameters'. Then, a moving average type of approach is in order. This involves fitting the function to the first n observations (n is the 'order of the average') obtaining one set of estimates, then fitting the function to n more observations where one observation at the beginning is dropped and one at the end added. This can be repeated until the time period is exhausted. These parameter estimates provide a 'smoothed' time series for each parameter in the function.

R sets of sampling errors, etc.† The problem of employing these statistics to measure technological change, *inter alia*, is taken up in the next section.

IMPLEMENTING EPOCHAL PARAMETER ESTIMATES TO MEASURE TECHNOLOGICAL CHANGE

The total change in output is decomposable into three forces: (*a*) the change in inputs, (*b*) neutral technological change, and (*c*) non-neutral technological change. Knowing the values of the variables for any two time points in which we are interested, together with the epochal estimates of the production function, the influence of each of the forces (*a*)–(*c*) on the total change in output can be quantified. In fact, the actual distribution of forces affecting ΔX can be approximated by the estimated distribution of forces to the degree that the epochal production functions fit the data. We proceed as follows.

First, the notation. In the Cobb–Douglas form (8.2), the inputs, combined for purposes of measuring their influence on the change in output, are denoted by F; the term through which neutral technological change operates is the efficiency parameter A (economies of scale are discussed separately below); and the term through which non-neutral technological change operates is denoted by B and refers to the parameters a and b. As before, the subscript r denotes an epochal estimate; for example, B_r represents the estimates of a and b for the rth epoch, and F_r represents the value of labour and capital for a time point in the rth epoch. The identity (8.3) may then be written in this notation as

$$\Delta X = X(A_r, B_r, F_r) - X(A_{r-1}, B_{r-1}, F_{r-1}), \qquad (8.6)$$

where ΔX is the change in output between a time point in r and $r - 1$.

A new and expanded identity can be formed from (8.6),

$$\begin{aligned}\Delta X = &\; X(A_r, B_r, F_r) - X(A_{r-1}, B_r, F_r) \\ &+ X(A_{r-1}, B_r, F_r) - X(A_{r-1}, B_{r-1}, F_r) \\ &+ X(A_{r-1}, B_{r-1}, F_r) - X(A_{r-1}, B_{r-1}, F_{r-1}). \quad (8.7)\end{aligned}$$

† Using the Cobb–Douglas function, the same regression form is specified in each epoch. This may lead to specification bias since, in general, one cannot expect the elasticity of substitution of labour for capital to be equal to unity for R epochs. However, this restriction is relaxed when using the CES production function.

This identity can be written in six different ways depending on whether we begin differencing (8.6) with A_r, B_r, F_r, A_{r-1}, B_{r-1}, or F_{r-1}. Since there are three terms in the six different ways of writing (8.7), there are eighteen terms in all. Among these eighteen terms would be:

$$X(A_r, B_r, F_r) - X(A_{r-1}, B_r, F_r), \tag{i}$$

$$X(A_r, B_{r-1}, F_r) - X(A_{r-1}, B_{r-1}, F_r), \tag{ii}$$

$$X(A_r, B_r, F_{r-1}) - X(A_{r-1}, B_r, F_{r-1}), \tag{iii}$$

$$X(A_r, B_{r-1}, F_{r-1}) - X(A_{r-1}, B_{r-1}, F_{r-1}). \tag{iv}$$

These terms represent the finite differences in (8.7) and its five counterparts where the differences are taken with respect to A. The forms (i) and (iv) each appear twice and (ii) and (iii) each appear once among the eighteen terms. Therefore, a good estimate of the contribution of the change in X attributable to epochal change in A would be a weighted average of the forms (i)–(iv), with (i) and (iv) receiving twice the weight of (ii) and (iii). Forms similar to (i)–(iv) are included in the eighteen terms. Therefore, we can evaluate the effect on the total change in output of epochal changes in A, B and F. Since these finite differences are identities, the sum of the weighted averages of the estimate of ΔA, ΔB, and ΔF approximate the actual ΔX to the degree that the difference in the epochal estimates of the production function approximate the actual difference in output. Had we wished to determine the separate influence of epochal differences in A, α, β, N and C, then (8.7) would have five terms which would have been differenced in ten ways. In any case we are equipped with a device which permits us to add up any number of influences on the change in output (or any other focal variable, for that matter). The finite differencing framework for n terms is presented in Appendix C.†

† In the Brown–Popkin article ('A Measure of Technological Change and Returns to Scale', *The Review of Economics and Statistics*, vol. 42) a total differential of the Cobb–Douglas production function was taken where not only the factor inputs but the parameters had a time dimension. The total differential was then evaluated with epochal estimates of the Cobb–Douglas production function. Since these involve discrete differences over long periods of time, the neighbourhood rule is violated. Hence, the estimate of the total change in output deviated too far from the actual change in output. The finite differencing method outlined immediately above eliminates this difficulty.

THE EVALUATION OF ECONOMIES
OR DISECONOMIES OF SCALE

The percentage change in output attributable to the exploitation of economies or diseconomies of scale may be measured as follows. Assume that firms are operating in the range of economies of scale, $a_r + b_r > 1$; where these are the estimates of the elasticity of production with respect to labour and capital, respectively, in the rth epoch. Alternatively, assume that these same firms are operating under constant returns, i.e. with coefficients $a^r = a_r/(a_r + b_r)$ and $b^r = b_r/(a_r + b_r)$. Since non-neutral technology is unchanging within epoch r, it is possible to ask and answer the following question: given the actual change in inputs in the rth epoch, what is the excess output of firms operating in the range of increasing returns over the same firms using the same inputs operating under constant returns?

Operationally, the measurement of the effect of changes in returns to scale involves the following steps. By the finite difference method, the effect on the change in output of a variation in F_r is computed using a_r and b_r. Call this component ΔX_F. Then the effect of a change in output of a change in F is computed, again by the finite difference method, but using a^r and b^r; call this $\Delta X_{F'}$. The difference $\Delta X_F - \Delta X_{F'}$ represents the change in the excess output of firms operating in the range of increasing returns over the same firms using the same inputs operating under constant returns. This complexity is the cost of using the Cobb–Douglas function. It will be shown in the following chapter that such an elaborate procedure to measure the effect of returns to scale separately from technological change is unnecessary when the CES production function is specified.

VALUE-ADDED MEASURES AS
A SOURCE OF SPECIFICATION ERROR
IN STRUCTURAL ANALYSIS

In a statistical structural change analysis, it is assumed that the relevant variables are included and that the general form of the function remains unchanged even though its values may be altered. Thus, if a Cobb–Douglas relation is specified, one usually tests whether the elasticities have changed through time, not whether the function has changed from a Cobb–Douglas to, say, a Leontief production function.

The difficult part of the assumption is the assurance that all relevant variables are explicitly accounted for. For one may find that a structural change has occurred, for example, because an input has been omitted which may have been unimportant in an early part of the period under consideration, but has become relatively more important as a function of time. The occurrence of a structural change is then spurious.

In estimating the degree of homogeneity of a production function—and hence the degree of returns to scale—especial care should be taken to include all the factors of production whose services contribute to the current production. If one or several is omitted the estimate of the degree of returns to scale is biased upward.†

In this context a problem with intermediate inputs arises. The analyst, attempting to avoid the problem, may employ national income and product estimates. For one of the advantages of operating within the national income framework is that intermediate inputs can be neglected, since the national output series are calculated net of intermediate goods. However, there is a cost to using the national output measures. It involves a specification error, the seriousness of which is difficult to evaluate. Nevertheless we can offer some hypotheses concerning it.

Consider as a first approximation a linear production function in which labour and intermediate goods (I) are the only factors

$$X = f(N, I), \tag{8.8}$$

where all variables are index numbers with a common base period. If we use a value-added output measure we have

$$X - I = \alpha N + \bar{v}, \tag{8.9}$$

or
$$X = \alpha' N + I + \bar{v}, \tag{8.10}$$

where $\bar{v}$ is an error term. The error term is introduced to show that (8.9) and (8.10) do not hold exactly. This assumes that the coefficient on intermediate factors is unity. Of course, the correct specification is
$$X = \alpha N + \beta I + v, \tag{8.11}$$

where β is to be determined empirically. Suppose that the incorrect specification (8.10) is confronted with data by least

† This has been emphasized by Z. Griliches, 'Specification Bias in Estimates of Production Functions', *Journal of Farm Economics*, vol. 39 (1957), pp. 8–20.

squares rather than the correct specification (8.11). Then, using a theorem derived by Henri Theil,† it can be shown that the expectation of the estimate of α' in (8.10) is

$$E(\alpha') = \alpha + (\beta - 1)\,p_1, \qquad (8.12)$$

where p_1 is the least-squares regression coefficient in the relation,

$$I = p_0 + p_1\,N, \qquad (8.13)$$

since all variables are index numbers $\beta < 1$, and since intermediate inputs are positively correlated with labour inputs $p_1 > 0$. Hence $(\beta - 1)\,p_1 < 0$, and the estimate of α in (8.10) is biased downward. This, of course, would bias upward an estimate of technological change. However, the production function (8.8) is quite inadequate to begin with so that these results are only suggestive.

To examine the specification bias in a Cobb–Douglas production function introduced by value-added measures, it is necessary to formulate a different value added relation—namely, gross output divided by intermediate inputs X/I. This is really an intermediate input productivity index. Denoting logarithms of variables by lower-case letters, a Cobb–Douglas production function restricted to constant returns to scale is

$$x - i = \alpha n + (1 - \alpha)\,c + \bar{v} \qquad (8.14)$$

or

$$x - c = \alpha(n - c) + i + \bar{v}. \qquad (8.15)$$

This is the form that is estimated. However, the proper specification is

$$x - c = \alpha'(n - c) + \beta(i - c) + v. \qquad (8.16)$$

Again, using Theil's theorem, the expectation of the estimate of α in (8.15) is

$$E(\alpha) = \alpha' + p_1\beta - p_2, \qquad (8.17)$$

where p_1 and p_2 are the regression coefficients derived from the auxiliary least-squares regressions

$$(i - c) = p_0 + p_1(n - c) + \text{disturbance} \qquad (8.18)$$

$$i = p_0' + p_2(n - c) + \text{disturbance}. \qquad (8.19)$$

First, we note that β in (8.16) is positive and probably so is p_1 in (8.18) (a rise in labour inputs is associated with a rise in the inputs of intermediate goods for any given technology if output is allowed to vary). This imparts an upward bias to the estimate

† 'Specification Errors and the Estimation of Economic Relationships', *The Review of the International Statistical Institute*, vol. 25 (1957), p. 43.

of α in (8.15). On the other hand, p_2 in (8.19) may be positive or negative depending on whether a rise in capital intensity, which is denoted by $(n-c) < 0$, is associated with a saving or using of intermediate inputs. If a rise in capital intensity is associated with a fall in the rate of utilization of intermediate goods, then $p_2 < 0$. Of course, different industries would probably yield different signs for p_2, but in general one would presume that it is positive. Hence, in (8.17) there are two con-flictingbi ases in the estimate of α in (8.15), and hopefully they may be mutually cancelling.

Unfortunately, this last exercise is also only suggestive, since the empirical economist has little choice in the specification of the value-added measure. These measures are usually of the form $X-I$, not X/I. Hence, the extent to which a value added measure in the form $X-I$ biases estimates of a Cobb–Douglas (or the CES) production function is difficult to say. Yet if we are interested in technological progress, then it is the changes in the parameter estimates that are important. If the specification bias is invariant through time then it will not affect our measure of technological change. The introduction of technological change into the discussion raises another source of specification error in the use of the value-added measures. For we must con-sider the effect on the parameter estimates in the unspecified relation of holding constant the coefficient on the intermediate inputs. If it has been changing due to technological progress in the correctly specified relation, our estimates of the parameters in the incorrect relation will be unstable.

Thus, suppose that we wish to measure α in

$$X - I = \alpha N + \bar{v}$$

or
$$X = \alpha N + I + \bar{v}, \tag{8.20}$$

where $X - I$ is value added. The correct relation is

$$X = \alpha' N + \beta_t I + v', \tag{8.21}$$

where β_t varies through time due to technological progress, for example, the saving of fuel inputs. The variable coefficient β_t can be stated as an explicit, known function of time, but we do not gain anything in this context. We find that the expectation of α in (8.20), the incorrect relation that is estimated, is

$$E(\alpha) = \alpha' + \beta_t p_1 + p_2, \tag{8.22}$$

where p_1 and p_2 are derived from the auxiliary least-squares regressions,

$$N = p_0 + p_1 I + \text{disturbance}, \tag{8.23}$$

$$I = p_0' + p_2 N + \text{disturbance}. \tag{8.24}$$

It is seen from (8·22) that because of structural change in the relation of intermediate inputs to output, the estimate of the coefficient on *labour* is subject to variation, even though α', the correct coefficient of labour, is stable. In general, unstable coefficients on variables that are omitted or incorrectly specified can produce instability in the coefficients of the variables that are included. Of course, if the omitted or uncorrectly specified variables possess stable coefficients, then assuming no structural change among the included variables their coefficients will be stable.

The statistical analysis of structural change in the production function outlined above reflects structural instability of omitted or incorrectly specified variables. It does this because it measures the total shift in the production function. Hence in this respect the instability (if it exists) produced by the incorrect specification of the intermediate input offers no difficulty. However, it complicates the interpretation of the estimates of structural changes of coefficients on the included variables. For instance, an estimate of a labour-saving technological change may partially or wholly result from instability in the coefficient on the omitted intermediate input variable. Unless further analysis—an analysis that includes the intermediate inputs explicitly—indicates this is not the case, all one can say is that the estimates of structural change have a particular configuration *within the value-added framework that has been used*. In sum, in using value-added measures such as the national income accounts, one obtains certain benefits—namely, the simplification in analysis that results from having to consider only two inputs, capital and labour—but their cost is the partial obfuscation of the estimates of structural change.†

† An additional benefit obtained from operating within a national income framework is that the output quantities are adjusted for changing quality, to the extent that this can be done in the present stage of index number development. See *National Income, A Supplement to the Survey of Current Business*, 1954 edition, U.S. Department of Commerce, Office of Business Economics, Washington, D.C., p. 154.

SUMMARY AND EVALUATION

The objective of the present chapter is to develop a measure of technological change which permits the decomposition of the Abramowitz Residual into its components, i.e. into neutral technological progress, non-neutral technological progress and economies or diseconomies of scale. It was asserted that a direct estimation of the parameters of a production function is required to accomplish the aim. This assertion appears to be justified even in view of the deficiencies of the methods set out in the present chapter.

The first direct set of estimates of a Cobb–Douglas type production function which were used primarily for the quantification of technological change were made by Professor Tinbergen. These estimates were based on the assumption that all technological progress was of the neutral type. By including an exponential trend term in the two-factor-of-production Cobb–Douglas relation, Professor Tinbergen is able to quantify changes in the parameter which represents neutral technological progress.

A generalization of Prof. Tinbergen's method involves adding up the effect of the changes of all parameters in the Cobb–Douglas production function—changes which represent neutral as well as non-neutral technological change. The method requires that technological epochs be isolated; these are periods of time within which no non-neutral technological progress has occurred. By employing stability analysis, these technological epochs can be isolated (if they exist) in a relatively objective manner. Having obtained epochal estimates of the parameters in the Cobb–Douglas relation, the necessary data is at hand to implement a finite differencing procedure to evaluate the effect on the change in output of changes in labour and capital inputs, of non-neutral technological changes, and of neutral technological changes. Only between epochs can the effect on output of non-neutral technological changes be evaluated, by definition of the epochs themselves. Within a technological epoch, it is possible to quantify the effect on output of the industry or economy operating in the range of diseconomies or economies of scale compared to the effect on output of the industry or economy operating in the range of constant returns to scale. The method of adding up the separate forces affecting output permits the estimation of the distribution of these forces, with an accuracy equal to the closeness of fit of the production function.

There are various deficiencies inherent in the measures discussed in the present chapter aside from the adequacy of data. They are listed below together with my own evaluation of their seriousness.

(1) The Cobb–Douglas relation is deficient, since it specifies a constant elasticity of substitution between capital and labour equal to unity. This involves a serious (for certain purposes) specification error and the adequacy of the Cobb–Douglas relation should be tested for a unitary elasticity for any data to which it is being applied. A method of testing for unitary elasticity of substitution is set out below.

(2) The impossibility of identifying the estimates when using cross-section data has been touched on, with the conclusion that cross-section data is useless except for very limited purposes in the present context. However, there is also an identification problem using the time-series data. This involves the high collinearity between capital data and employment or man-hours data. According to E. H. Phelps Brown,† the Cobb–Douglas relation 'can describe the relations between the historical rates of growth of labour, capital and the product, but the coefficients that do this do not measure marginal productivity'. I think this is an unnecessary conclusion. In the first place, the inclusion of a trend term in the regression reduces the confluence almost in all cases. Secondly, a good statistical fit can withstand a large amount of collinearity without impairing the significance of the structural estimates. And, thirdly, there are well-known tests for the presence and effects of collinearity on parameter estimates which should be made prior to utilizing the estimates for any purpose.

(3) It can be argued that the measure of non-neutral technological progress is not 'pure', since a firm operating in the range of increasing returns in epoch r and decreasing returns to scale in epoch s ($s = r + 1$) may prove to have negative non-neutral technological cl ange by the measure. But no rational entrepreneur would choose a technology that yielded less rather than more output with the same inputs. Since he chose the latter, it is revealed superior to the former technology; therefore,

† 'The Meaning of the Fitted Cobb–Douglas Function', *Quarterly Journal of Economics*, vol. 71 (November 1957), p. 551.

the measure of non-neutral change may not be accurate. The difficulty lies in the nature of the Cobb–Douglas relation. A functional form that permits the representation of returns to scale in a parameter or set of parameters separately from other parameters, changes in which represent non-neutral technological change, avoids this difficulty. The CES production function does just that as was indicated in Chapter 4, and to which we return in the next chapter.

(4) As shown above, the use of value-added measures may be very disturbing to the analyst attempting to quantify technological change. For the interpretation of the structural change is clouded when the possibility of variations in the parameters on intermediate inputs is admitted. However, the advantages of using the published national income data or output data, which are a type of value-added measure, are so great that they outweigh the potential specification error introduced by their improper specification of intermediate inputs. Certainly, for specific problems, the output measure should be gross of all inputs, but this is for the analyst to decide.

(5) Even though the finite differencing method goes a considerable distance towards resolving the adding-up problem—the problem of quantifying the separate influence on the change in output of the separate forces—it involves a certain arbitrariness. This is the problem of initial or terminal year weights. The arbitrariness results from distributing the interaction or residual between measures that use initial and year-end weights by an averaging process. However, by focusing on the shortest periods possible, this arbitrariness can be minimized.

9

THE MEASUREMENT
OF TECHNOLOGICAL CHANGE
IN A CES WORLD

The present chapter has two general purposes. The first part presents three different methods of obtaining parameter estimates of the CES production function. Although the orientation of the present work is not toward statistical methodology, this extension into it is justified because of the relatively unmanageable nature of the CES production function. The second part of the chapter discusses the way in which technological change can be represented statistically by the CES function. This is treated somewhat briefly because the previous chapter contained an extensive discussion of the measurement of technological change and the same principles apply here.

FITTING THE CES
PRODUCTION FUNCTION

Consider the logarithmic transform of the CES production function:

$$\log X = \log \gamma - v/\alpha \log (\kappa C^{-\alpha} + (1 - \kappa) N^{-\alpha}), \qquad (9.1)$$

where X is the output, C is capital, N is labour and where γ is the technological efficiency parameter, κ is the capital intensity parameter, v represents the degree of returns to scale associated with any given technology and $\alpha = -[1 - (1/\sigma)]$, σ being the elasticity of substitution. The problem is to obtain an estimate of the parameters, γ, v, α and κ, given data on output, capital and labour inputs. A simple least-squares procedure cannot be applied directly to (9.1) since the term $(\kappa C^{-\alpha} + (1 - \kappa) N^{-\alpha})$ contains parameters which are to be estimated. Until the estimates of κ and α are made, it is not possible to regress $\log X$ on $\log (\kappa C^{-\alpha} - (1 - \kappa) N^{-\alpha})$. Therefore, the estimates of the parameters of (9.1) must be obtained by other methods.

One method that has been used involves specifying a side relation (to be described presently) which contains κ and α as parameters. A confrontation of this side relation with data will yield estimates of κ and α. These estimates are then inserted into (9.1) and a new variable is defined

$$\hat{V} = (\hat{\kappa} C^{-\hat{\alpha}} + (1 - \hat{\kappa}) N^{-\hat{\alpha}}).\tag{9.2}$$

The following relation can then be directly fitted to data

$$\log X = \log \gamma - v/\alpha \log \hat{V},\tag{9.3}$$

and estimates of γ and v can be obtained.

In order to obtain estimates of κ and α, we can use the CES expansion path function, which is the side relation referred to above;[†] in logarithmic form it is

$$\log \frac{N}{C} = \sigma(1 - \lambda) \log \kappa' + \sigma \log \frac{q}{w} + \lambda \log \left(\frac{N}{C}\right)_{-1},\tag{9.4}$$

where q/w is the ratio of the rental value of capital to the wage of labour, $\kappa' = \kappa/(1 - \kappa)$, and λ is the rigidity parameter. Equation (9.4) and variants of it have been tested empirically by cross-section and time-series data for the variables.[‡]

[†] See K. Arrow, H. B. Chenery, B. Minhas, and R. Solow, 'Capital–Labor Substitution and Economic Efficiency', *The Review of Economics and Statistics*, vol. 43; M. Brown and J. S. de Cani, 'Technological Change and the Distribution of Income, *International Economic Review*, vol. 4; R. I. McKinnon, 'Wages, Capital Costs and Employment in Manufacturing: A Model Applied to 1947–58 U.S. data', *Econometrica*, vol. 30; J. A. Minasian, 'Elasticities of Substitution and Constant–Output Demand Curves for Labor', *The Journal of Political Economy*, vol. 49 (June 1961), pp. 261–70; B. S. Minhas, 'The Homohypallagic Production Function, Factor Intensity Reversals, and the Heckscher–Ohlin Theorem', *Journal of Political Economy*, vol. 70 (April 1962), pp. 138–56; R. E. Lucas, *Substitution Between Labor and Capital in U.S. Manufacturing*: 1929–1958 unpublished doctoral dissertation, 1963, University of Chicago; R. K. Diwan, 'An Empirical Estimate of the Constant Elasticity of Substitution Production Function', paper presented to the 1963 European Meeting of the Econometric Society, Copenhagen; R. W. Resek, 'Neutrality of Technical Progress', *The Review of Economics and Statistics*, vol. 45.

[‡] For example, Arrow *et al.* use international cross-section data on the marginal product and marginal rate of substitution side relations of the CES function; Minasian uses industrial cross-section data for the United States on the marginal product side relation; P. Nelson employs cross-section data by state and uses a variant of the expansion path side relation. Time series have been used also: by McKinnon on the marginal product side relation; by Lucas on both side relations; by Brown-de Cani on the marginal rate of substitution side relation; and by Diwan on the same side relation.

The estimates of the elasticity of substitution are the focal points in these studies. Since different classifications and data sources are employed by them, only the broadest comparisons between the studies is possible. Nevertheless, the following pattern is apparent: the cross-section data yield higher values for the elasticity of

The expansion path side relation (9.4) can be fitted to data by the method of least squares or by a consistent estimating procedure. All studies referred to here have applied least squares to a side relation of the CES production rule. The assumption underlying the use of classical least squares is that the error is normally distributed, in which case the estimates of the parameters are maximum-likelihood estimates. An important source of bias in the estimates of the parameters of the side relation is the degree of correlation of the residuals of (9.4), say, with the explanatory variables q/w and $(N/C)_{-1}$. If relative factor prices are taken as parameters by firms on which they base their relative factor inputs, then this source of bias will be minimal. But if the decision on relative factor inputs also influences relative factor prices, then simultaneous equation bias is introduced. That is, the influences from the supply side are interjected into the estimates of the demand equation, (9.4). One method of minimizing simultaneous equation bias is to specify the relations at a low level of aggregation; for example, at the firm level it is more likely than at the industry level, say, that relative factor

substitution than do time series—the central value for the cross-section elasticity exceeds unity by a small amount, and for the time-series elasticity it is less than half of that.

Lucas attempts to explain the discrepancy by computing a long-run elasticity, using a distributed lag framework, on time-series data. This would tend to narrow the gap between the two types of estimates. However, no attempts to reconcile them have proved successful.

Although there may exist theoretical and statistical explanations which reconcile the estimates of the elasticity of substitution, the discussion in Chapter 5 implies that they are irreconcilable, in principle. For the cross-section estimates are derived from the relation between relative factor prices and factor proportions *at a point in time*. And, at each point in time, the factor proportions for the firm or industry are relatively fixed. Of course, factor proportions between firms will vary, depending on where the firms happen to be in their quest for an equilibrium position. However, relative factor prices will not vary as much between firms, since general market forces tend to force them to equality. Hence, a small percentage change in relative factor prices may be associated with large percentage changes in the relative factor proportions that are fixed for each firm. In contrast, the time-series tests combine factor proportions that vary through time with relative factor prices; and presumably factor proportions vary through time, at least in the long-run case, in response to changes in relative factor prices. There is no reason to expect the time-series elasticity to be high or low—it is what technology stipulates it to be. On the other hand, if firms happen to be caught with fixed proportions at one point on their path to equilibrium rather than another point, then two measures of the cross-section elasticity may be different with no change in technology and no change in relative factor prices. In short, time-series and cross-section estimates of the elasticity of substitution may refer to two different phenomena.

inputs are influenced by relative factor prices. A low level of aggregation also reduces aggregation bias, which in a double logarithmic function could be quite large.[†]

Having obtained estimates of σ and κ from (9.4) these can be utilized by defining the variable V in (9.2). However, a prior decision must be made as to whether one requires long- or short-run estimates of the production function. Since (9.4) is a short-run version of the expansion path, the estimates of the parameters yield short-run parameter estimates, and by a suitable transformation they can also be made to furnish long-run parameter estimates. As discussed in Chapter 5, the short-run parameter estimates are $\hat{\sigma}$ and $\hat{\kappa}^{(1-\hat{\lambda})}$. These can be used to define a short run V, call it V_s. Then, a regression of $\log N/K$ on V_s will yield short-run estimates of the remaining parameters in the CES, i.e. it will yield $\hat{\gamma}$ and $\hat{\kappa}$.

If a long-run production function is required, it is necessary to transform the short-run parameter estimates of (9.4) under the assumption that the long-run parameter estimates are $\hat{\kappa}'$ and $\hat{\sigma}/(1-\hat{\lambda})$.[‡] Alternatively, one can fit the CES production with the short-run estimates of σ and κ, and then obtain a long-run estimate of output by evaluating the function with given labour and capital inputs and with the *long-run* estimates of σ and κ (see Chapter 5).

It may be necessary to include a trend term in (9.4). The fitting equation would then be,

$$\log N/C = (1 - \lambda) \log \kappa' + \sigma \log q/w + \lambda \log (N/C)_{-1} + \alpha t. \quad (9 \cdot 5)$$

Here the parameter estimate on t would represent the rate at which the capital intensity parameter κ' changes. If the para-

[†] McKinnon ('Wages, Capital Costs and Employment in Manufacturing...', *Econometrica*, vol. 30, pp. 512–14) has a discussion of bias resulting from two kinds of specification error in the CES side relation, single equation bias and serial correlation. The seminal paper on specification error and aggregation bias is by H. Theil, 'Specification Errors and the Estimation of Economic Relationships', *The Review of the International Statistical Institute*, vol. 25. Also, see Z. Griliches, 'Specification Bias in Estimates of Production Functions', *The Journal of Farm Economics*, vol. 39 (no. 1, 1957). Assuming that the supply relations are influential in determining relative factor prices, then a consistent estimating procedure, for example, two-stage least squares, can be employed. See H. Theil, *Economic Forecasts and Policy* (North-Holland Publishing Co. 1960), chap. 6; and R. E. Lucas, *Substitution Between Labor and Capital in U.S. Manufacturing: 1929–1958*.)

[‡] These long-run estimates as well as in some of the short-run coefficients suffer from the bias of a ratio estimate; for example, the long-run elasticity of substitution is derived by multiplying $\hat{\sigma}$ by $(1 - \hat{\lambda})$. The usual correction should be made for this bias.

meter estimate of t is positive, then the technological change is capital-using; if it is negative, technological progress from (9.5) is capital-saving. I will discuss this below within the context of the representation of technological change in the CES production function.

One of the deficiencies of the CES production function that was mentioned above in Chapter 4 is that the capital intensity parameter κ is not invariant to units of measurement of the variables in (9.4) or (9.5).† Of course, σ and λ are not subject to this qualification. However, the estimate of κ does enter the construction of the new variable V, and, depending on the choice of the units of measurement of the variables, it is possible to make V whatever we would like it to be. The solution is quite simple: whenever κ' or γ become focal parameters, then the analysis should proceed in terms of their relative changes.

Even when relative changes in the parameters and variables are under consideration, and the arbitrariness associated with κ' and γ is eliminated, there are some situations when the size of the ratio N/C is crucial. It becomes expedient then to measure the variables as index numbers with a common base period. Let $N = nN_0$, $C = cC_0$, $Q = qQ_0$ and $w = w'w_0$, where the symbols with zero subscripts are base-year figures and n, c, q, and w' are dimensionless, i.e. index numbers. Now define

$$\kappa'^* = \kappa'(N_0/C_0)^\sigma (w_0/Q_0),$$

and combine the logarithmic transform of this with (9.4); we obtain

$$\log n/c = \sigma(1 - \lambda) \log \kappa'^* + \sigma \log (q/w') + \lambda \log (n/c)_{-1}. \quad (9.6)$$

Since n, c, q, w', λ, and σ are dimensionless, $\log \kappa'^*$ will be in units of the labour–capital ratio and the wage–capital rental ratio of the base year.‡

This method of fitting the CES function to data can be summarized as follows: a side relation is derived from the theory of the firm; it is confronted with data and two parameters are estimated, one of which is the elasticity of substitution; inserting

---

† 'It is easily seen that κ can never exceed unity for any choice of units of N, C, etc. This holds for whatever is obtained as an estimate of κ', so long as it is positive; for $\kappa = \kappa'/(1 + \kappa')$, which is always less than unity.

‡ A discussion of dimensions of variables is found in R. G. D. Allen, *Mathematical Analysis for Economists*, pp. 9–16.

these estimates into the CES function proper, a new time series is generated on which output is regressed in a log-log relation. This yields the remaining parameters.

A SECOND METHOD OF FITTING
THE CES PRODUCTION FUNCTION

This method estimates the parameters of the CES production function directly, i.e. without the specification and estimation of side relations. Its principal advantage is that it requires the acceptance of one theory instead of two. That is, the first method posits a side relation which is derived from the theory of marginal productivity under the assumption of cost minimization; it also posits the production function itself, which in its abstractness is a kind of theory. The present method posits only the production function, only one theory. In so doing it permits the estimation of all covariances, whereas in the first method, for example, the covariance between v and $\hat{\alpha}$ could not be found directly.

The least-squares estimation of non-linear equations can be obtained by two approaches. In the more common procedure, the model is linearized by a first-order Taylor series approximation about the initial guesses of the parameters. The usual normal equations are derived and corrections of the parameter estimates are calculated by iteration until convergence criteria are satisfied. Another procedure is to apply various modifications of the method of steepest descent. Both procedures embody difficulties, however; the Taylor series approximation—sometimes called the Gauss–Newton method—may not converge, and the gradient method may require an inordinate number of iterations for convergence. Here the former procedure is outlined, but the reader may wish to consult several sources before he tries his hand.†

† M. Berman, E. Shahn and Marjory F. Weiss, 'The Routine Fitting of Kinetic Data to Models: A Mathematical Formalism for Digital Computers', *Biophysical Journal*, vol. 2 (1962), pp. 275–87; H. O. Hartley, 'The Modified Gauss–Newton Method for the Fitting of Non-Linear Regression Functions by Least Squares', *Technometrics*, vol. 3 (May 1961), pp. 269–80; R. W. Marquardt, 'An Algorithm for Least-Squares Estimation of Non-linear Parameters', *Journal of the Society of Industrial Applied Mathematics*, vol. 11 (June 1963), pp. 431–41; K. Levenberg, 'A Method for the Solution of Certain Non-Linear Problems in Least Squares', *Quarterly Journal of Applied Mathematics*, vol. 2 (1944), pp. 164–8; and A. P. Barten and Tjan Hok Soei, 'Estimation of a Non-Linear Relationship in a Complete Economic Model', Report 6126, Econometric Institute, Netherlands School of Economics (November 1961).

Let $r = v/\alpha$ and $G = [k_0 C^{-\alpha_0} + (1 - k_0) N^{-\alpha_0}]$, where the zero subscripts indicate initial guesses. (These can be taken from the estimates of the side relation, see above.) Then the first-order Taylor series approximation to the CES production function can be written as

$$\langle X \rangle = f_0 + \frac{\partial X}{\partial \gamma} (\gamma - \gamma_0) + \frac{\partial X}{\partial \kappa} (\kappa - \kappa_0) + \frac{\partial X}{\partial \alpha} (\alpha - \alpha_0) + \frac{\partial X}{\partial r} (r - r_0)$$

$$= f_0 + G^{-r_0}(\gamma - \gamma_0) + r_0 \gamma_0 G^{-r_0-1}[C^{-\alpha_0} - N^{-\alpha_0}] (\kappa - \kappa_0)$$

$$- r\gamma G^{-r_0-1}[\kappa_0 C^{-\alpha_0} \log C + (1 - \kappa_0) N^{-\alpha_0} \log N] (\alpha - \alpha_0)$$

$$+ \gamma_0 G^{-r_0} \log G(r - r_0), \tag{9.7}$$

where the brackets $\langle\ \rangle$ denote predictions based on the linearized model as distinct from those derived from the original CES production function, and f_0 is the original function evaluated at the initial guesses. The function X is now formed as follows:

$$Z = \Sigma[X_i - \langle X_i \rangle]^2,$$

where i is an observation index. It is seen that the elements of the correction vector—namely, $(\gamma - \gamma_0)$, $(\kappa - \kappa_0)$, $(\alpha - \alpha_0)$ and $(r - r_0)$ —enter linearly in Z and hence can be found by application of least squares; i.e. by equating to zero the partial derivatives of Z with respect to each member of the correction vector. The estimated correction vector is then applied to Z a second time, new least-squares estimates obtained, and so on, until the successive differences in the parameter estimates satisfy a convergence criterion.

There are several factors responsible for failure to converge,† but it should be noted that, if convergence is obtained, the parameter estimates and their standard errors *are* the parameter estimates and standard errors of the original non-linear equation even though they are obtained by a linearized model. This can be seen from (9.7), in which the elements of the correction vector vanish at the point of convergence, leaving the original function evaluated at the converged values of the parameters. Hence, this method can yield parameter estimates of the CES production function directly, provided that the initial guesses of the parameters are in the neighbourhood of the true parameters.

There are many advantages to the employment of this method of fitting the CES production function, so that in spite of the time and energy it requires, it should be encouraged.

† M. Berman *et al.*, *op. cit.* p. 281.

A THIRD METHOD OF FITTING
CES PRODUCTION FUNCTION

This method uses a variant of the CES production function. The function, suggested by Robert Solow, is more general than (9.1) in that it does not specify homogeneity as the CES production function does.† The empirical situation determines whether this new function is homogeneous or not; moreover, it can be homogeneous of any degree. A variant of the Solow function has been fitted by J. G. M. Hilhorst to cross-section and time-series data for 27 Dutch industries.‡ Using our notation, the function is

$$X = (AN^a + BC^b)^{1/c}, \tag{9.8}$$

where A, B, a, b and c are parameters to be estimated. If $a = b$, then

$$X = [(AN^a + BC^a)]^{1/c}, \tag{9.9}$$

and the function is homogeneous of degree a/c. In this case, economies of scale would be indicated by $a/c > 1$, diseconomies by $a/c < 1$. Moreover, if $a = b = c$, then the function is linear homogeneous and becomes the CES production rule where $a = [(1/\sigma) - 1]$. It can be non-homogeneous for $a \neq b$.

In order to fit (9.8) to data, Hilhourst finds the marginal rate of substitution of labour for capital and equates it to the relative factor price ratio

$$\frac{\partial X/\partial C}{\partial X/\partial N} = \frac{q}{w} = \frac{b}{a}\frac{B}{A}\frac{C^{b-1}}{N^{a-1}}.$$

He combines this with (9.8), and depending on how the result is written, two equations can be obtained, which in logarithmic form are

$$\log X = \frac{1}{c}\log A + \frac{a}{c}\log N + \frac{1}{c}\log\left(\frac{a}{b}\frac{qC}{WN} + 1\right), \tag{9.10}$$

$$\log X = \frac{1}{c}\log B + \frac{h}{c}\log C + \frac{1}{c}\log\left(\frac{b}{a}\frac{WN}{qC} + 1\right). \tag{9.11}$$

These are the estimating equations, and all parameters can be estimated by iteration. First, set $a = b$ in the brackets to derive an estimate of the remaining parameters. This yields a first estimate of a and b, which is inserted in the brackets for a second application of least squares, etc., until a/c and b/c do not change

† 'A Contribution to the Theory of Economic Growth', *Quarterly Journal of Economics*, vol. 70 (February 1956), pp. 65–94.
‡ 'Measurement of Production Functions in Manufacturing Industry', *Statistical Studies*, no. 13.

in successive rounds. Hilhorst finds that the process converges rapidly. Of course, this method can be used to estimate the parameters of the CES. It has an advantage in that data on income shares is required rather than factor price data, and the latter are somewhat less reliable than the former. However, the work involved is considerably greater than that required for the first method of estimating the CES function. But this procedure presents an alternative to the CES function. As such it can be used to refute the CES theory. Also, by testing Hilhorst's function, it is possible to determine whether a given body of data generates a homogeneous or non-homogeneous production function and in this way throw empirical light on the proportionality controversy.†

In sum, it is clear that Hilhorst's procedure represents an additional method for fitting the CES production function to data. That it is subject to the same difficulties as the other two methods is also clear without detailing them. ‡

† This revolves around whether the production function is homogeneous or not. For a recent view and a bibliography, see H. Leibenstein, 'The Proportionality Controversy and the Theory of Production', *Quarterly Journal of Economics*, vol. 69 (November 1955), pp. 619–25.

‡ We can mention here that the CES function satisfies the Nataf conditions for aggregation (see A. A. Walters, 'Economics of Scale in the Aggregate Production Function', *Discussion Paper, Series A, University of Birmingham*, no. 29, pp. 9–10), so that no economic inconsistency results in using the CES function at a macro level if the micro production functions are also of the same form. The statistical aggregation properties of the CES function have as yet not been worked out though it is a simple matter to indicate the statistical aggregation properties of the CES side relation by means of Theil's specification theorem, since it is linear in the logs. Suppose that the true relation is

$$\mu = \sum_i \sigma_i \rho_i + \sum_i \lambda_i \mu_{i-1}$$

where $\quad \mu = \log \frac{N}{C}, \quad \rho_i = \log \left(\frac{q}{w}\right)_i \quad$ and $\quad \mu_{i-1} = \log \left(\frac{N}{C}\right)_{i-1}.$

However, we do not estimate this directly but obtained least squares estimates of the macro relation,

$$\mu = \sigma\rho + \lambda\mu_{-1}.$$

Now, the expectation of σ is

$$E(\sigma) = \sum p_i \sigma_i + \sum p_i' \lambda_i,$$

where the p_i are the regression coefficients derived from the relation of each of the ρ_i and ρ, and the p_i' are the coefficients derived from the regression between ρ_i and μ_{i-1}. It can be shown that $\sum_i p_i = 1$ and $\sum_i p_i' = 0$, so that the expectation of σ is a weighted average of the micro σ's *plus* a weighted sum of the micro λ's. where the weights of the latter sum to zero. Hence, little bias results if the covariance is small between the micro ρ's and the macro variable $\mu-1$.

MEASURING TECHNOLOGICAL CHANGE
WITH THE CES PRODUCTION FUNCTION

The immediate problem is to isolate technological epochs using the CES production function. As a first approximation, a technological epoch is defined here to be a period of time within which no non-neutral technological change has occurred—i.e. a period of time within which the parameters of the expansion path (9.4) are stable. Neutral technological changes can occur between and within epochs. The statistical determination of the epochs for equation (9.4) is essentially the same as the Cobb–Douglas production function which was discussed in some detail in the previous chapter. Hence I will only sketch out the procedure here.

An overall time period is chosen and equation (9.6) is fitted to an arbitrarily small period of time, the number of observations exceeding the number of parameters in (9.6) at the beginning of the overall period. This yields one set of estimates. Another arbitrarily small period of time contiguous to the first set of observations is used for a second fit of the equation, yielding a second set of estimates. A third fit is obtained from the combined observations of the two contiguous time periods. Then an F test is used to determine whether a structural change has occurred between the first and second time periods. If none has occurred the procedure is repeated on successive contiguous time periods. But if a structural break is uncovered the procedure is repeated, beginning with the observation that occurs just after the structural break. In this way technological epochs using the CES function may be uncovered. A less powerful method of isolating epochs is the following: the expansion path function is fitted to an arbitrarily small number of observations, say n observations, at the beginning of the overall period just as before; another fit is obtained for $n + 1$ observations, and an F test is performed to determine whether the $(n + 1)$st observations are generated by the same structure as the n observations and so on. This is less work than the first method, but its power is also smaller.

Suppose that two time periods have been uncovered within each of which we can say that the parameters of the expansion path function in the first time period differ from the parameters in the second time period. In other words, we have obtained estimates of α, κ and λ for two epochs. We must still obtain estimates for γ and ν in order to have a full complement of parameter estimates of the CES production function. To do this, a new variable V is formed for each epoch

$$\hat{V} = [\hat{\kappa} C^{-\hat{\alpha}} + (1 - \kappa) \, N^{-\hat{\alpha}}],$$

where $\hat{\kappa}$ and $\hat{\alpha}$ can be either long- or short-run estimates depending on the particular problem under consideration. Then output can be regressed on this new time series (see equation (9.3)) from which $\hat{\gamma}$ and $\hat{\nu}$ are derived for each epoch. Of course one can add a trend term which would be interpreted as neutral technological change within epoch. The epochal changes in $\hat{\gamma}$ and $\hat{\nu}$ denote neutral technological progress between epochs. In sum there are two sets of estimates of all parameters in the CES production function.

The meaning of a technological epoch is unambiguous when the expansion path (9.6) is under consideration. But if a trend term is added to (9.6), and its coefficient is significantly different from zero, then the previous definition of a technological epoch must be modified. For if the coefficient on the trend term is significant then κ' and κ must be changing, which means that non-neutral technological change is occurring in a gradual rather than discrete manner. Even if the function which includes the trend remains stable, non-neutral technological change is occurring and thus no technological epoch can be defined in the previous sense of the term. Hence, non-neutral technological change is occurring gradually, and this must mean that transition periods (see Chapter 5) are of such length and character as to blunt the appearance and disappearance of an epoch. In this case, one simply defines the variable V as follows:

$$\hat{V} = [\hat{\kappa} \, e^{\hat{g}t} c^{-\hat{\alpha}} + (1 - \hat{\kappa} \, e^{\hat{g}t}) \, n^{-\hat{\alpha}}],$$

where $\hat{\kappa}$ and $\hat{\alpha}$ can either be short- or long-run estimates $\hat{\kappa} \, e^{g}_t = \hat{\kappa}' \, e^{\hat{g}t} / (1 + \hat{\kappa}' \, e^{\hat{g}t})$, and g is the coefficient on the trend term when equation (9.6) is fitted with a trend. Then the regression of $\log X$ and $\log \hat{V}$ is performed in a straightforward manner.

Suppose that equation (9·6) were fitted to data with a trend included in it, and a stability analysis revealed the existence of a structural break. This implies that non-neutral technological progress is proceeding in a gradual manner but that two different technologies are presented in the data. Such a result is the most general type of non-neutral technological change that can be represented by production function analysis.

The inclusion of the trend term in the CES side relation is intended also to account for obsolescence, since we are assuming that the services of capital are approximated by a net capital stock measure. Recall that when a net capital stock measure is used, and when the obsolescence component of depreciation is non-zero, then the trend in the relationship depicts embodied technological progress as well as the disembodied type, if it exists (see Chapter 6). For, if gross investment is positive, the trend term in a net capital stock model reflects the productivity increases resulting from the introduction of new and technically superior capital items. Now gross investment can be positive because of a change in relative factor prices; and it may also be required in order for the firm to achieve its equilibrium labour–capital ratio (see Chapter 5). Hence, even if there is no change in the current factor-price ratio, the firm may be investing currently, in response to previous changes in relative factor prices, simply in order to reach its equilibrium expansion path. There will result a productivity increase, and to account for this a trend term is required in the side relation in order to maintain stability of the coefficient on the distributed lag term.

Now suppose that the second method of fitting the CES production function were employed. The representation of technological change would proceed in the same way as if the first method were employed to fit the function to data. It would even be possible to handle the case where non-neutral technological change is proceeding gradually. However, the requisite modifications of the CES function would vastly complicate it.

Having significant epochal estimates of the parameters of the CES production function by whatever method is used to obtain them, we can measure the three forces affecting the total change in output. These are the change in inputs, neutral technological change and non-neutral technological change. Using the epochal estimates of the parameters of the CES production function, the finite differencing method yields a measure of the three forces affecting the total change in output. Since the finite differencing procedure for the CES function is the same as that used on the Cobb–Douglas function in the last chapter (also see Appendix C) it is unnecessary to repeat it.

The use of the CES function to represent technological change is more general than that obtained by using the Cobb–Douglas function. For it can represent all technological characteristics of the Cobb—Douglas as well as measure the change in the elasticity of substitution—something that the Cobb–Douglas cannot do. The cost of its generality is the burden of fitting it.

PART III

EMPIRICAL INVESTIGATIONS OF TECHNOLOGICAL PROGRESS

10

TECHNOLOGICAL PROGRESS
IN THE UNITED STATES
1890–1960

This chapter presents an attempt to measure the general factors affecting economic growth in the private domestic non-farm sector of the United States for the period 1890–1960. It represents an application of some of the measurement techniques developed in Chapter 8. Specifically, it asks what part of economic growth in a broad sector of the United States economy is attributable to the growth in the inputs of labour and capital, to non-neutral technological progress and to neutral technological change, including in the latter changes in the degree of returns to scale. This decomposition is only a first step towards the explanation of these forces, and to the explanation of economic growth itself. The important task that remains to be done is the explanation of these measures themselves, thus leading to a general theory of economic growth.

The measurement procedure involves the estimation of the Cobb–Douglas production function and the structural breaks that have occurred in it within the overall time period under consideration. The estimating form of the function used below is

$$\Delta \log X = \beta \Delta \log N + \gamma \Delta \log C + \alpha, \qquad (10\cdot1)$$

where X is gross private domestic output, N represents man-hours employed in that sector and C is the *utilized* capital stock (plant, equipment and inventories). Since the properties of (10.1) are set out in Chapter 3, it is unnecessary to discuss them here.

In the first section of the present chapter a method is developed of abstracting from the effect of cyclical variations on the estimates of the structural breaks in the production function. The actual search for epochal breaks is then taken up in the third section. Epochal estimates of the production function are presented and discussed in the third section, and finally the fourth section contains the computations of the sources of change in gross private domestic output. This last section concludes with a preliminary attempt to rationalize the changes in the rate of technological progress. The reader not interested in the detailed derivation of the measures may wish to pass directly to the last section.

THE PROBLEM OF CYCLICAL FLUCTUATIONS IN THE ESTIMATION OF STRUCTURAL CHANGE

We are concerned here with the problem of abstracting from the effects of cyclical fluctuations in output, capital and labour on estimates of the structural breaks in the production function. For if the estimates of the structural discontinuities are dependent on the characteristics of the business cycle then they are inaccurate indications of changes in the production function due to technological progress, which is of course what we want to measure.

The obvious way to abstract from the effects of the cycle on estimates of structural change is to include in the estimating form a cyclical variable directly alongside the labour and capital inputs. However (10.1) already contains a cyclical variable, for a capacity utilization variable is combined with the capital stock data to yield a measure of utilized capital services (see Appendix D).

But it can be argued that the rate of utilization of industrial resources over the cycle affects the production relation in two ways. In the first place, the available capital should be adjusted for utilization, as is done in (10.1), because actual output depends on the quantity of utilized services of capital, not the available services. Secondly, as the utilization rate increases, the efficiency of all factors of production increase, since, presumably, the optimal combination of factors is associated with higher rather than with lower levels of capacity utilization. Hence, the second way in which the utilization rate affects the production relation implies that it has a neutral effect on all factors, in contrast to the first in which only the capital input is influenced. This, in turn, implies that a utilization or cyclical variable should be specified alongside the labour and capital variables in our estimating form.†

---

† In the Cobb–Douglas form, the two adjustments collapse to one—thus

$$\log X = a + \beta \log N + \gamma \log sC' + \alpha' \log s$$

Several regression estimates of the Cobb–Douglas form were obtained in which the capacity utilization rate appeared twice, as a utilization adjustment of the capital stock variable, and alongside the utilized capital stock and labour variables. For one of several reasons these experiments were rejected; for example, in two cases, the estimates of the labour elasticity were negative, and in one case the estimate of the capital elasticity was not significantly different from zero. In view of these negative experiments an alternative method of abstracting from the cyclical effects is required.

An iterative procedure can be developed to eliminate the cyclical effects as follows. First, the Cobb–Douglas estimating form (10.1) is fitted to observations for the overall period 1890–1960 using an initial guess on the value of the utilization index s. If the residual error of this regression is correlated with capacity utilization, the adjustment for capacity utilization is clearly inadequate, and it is necessary to adjust that variable. The original adjustment for capacity utilization of the capital stock variable is inadequate by an amount that is equal to the contribution by the capacity utilization variable to the explanation of the residual. Symbolically, the residual of the first difference of (10.1) is $\Delta \log u$, say, and if the cyclical influence is still present in the estimate of (10.1) even though we have adjusted the capital stock by s then the correlation between $\Delta \log u$ and $\Delta \log s$ must be significant. It is then necessary to refit (10.1) with a modified utilization index $(1 + w_1) \log s$, where w_1 is the regression coefficient of the relation between $\Delta \log$ and $\Delta \log s$; i.e. defining α' to include the trend, we fit

$$\Delta \log X = \alpha' + \beta' \Delta \log N + \gamma' \Delta[(1 + w_1) \log s + \log C'],$$

which yields the error $\Delta \log u'$. Again, the test for residual cyclical effects is made

$$\Delta \log u' = w_0 + w_2 \Delta \log s,$$

and if the correlation is still significant the Cobb–Douglas form is re-estimated as follows:

$$\Delta \log X = \alpha'' \Delta \log N + \gamma''[(1 + w_1 + w_2) \log s + \log C'],$$

yielding the error $\Delta \log u''$.

can be written as $\quad \log X = a + \beta \log N + \gamma \log C' + (\alpha' + \gamma) \log s,$

where s is the utilization index. However, there is a statistical difference between the estimates of the two forms even though they reduce to the same specification.

The new capacity utilization term is

$$\left(1 + \sum_i^n w_i\right) \log s,$$

where n is the number of iterations required to eliminate the correlation between the residual of the production function in which the capital stock variable is adjusted for utilization and the utilization variable itself. Hence, we obtain a new capacity utilization variable.

The original guess of the utilization index s includes the influences of changes in labour, capital and neutral and non-neutral technology (see Appendix D). Our final index holds constant all but non-neutral technological change, since the other factors are included explicitly in the production function. As such it is more accurate as a pure measure of capacity utilization than alternative indexes.†

The procedure for eliminating the cyclical influence is executed by obtaining an estimate of the Cobb–Douglas form (10.1) for the period 1890–1960, where the initial guess of the capacity utilization variable is obtained by The Wharton School method (Appendix D); the regression is

$$\Delta \log X = 0\cdot0042 + 0\cdot3838\, \Delta \log N + \underset{10\cdot0008}{0\cdot6890\, \Delta\, (\log s + \log C')},$$
$$\underset{2\cdot7744}{\quad} \underset{4\cdot0725}{\quad}$$

$$R^2 = 0\cdot8420, \quad \text{D–W} = 1\cdot406,$$

where the underlined numbers beneath the coefficients are T ratios and D–W denotes the Durbin–Watson statistic. The residuals of this regression are regressed, in turn, against $\Delta \log s$ to yield

$$\Delta \log u = -0\cdot0007 + 0\cdot3557\, \Delta \log s,$$

with an $r^2 = 0\cdot3612$. There is an indication from these results that the initial utilization adjustment does not eliminate all of the influence of the cycle in the estimate of the production function. Thus, the utilization index is modified by taking the sum: $\log s + 0\cdot3556 \log s$, which is the second approximation to the

† For a discussion of the various existing measures of capacity utilization, see 'Measures of Productive Capacity', Hearings Before the Subcommittee on Economic Statistics of the Joint Economic Committee, 87th Congress (May 1962), U.S. Government Printing Office, Washington, D.C.

capacity utilization variable. The Cobb–Douglas form is re-estimated with this variable for the overall time period, and the result is

$$\Delta \log X = 0 \cdot 0061 + 0 \cdot 3253 \, \Delta \log N + \; 0 \cdot 5521 \, \Delta \, (1 \cdot 3556 \log s + \log C')$$
$$\quad\quad\quad\quad 4 \cdot 4913 \quad 3 \cdot 6860 \quad\quad\quad 11 \cdot 4081$$

$$R^2 = 0 \cdot 8873, \quad \text{D–W} = 1 \cdot 4900.$$

The residuals of this regression, when regressed against $\Delta \log s$, yield a coefficient of determination that is not significantly different from zero. Thus the second approximation to the utilization variable has effectively eliminated the influence of cycle from the overall estimate of the Cobb–Douglas form.

The new utilization variable can now be employed in the search for structural breaks, and we are reasonably assured that any breaks we are able to isolate are probably not attributable to cyclical influences.

Before proceeding to the structural change analysis a brief comment on the last estimate of (10.1) is warranted. Note that the regression is quite respectable: the coefficients have the correct signs, they are highly significant (the capital coefficient is over 11 times its standard error), the coefficient of determination is unusually high for a regression in first differences, and the degree of serial correlation is not worrisome. True the relative sizes of the labour and capital elasticities of production are different from what we would expect on the basis of their relative income shares, but this is a technological relationship and market influences may explain the discrepancy. We should also note that the elasticities sum to less than unity, thus implying that the economy operated under decreasing returns to scale throughout the period. But the important point is that, on the basis of these traditional criteria, the estimates appear to be acceptable as they stand, and yet it is shown below, using the same form and the same data, that several structural breaks occur in the period from which the observations for the regression are drawn. Hence, significant and theoretically reasonable estimates of coefficients may well be consistent with the presence of structural change, and we cannot use the customary statistics as evidence for the absence of such changes. Though this point is well known, it should be underscored.

THE SEARCH FOR EPOCHS

The search for epochs is begun by estimating (10.1) with observations drawn arbitrarily from the period 1890–99. The residual variance of this estimate is given in line 1 of Table 10.1. Are the observations from the contiguous sub-period 1900–06 generated by the same structure that yielded the initial set of observations? To answer this, two additional estimates of (10.1) are required, one for the period 1900–06 and the second for 1890–1906. The residual sums of squares of all three estimates are presented in Table 10.1. An F test with 11 and 3 degrees of freedom (column 2) indicates that the null hypothesis—i.e. both sets of observations, 1890–99 and 1900–06, derive from the same regression model—cannot be rejected at the 5 per cent level of significance. For in order to infer that the 1900–06 observations were produced by a different production function F would have had to be at least 3·59. The calculated F is 1·99 and is well below this limit.† Note that the arbitrariness in selecting the initial and the second sets of observations is not bothersome, for if a structural break occurs it is possible to employ the method set out in Chapter 8 for isolating the year or years in which it occurred.

TABLE 10.1. *Residual sum of squares* (R.S.S.) *of the Cobb–Douglas production function for the period 1890–1906, and the theoretical and calculated F ratios*

	R.S.S.	Degrees of freedom	Calculated F	Theoretical F
1890–99	8·3439^{-4}	—	—	—
1900–06	3·3255^{-4}	$\dfrac{17\text{–}6}{3}$	1·99	3·59
1890–06	17·9866^{-4}	—	—	—

† The choice of a 5 per cent level of significance permits the rejection of the null hypothesis more readily than if a 1 per cent level of significance, say, were selected. The justification for this is that the autocorrelation in time-series data builds into the estimates an inherent structural rigidity which would tend to increase Type II error. See R. L. Anderson and T. A. Bancroft, *Statistical Theory in Research* (McGraw-Hill Book Co., 1952), chap. 11. Hence the selection of the 5 per cent level is an attempt to compensate for this property of time-series data—it is an expression of our relative willingness to reject the null hypothesis even when the deviation from the null hypothesis is not large. It is my belief that in the present context conservatism in the choice of significance level—i.e. condoning the rejection of the null hypothesis only when the actual deviation from it is relatively large—is unjustified.

We are reasonably confident that the observations of the period 1890–1906 are generated by the same structure. But are the observations from the contiguous sub-period 1907–13. generated by that structure? Table 10.2 provides sufficient information for an F test of the null hypothesis that the 1907–13 observations are drawn from the same sample as the 1890–1906 observations (given that we have not rejected the null hypothesis that the 1900–06 observations are homogeneous with those of 1890–1900). Since the calculated F would have to be at least 3.29, and since it is 4.28, it is necessary to reject the null hypothesis that the observations from 1907 to 1913 are homogeneous with those of 1890–1906. Hence we have the first structural break, and though it is possible to estimate the year or years in which it occurred we date it between 1906 and 1907.

TABLE 10.2. *Residual sum of squares* (R.S.S.) *of the Cobb–Douglas production function for the period 1890–1913, and the theoretical and calculated F ratios*

	R.S.S.	Degrees of freedom	Calculated F	Theoretical F
1890–1913	$22 \cdot 1103^{-4}$	—	—	—
1890–99	$8 \cdot 3439^{-4}$	—	—	—
1900–06	$3 \cdot 3255^{-4}$	$\dfrac{24-9}{3}$	$4 \cdot 28$	$3 \cdot 29$
1907–13	$0 \cdot 2398^{-4}$	—	—	—

TABLE 10.3. *Residual sum of squares* (R.S.S.) *of the Cobb–Douglas production function for the period, 1907–20, and the theoretical and calculated F ratios*

	R.S.S.	Degrees of freedom	Calculated F	Theoretical F
1907–20	$5 \cdot 2158^{-4}$	—	—	—
1907–13	$0 \cdot 2398^{-4}$	$\dfrac{14-6}{3}$	$0 \cdot 09$	$4 \cdot 07$
1914–20	$4 \cdot 7880^{-4}$	—	—	—

The procedure used for uncovering the first structural break can be repeated, starting with the observations from 1907 to 1913. The question now is: are the observations of 1914–20 homogeneous with those of 1907–13? In Table 10.3, it is seen that the null hypothesis cannot be rejected; hence the two sub-periods are homogeneous. However, the F tests in Table 10.4, which covers the period, 1907–27, indicate that a structural break did occur between sub-periods 1907–20 and 1921–27. It is dated between 1920 and 1921.

TABLE 10.4. *Residual sum of squares (R.S.S.) of the Cobb–Douglas production function for the period 1907–27, and the theoretical and calculated F ratios*

	R.S.S.	Degrees of freedom	Calculated F	Theoretical F
1907–27	18.6554^{-4}	—	—	—
1907–13	0.2398^{-4}	$\dfrac{21-9}{3}$	3.62	3.49
1914–20	4.7880^{-4}	—	—	—
1921–27	4.8926^{-4}	—	—	—

TABLE 10.5. *Residual sum of squares (R.S.S.) of the Cobb–Douglas production function for the period 1921–33, and the theoretical and calculated F ratios*

	R.S.S.	Degrees of freedom	Calculated F	Theoretical F
1921–33	7.0925^{-4}	—	—	—
1921–27	4.8926^{-4}	$\dfrac{14-6}{3}$	0.34	4.07
1928–33	1.3950^{-4}	—	—	—

Continuing the search for epochs beginning in 1921, we inquire whether the observations drawn from 1928 to 1933 are homogeneous with those of 1921–27. An F test calculated with the R.S.S. for those years, shown in Table 10.5, indicates that no structural break occurred in the period. A test for homogeneity of the observations from 1934 to 1939 with those of 1921–33, Table 10.6, also reveals the absence of a structural break. Hence, the observations from 1921 to 1939 appear to be generated by the same structure.

TABLE 10.6. *Residual sum of squares (R.S.S.) of the Cobb–Douglas production function for the period 1921–39, and the theoretical and calculated F ratios*

	R.S.S.	Degrees of freedom	Calculated F	Theoretical F
1921–39	17.3462^{-4}	—	—	—
1921–27	4.8926^{-4}	$\dfrac{21-9}{3}$	3.14	3.49
1928–33	1.3950^{-4}	—	—	—
1934–39	3.4444^{-4}	—	—	—

The procedure can now be varied by beginning in the terminal year and working backward toward the 1921 structural break. Consider the null hypothesis that the observations from the period 1947 to 1953 are homogeneous with those of the period 1954–60. From Table 10.7, the calculated F is 2.53; in order to reject the null hypothesis, F would have had to be 4.35, so that there is little basis for its rejection. A test for the inclusion of the period that includes the war years, 1940–46, is executed in Table 10.8. It is evident from this table that the war period cannot be said to possess a structural break with reference to the post World War II period.

TABLE 10.7. *Residual sum of squares* (R.S.S.) *of the Cobb–Douglas production function for the period 1947–60, and the theoretical and calculated F ratios*

	R.S.S.	Degrees of freedom	Calculated F	Theoretical F
1947–60	$3·9152^{-4}$	—	—	—
1947–53	$1·2358^{-4}$	$\dfrac{13-6}{3}$	2·53	4·35
1954–60	$0·6407^{-4}$	—	—	—

TABLE 10.8. *Residual sum of squares* (R.S.S.) *of the Cobb–Douglas production function for the period 1940–60, and the theoretical and calculated F ratios*

	R.S.S.	Degrees of freedom	Calculated F	Theoretical F
1940–60	$17·4725^{-4}$	—	—	—
1947–53	$1·2358^{-4}$	$\dfrac{20-9}{3}$	1·43	3·59
1954–60	$0·6407^{-4}$	—	—	—
1940–46	$10·6952^{-4}$	—	—	—

However, a structural break does occur around 1940. For it is possible to reject the null hypothesis that the observations from 1933 to 1939 are similar to those of 1940–60 from a test of the R.S.S. in Table 10.9. The calculated F 3.45 exceeds the theoretical F at 15 and 3 degrees of freedom. Apparently, the war years ushered in a new type of technology that remained roughly invariant throughout the post-World War II period. We date this structural break between the years 1939 and 1940, recalling again that a more intensive application of the methods presented in Chapter 8 would enable us to isolate in a less arbitrary manner the years in which the break occurred.

TABLE 10.9. *Residual sum of squares* (R.S.S.) *of the Cobb–Douglas production function for the period 1933–60, and the theoretical and calculated F ratios*

	R.S.S.	Degrees of freedom	Calculated F	Theoretical F
1933–60	27·4798^{-4}	—	—	—
1940–46	10·6952^{-4}	—	—	—
1947–53	1·2358^{-4}	$\dfrac{27-12}{3}$	3·45	3·29
1954–60	0·6407	—	—	—
1933–39	3·6911	—	—	—

To sum up, three structural breaks in the Cobb–Douglas production function in the private domestic non-farm sector are evident in the overall period 1890–1960. They are dated roughly between 1906 and 1907, 1920 and 1921, and between 1939 and 1940. These breaks permit us to define, approximately, four technological epochs. They are 1890–1906, 1907–20, 1921–39, and 1940–60. These are technological epochs in the same sense in which the Schumpeterian waves are epochs; they are isolated, however, by methods that are distinctly non-Schumpeterian.

Before proceeding to utilize the epochal estimates, a brief check on one of the F tests should be made. In Table 10.6 the observations of the period 1921–39 are seen to be homogeneous, yet the calculated F statistic 3·14, is just within the bound set by $F(12, 3)$. Could it be that a different type of test, and a different grouping of observations, would yield a structural break in the neighbourhood of 1933? An answer to this can be provided by estimating the Cobb–Douglas production function for the period 1921–27, which yields a R.S.S. of 2·3767^{-4}. An estimate of the Cobb–Douglas function for 1921–1929 is obtained which produces a R.S.S. of 4·8926^{-4}. The F ratio is

$$\frac{5\cdot3767 - 4\cdot8926}{5\cdot3767}(9-3) = 2\cdot70,†$$

but the tabulated F for 6 and 2 degrees of freedom at the 5 per cent level of significance is 5·14, so that the observations from 1928 and 1929 appear to be homogeneous with those of 1921–27. This procedure can be continued adding 2 years at a time until we pass through the 1933 neighbourhood. The results are

† See Chapter 8.

included in Table 10.10. The calculated F's are well within the appropriate limits so that this test and this grouping of observations supports the initial finding that a structural break did not occur in the early 1930's. These tests notwithstanding, a structural break in the early 1930's may still exist in the data but, if it does, its presence must be detected either by more powerful tests than those used here or by a more meticulous application of the variance analysis.

TABLE 10.10. *Subsidiary F tests for a structural break in the Cobb–Douglas production function in the period 1927–35*

	R.S.S.	Degrees of freedom	Calculated F	Theoretical F
1921–27	4·8926	9–2	2·70	5·14
1921–29	5·3767	2		
1921–29	5·3767	11–3	0·64	4·26
1921–31	6·4092	2		
1921–31	6·4092	13–3	0·48	4·10
1921–33	7·0925	2		
1927–33	7·0925	15–3	0·53	3·88
1921–35	7·7813	2		

The epochal estimates can be questioned for another reason, for the inclusion of observations taken during a war period may not be justified for the purposes of production estimation. The argument for the exclusion of the war years asserts that not only are technological constraints on production present during such a period, but there are other requirements (governmental restrictions, etc.) that must be satisfied which are unrelated to the technology of the firm. One consequence of these extra-technological constraints is that the capacity utilization adjustment may be significantly biased, the direction of which is difficult to assess in individual cases. Hence, we shall proceed with a second set of epochal estimates which exclude the two world war periods. However, it is not simple to execute this, since one of the war periods falls within an epoch, part of which cannot be allocated to a contiguous epoch. That is, the observations taken from the period 1907–13 cannot be combined with those of 1890–1906, since they are not homogeneous (see Table 10.2). If we wish to exclude the war years, then we must ignore completely the second epoch. This dilemma should not overly disturb us, however, since the data in the early part of the overall period are probably not as reliable as we would wish; indeed, the further back in time we venture with the data the less reliable they are. Thus, our arbitrary action of ignoring the whole epoch 1907–20 may not reduce—it may even increase—the accuracy of the measures of technological progress derived below. There is no such problem with respect to World War II; there, all that needs be done is to eliminate the war years from the fourth epoch. The second set of epochal estimates are then: 1890–1906, 1921–39, and 1947–60.†

A comparison of the epochs estimated above with those obtained from a search of the technical literature for 'crucial' changes in technology is not feasible. The difficulty with this, aside from the burden of work involved, is that *any* estimate of a structural break in the production function could probably be supported by such evidence. There are important questions that can be answered to some extent by a search of the technical literature, for example, the determination of the lag between an invention and its implementation in the production process— but the reliance on this research device to uncover, or even support, estimates of structural breaks is unwarranted in view of its potential arbitrariness.

It is to be recalled that the structural breaks uncovered here may not be invariant to a replacement of the Cobb–Douglas production function with, say, the CES function. The size of this potential specification error is difficult to assess, and until our experiment is replicated with the CES function it is impossible to treat it. We should also note that we are ascribing the structural breaks to discrete changes in the production function—i.e. to

---

† In the Brown–Popkin study two structural breaks between 1918 and 1919, and between 1937 and 1938, are isolated in the overall period 1890–1958. 'A Measure of Technological Change and Returns to Scale', *The Review of Economics and Statistics*, vol. 44. The data there cover the private domestic non-farm sector of the United States, the same as those used in the present effort, except that the Brown–Popkin study employed J. Kendrick's preliminary estimates. In the earlier work, the testing for breaks was done by means of tolerance interval tests on the level form of the Cobb–Douglas production function rather than by the covariance analysis of the first difference form of the Cobb–Douglas function which is used above. In spite of these differences, the breaks discovered in the earlier work are close to those obtained above except for the discontinuity in 1907–08. Hence, the only major difference between the two sets of results is the presence of the 1907–08 interruption uncovered in the present study. This can be attributable to any number of reasons, but since the results of the present study take precedence over the Brown-Popkin results it is unnecessary to pursue the comparison further.

discrete changes in technology. Yet due to the aggregate nature of our data these breaks may be attributable to variations in the relative sizes of the industries within the aggregate, assuming that all industries do not have the same capital–labour ratios. Again, until the experiment is replicated at a lower level of industrial detail we must attribute the structural breaks found here to changes in technology and industry mix, the proportions of each being unknown.

EPOCHAL ESTIMATES OF AN AGGREGATE PRODUCTION FUNCTION

The estimates of the Cobb–Douglas production function for the four epochs including the war years are shown in Table 10.11. A cursory inspection reveals that the parameter estimates do differ between epochs as one would expect from the results of the stability tests executed above. The extent of their differences is indicated in column 8, which contains the ratio of the labour elasticity of production to the sum of the production elasticities, called the 'relative labour production elasticity'.†

The trend of the ratios in column 8 reveals that capital-using technological progress occurred beginning in the first epoch (the marginal product of labour $\beta(X/N)$ has fallen relative to the marginal product of capital $\gamma(X/C)$ for each labour–capital ratio). In view of the enormous increase in roundabout techniques introduced in the 1920's, this result is not surprising. But the slight rise in the relative labour production elasticity from the third to the fourth epoch is unexpected, for this signifies a labour-using technological change. Such a result is unexpected when viewed alongside the empirical accounts in the 1950's of

† Note that if the production elasticities truly represented the income shares of the respective factors of production, then the ratio in column 8 of Table 10.11 would be approximately equal to 0·65, since property income is about 35 per cent of income originating and labour income comprises about 65 per cent. But market forces can force the ratio of income shares to deviate from the ratio of production elasticities; also, the elasticity of substitution of labour for capital may not be unity as specified in the Cobb–Douglas function. For these reasons, as well as the aggregation problem, it is misleading to use these particular estimates in the analysis of income shares (see Chapter 12). However, market forces do not enter into our estimates of technological progress so that the changes in the estimates of the production elasticities can be used for the analysis of technological change in an approximate manner.

TABLE 10.11. *Epochal estimates of the Cobb–Douglas production function with war years*

Epochs	$\hat{\beta}_r$	$\hat{\gamma}_r$	$\hat{\alpha}_r$	$\bar{R}^2$	D–W	$\hat{\beta}_r + \hat{\gamma}_r$	$\dfrac{\hat{\beta}_r}{\hat{\beta}_r + \hat{\gamma}_r}$
(1)	(2)	(3)	(4)	(5)	(6)	(7)	(8)
(1) 1890–1906	0·6904 3·0016	0·4156 4·5047	0·0018† 0·5287	0·867	1·977	1·1060	0·624
(2) 1907‡–20	0·1272 2·5843	0·7347 3·0538	0·0018 5·1583	0·998	2·395	0·8619	0·148
(3) 1921–39	0·3829 2·3622	0·5046 5·0394	0·0077 3·0268	0·928	1·810	0·8875	0·431
(4) 1940–60	0·4531 2·5825	0·4891 3·7431	0·0069 2·6790	0·775	1·277§	0·9422	0·481
(4) 1940‖–60	0·5282 2·3381	0·4243 2·4297	0·0059 3·8121	0·998	1·944	0·9525	0·554

† Not significant at the 5 per cent level.
‡ Estimates derived from the level form of the Cobb–Douglas function.
§ Null hypothesis that residuals are independent is rejected.
‖ The unacceptable Durbin–Watson statistic for the regression run on logarithms of the observations from 1940 to 1960 indicates that certain systematic variables are influencing it. There is reason to believe that technological behaviour in the war years is not adequately characterized by the Cobb–Douglas function, since their omission yields an acceptable Durbin–Watson statistic (see Table 10.12). Since the present study is not primarily concerned with war technologies, it is justified in abstracting from their influences. This can be accomplished here by implementing the correction procedure developed by H. Theil and A. L. Nagar, 'Testing the Independence of Regression Disturbances', *Journal of The American Statistical Association*, vol. 56 (December 1961), pp. 803–5. The procedure involves the re-estimation of the *level* form of the regression on the observations from 1940 to 1960 by taking account of the autocorrelation in the residuals as expressed in the Durbin–Watson statistic. Even though the null hypothesis that the residuals are independent is not rejected when the Theil–Nagar correction is applied (provided the error in the relation follows a first order autoregressive relation), the authors warn that the standard errors of the coefficients are probably understated, on the average. Hence, on this basis it is difficult to assert with confidence that the movement of $\beta_r/(\beta_r+\gamma_r)$ from 0·431 in the third epoch to 0·554 in the fourth is a real one. But the information in Table 10.12, below, supports the assertion that the change was a real one.

technologically displaced labour, although it is not inconsistent with these accounts. In any event, the present writer expected a decrease in the relative labour elasticity, not an apparent rise.

The downward pattern of returns to scale over the period 1890–1960 can be traced in column 7. There were increasing returns to scale during the first epoch, but during the rest of the period the system clearly operated under decreasing returns.

(Within the margin of error, the sums of the production elasticities do not differ between the second, third or fourth epochs.) Since there has been scepticism of the estimates of returns to scale in time-series applications of Cobb–Douglas functions, it is necessary to summon supplementary support for the present results—i.e. besides the care we have taken to eliminate the influence on these estimates of non-neutral technological change. Clearly, no acceptable test of returns to scale can be executed until the CES function is estimated with sufficiently detailed industry time-series data, keeping non-neutral technological change constant and adhering to the usual statistical standards. In lieu of this the following test is offered within the present framework: holding technology constant we should expect smaller returns to scale—or even greater decreasing returns—when the economy is operating at very high levels of activity, for example, during war periods, than when it is operating at lower levels of activity; hence, the sum of the production elasticities should be smaller during the periods 1914–20 and 1940–46 than during the periods 1907–20 and 1940–60, respectively. For the period 1914–20, the sum of the elasticities is estimated to be 0·5600, whereas for the epoch in which World War I occurred the sum is 0·8619; during World War II (1940–46) the production elasticities sum to 0·9043, while they are equal to 0·922 for the period 1940–60. Apparently, the degree of returns to scale was not reduced as much in World War II as it was in World War I. These comparisons indicate that when the economy moves from very high to lower levels of activity, returns to scale tend to rise. Such may not be the case when the economy falls from just a high to a lower level of activity, for in the high activity periods 1921–26 and 1921–31 our estimates of returns to scale are higher than the estimate for the depressed period 1932–39. This is not as ambiguous as it seems though, since economies of scale can hardly be achieved in capital intensive production processes when activity is at a very low level as it was during the 1930's. Hence, we can say that the movements in the estimated returns to scale at least do not confute our *a priori* expectations. Of course, the comparisons of returns to scale in various periods, holding constant non-neutral technological change, do not lend support to the estimates of the levels of the returns. For this supplementary data would be required.

When the war years are omitted from the epochal estimates of the aggregate production function, there is only one substantial change in the patterns we have just noticed. This pertains to the long-term rise in capital-using technology, which is evident when all observations are included, but is absent when the war years are omitted. In Table 10.12, column 8 shows that the relative labour elasticity has remained essentially the same from the first to the last epochs when the war years are omitted. Moreover, the increase in labour-using technology from 1921–39 to 1948–60 is larger than one would infer from a comparison of the relative labour elasticity in the last two epochs shown in Table 10.11. If, indeed, this result is found to represent technological progress and not a change in output mix, the implications are extremely far reaching. Needless to say, the point should be explored further.

TABLE 10.12. *Epochal estimates of the Cobb–Douglas Production function without war years*†

Epochs	$\hat{\beta}_r$	$\hat{\gamma}_r$	$\hat{\alpha}_r$	R^{-2}	D–W	$\hat{\beta}_r + \hat{\gamma}_r$	$\dfrac{\hat{\beta}_r}{\hat{\beta}_r + \hat{\gamma}_r}$
(1)	(2)	(3)	(4)	(5)	(6)	(7)	(8)
1890–1906	0·6904	0·4156	0·0018†	0·867	1·977	1·1060	0·624
	3·0016	4·5047	0·5287				
1921–39	0·3829	0·5046	0·0077	0·928	1·810	0·8875	0·431
	2·3622	5·0394	3·0268				
1947–60	0·6590	0·3791	0·0062	0·891	1·903	1·0381	0·635
	3·3895	3·3861	3·0099				

† All estimates are obtained from the first difference form of the Cobb–Douglas function. The second epoch, 1907–20, has been omitted, and so have the observations from 1940 to 1946 from the fourth epoch, 1940–60.

‡ Not significant at the 5 per cent level.

It is reasonable to expect that labour-saving techniques would be introduced during a war, and this is precisely what is found. For the period 1940–60 the relative labour elasticity is 0·481, but when the war years are excluded the relative labour elasticity rises to 0·635, thus confirming our notion that labour-saving techniques were introduced during World War II. Although these remarks are tentative in view of the fact that the output mix has not been held constant (*inter alia*), they are consistent with *a priori* expectations, and hence provide additional support for our estimates.

The pattern of returns to scale remains the same when the war years are excluded, although they rise more abruptly from 1921–39 to 1946–60. In the latter epoch, the economy even appears to have operated under increasing returns. Again, the only evidence on the level of the returns is what is shown here, but the invariance in the movement of returns to scale under different groupings of observations reinforces our confidence in the estimate of the movements.

The rates at which neutral technological change progressed over the period 1890–60 (indicated in column 4) also remain unchanged when the war years are excluded. The coefficient on the time trend in the first epoch is not significantly different from zero and then it rises to 0·0077 (or 2 per cent per year) in the period 1921–39, falling off slightly to 0·0062 (or 1·8 per cent per year) in 1946–60. Hence, even the Usherian type of technological change appears to have altered from the first to the second epochs in the rate at which it progresses.

The results in Table 10.12 satisfy standard statistical criteria. Except for the coefficient on the trend in the first epoch, the parameter estimates are highly significant. Moreover, the values for the Durbin–Watson statistic, column 6, do not permit the rejection of the null hypothesis that the residuals are independent. The relatively low $\bar{R}^2$'s for time-series estimates can be explained with reference to the fact that the fitting equations were transformed into first differences. Nevertheless, they also are highly significant.

The principal conclusion we can draw so far is that, staying within a Cobb–Douglas world at a fairly high level of aggregation, large structural changes did occur in the period 1890–1960. The approximations to structural changes upon which the conclusion is based are, of course, subject to refutation, yet to do so will require techniques and data that have yet to be applied to the problem.

SOURCES OF CHANGE
IN UNITED STATES OUTPUT

The epochal estimates of the aggregate production function provide the material for an allocation of the growth in United States output among its sources. Table 13 presents a decomposition on two alternative bases of the changes in the logarithm of output from 1890 to 1921 and from 1921 to 1960. The first part of the table decomposes output on the assumption that the economy was operating under constant returns to scale in all epochs. The elasticities of production used in this decomposition are taken from column 8 of Table 10.12. In the second part of Table 10.13 the decomposition is based on the actual estimated elasticities of production, columns 2 and 3 of Table 10.12. Both decompositions are obtained by means of the finite difference method.†

TABLE 10.13. *Decomposition of the growth in United States output under two assumptions concerning returns to scale*

I. Decomposition under assumption that constant returns prevail

		1890–1921	1921–60
1.	Private domestic non-farm output	0·5006	0·5769
2.	Increase in inputs	0·3814	0·2879
3.	Non-neutral technological progress	0·0496	−0·0756
4.	Change in the degree of returns to scale (II. 2+II. 3−I. 2−I. 3)	−0·0565	0·0802
5.	Neutral technological progress (I. 1−I. 2−I. 3−I. 4)	0·1261	0·2844

II. Decomposition under actual production elasticities

		1890–1921	1921–60
1.	Private domestic non-farm output	0·5006	0·5769
2.	Increase in inputs	0·3768	0·2761
3.	Non-neutral technological progress	−0·0023	0·0164

The contribution to the change in output of non-neutral technological change is positive for the period 1890–1921, under the constant returns assumption but it is negative for the later period. The analysis in Chapter 4 provides a rationale for this result, for one of the propositions derived there is that a labour-using technological change augments the rate of growth of out-

† As an illustration of the finite difference method, consider the value obtained, 0·3768, for the contribution to the change in log X of the change in inputs from 1890 to 1921. It is obtained by taking an average of two finite differences,

$$[\bar{\beta}\log\bar{N}+\bar{\gamma}\log\bar{C}]-[\beta\log N+\gamma\log C],$$

$$[(0·3829)\,(0·2367)+(0·5046)\,(0·5428)]-[0] = 0·3645,$$

$$[\bar{\beta}\log\bar{N}+\bar{\gamma}\log\bar{C}]-[\beta\log N + \gamma\log C],$$

$$[(0·6904)\,(0·2367)+(0·4156)\,(0·5428)]-[0] = 0·3890,$$

where the barred symbols denote 1921 values and the unbarred symbols are the 1890 values. Both the labour and capital inputs are indexes with 1890 = 100. Only two effects are finite differenced here; the third effect, neutral technological progress, is treated as a residual.

put only if labour is growing more rapidly than capital. Since capital grew more rapidly than labour throughout the whole period, and since the change in technology is estimated to be labour-saving from 1890 to 1921, the positive contribution of non-neutral technological change is to be expected. However, the estimated labour-using technological change from 1921 to 1960 should reduce the rate of output since capital is growing more rapidly than labour in that period also.†

In order to evaluate the effect on the change in output of the returns to scale factor, it is only necessary to subtract from the sum of lines 2 and 3 under the actual production elasticities decomposition the sum of lines 2 and 3 under the constant returns assumption. These two sums hold constant all effects except the sum of the elasticities, so that their difference must represent the effect which the change in the degree of returns to scale has on the change in output. From 1890 to 1921 this factor reduced the log of output by 0·0565, indicating that economies of scale in that period were insufficient to compensate for the reduction in the degree of returns to scale. But from 1921 to 1960 the returns to scale factor augmented the log of output by 0·0802. Hence the increase in the degree of returns to scale from 1921 to 1960 (the sum of the production elasticities rose from 0·8875 to 1·0381) was beneficial to economic growth.

Neutral technological progress was considerably larger in the second comparison than in the first, increasing the log of output by 0·2925 between 1921 and 1960 and only 0·1261 between 1890 and 1921. Of course, the change in the degree of returns to scale is also a neutral technological change, since it alters the production function without affecting the marginal rate of substitution between labour and capital. Taking the two effects together, then the total neutral technological change from 1890 to 1921 was only 0·0790 (0·1261–0·0565), but from 1921 to 1960, it was 0·3727 (0·2925+0·0802). The effect of total neutral technological progress rose roughly by a factor of 5 from the first comparison period to the second.

Total technological progress, the sum of lines 3–5 under the first decomposition in Table 10.13, rose substantially, about $2\frac{1}{2}$ times from the first comparison to the second. In fact, only

† The reason why we focus on the first part of Table 10.13 to provide the measure of non-neutral technological change rather than the second part which uses the actual estimated elasticities is discussed in Chapter 8, pp. 126–7.

from 1921 to 1960 did technological progress contribute more to the growth in output than the increase in inputs.† From 1890 to 1921, the increase in inputs was over 3 times as important as technological change. The relative importance of technological progress that has received much attention from economists (see Chapter 1) appears to be a phenomenon of the more recent rather than the more distant past. But even allowing for the large technological change effect in the second comparison, it is still not possible to say that the growth of inputs has a negligible effect on the growth of output.

The important results that emerge from Table 10.13 can be stated as follows: (1) the pace of technological progress, both neutral and non-neutral, has accelerated sharply in the latter part of the period under consideration; (2) aside from the change in the speed of technological advance, its internal composition has altered substantially from the first to the second part of the period, for the neutral component of this factor became much more important than the non-neutral component, and the signs of the non-neutral and returns to scale components changed from the earlier to the later part of the period.

Although these estimates are tentative they are sufficiently firm for us to pose the following unresolved questions. What factors influence the non-neutrality of technological progress? How can the switch be explained from a labour-saving technological change in the earlier part of the period to a labour-using technological change in the later part. What factors influence the rate of neutral technological advance and its components? In general, are the various types of technological change endogenous to the economic system—i.e. are these dependent on economic variables such as the relative supply of factors of production, expenditures on research, etc.‡

The explanation of the acceleration in neutral technological advance from the earlier to the later part of the period under consideration is a problem of first importance. For until an adequate explanation is forthcoming, this component of growth is not amenable to control; it follows from the large influence

† This result is consistent with those obtained by J. Kendrick, *Productivity Trends in the United States*, p. 82, table 7.

‡ See M. Brown and A. Conrad, where these problems are spelled out in a Cobb–Douglas framework ('Fundamental Economic Variables in a General System of Production', Division of Balanced International Growth, Netherlands Economic Institute).

neutral technological progress has on economic growth that the process of growth itself is not amenable to control until an acceptable explanation evolves.

The problem of explaining the rapid rise in technological advance in the latter part of the period may well turn out to be a very difficult one, indeed. For except for the rate of growth of output, there are no obvious variables which parallel the variation in neutral technology.† Since the rate of growth of output is generally inversely related to the degree of economies of scale, there may be a connection between the latter and the rate of neutral technological advance. In fact, the estimates derived above indicate that from 1921 to 1960 the degree of returns to scale was less than that estimated in the earlier part of the period. In lieu of a more obvious explanation of this phenomenon, the following tentative hypothesis is offered.

Reasoning by analogy, consider a profit maximizing firm which operates in a growing economy and which is about to encounter diseconomies of scale as a consequence of prospective plant expansion. As the economy grows, then the expected rate of increase of the firm's total costs must rise, provided that it duplicates its existing facilities in response to the rising demand. If the firm innovates, it may avoid the encounter with the range of diseconomies; for if the innovation is neutral or non-neutral, the long-run cost curve is lowered. Hence, it will innovate until the marginal returns of the new facilities in terms of its price (less amortization) is equal to the marginal returns of the existing type of facilities in terms of its price. For given prices of the prospective types of facilities, innovation will be greater the greater is the excess of the expected gross margins of the new facilities relative to the expected economies of scale associated with the existing capital items. Innovation may proceed at a more rapid rate in firms which are expected to experience or are experiencing diseconomies of scale than in those in which the degree of returns to scale is larger. The fact that neutral techno-

† It is difficult to uncover sufficiently reliable data on such obvious variables as educational attainments and research expenditures for the period 1890–1960. However, for shorter periods, various studies, many of them in the development stage, focus on these variables in explaining technological progress. Even though they do not span the whole period in question here, they may clarify the crucial relations between the fundamental variables and technological change, and thus, inferentially, an explanation of the rapid shift in technological progress beginning around 1920 may be forthcoming from this source. For a bibliography, see Brown and Conrad, *op. cit.*

logical advance was inversely related to the presence of economies of scale in the period under consideration provides only superficial support for the hypothesis of induced technological change.† For the empirical results themselves require support (recall that the measure of technological progress includes the effects of changes in the composition of output which are extraneous to the argument),‡ and the hypothesis contains implications that require clarification. I plan to return to the problem in a later work, but for the moment we have only an enigma and a suggestive hypothesis.

† The induced innovation hypothesis offered in the text differs from Hicks's induced invention theory (see *The Theory of Wages*, pp. 125–6). The latter conceives of the non-neutrality of innovations to be a function of the relative scarcity of a factor of production, whereas the hypothesis offered in the text relates technological progress, either neutral or non-neutral, to the degree of existing returns to scale.

‡ Benton Massell has found that nearly one-third of the aggregate measure of neutral technological progress in the period 1954–56 resulted from an inter-industry shift of resources; see his 'A Disaggregated View of Technical Change', *The Journal of Political Economy*, vol. 69 (December 1961), p. 555. One can infer that at the very least, one-third of our measure of technological progress for the period 1890–1960 is attributable to changes in the output mix.

11

TECHNOLOGICAL PROGRESS
AND EMPLOYMENT

Almost every economic theory, from the classicists to the
Keynesians, has focused on the problem of employment; and
almost every measure of social well-being involves employment
in some way. Yet, there is little consensus on the relative impact
of the various forces influencing it. That output has a substantial
effect on employment is fundamental in the Keynesian system.
On the other hand, the classicists, especially Ricardo, emphasized two factors influencing employment, the rate of saving
in relation to population growth (and the consequent substitution of capital for labour), and technological progress (usually
of a labour-saving type). Of course, the neoclassical system, in
its most general form, can potentially handle all of the forces
affecting employment.

In the process of determining the possibility of 'permanent'
technological unemployment, H. Neisser reviews the classical
and neoclassical position on technological unemployment.†
We may quote his principle conclusion: 'there is no mechanism
within the framework of rational economic analysis that...
would secure the full absorption of displaced workers and render
"permanent" technological unemployment in any sense impossible.' The implication is that when technological unemployment is present, only deliberate policy measures (or fortuitous
events) are able to eradicate it.

It follows that in order to implement such a policy it is
necessary to have reliable measures of the relevant quantities.
Our purpose here is to present a set of measures which are
designed to quantify the various forces affecting employment.

Since technology is only one of the several relevant forces, the
measures must isolate the separate effects on employment of the
change in output, the substitution of capital for labour *and*

† '"Permanent" Technological Unemployment', *American Economic Review*,
vol. 32 (March 1942), p. 71. This article presents an extremely lucid analysis of the
problems of displacement and absorption of workers resulting from technological
progress.

technological progress. The problem is essentially one of decomposing the total change in employment into its component changes. It is similar to that developed for measuring the effect of technological progress on output; for it involves the problem of 'adding up' the estimates of the changes in the technologically determined parameters of the relevant function. In the present case the relevant function is the demand for labour relation.

To construct a neoclassical demand for labour relation, one first postulates a production function which yields iso-product curves in the capital–labour plane. Under cost minimization the tangent of the iso-product curve is then equated to the tangent of the iso-outlay line, which gives the demand for labour and capital as a function of relative factor prices and output. The assumptions underlying this model are numerous, but perhaps the main ones are that both factor markets display the same degree of imperfection and that monopoly forces are independent of output and factor hire.†

When the iso-outlay lines are varied by a scale change, we obtain the change in the amount of labour demanded by the firm at different levels of output given technology and relative factor prices unchanged. When the slopes of the iso-outlay lines are shifted in any given way, the variation in the amount of labour demanded by the firm as relative prices change can be determined, given the level of output and technology.

Although we examined this extensively in Chapters 2–4 it is useful to repeat here how variations in technology affect the iso-product curves. There are four ways: (i) twisting them, i.e. changing the marginal rate of substitution of labour for capital at each combination of labour and capital (and for a given elasticity of substitution); and/or (ii) by re-scaling the iso-product curves so that for a given combination of labour and capital and for the marginal rate of substitution at that combination more or less output is obtained; and/or (iii) by altering the elasticity of substitution between capital and labour; and/or (iv) by packing the iso-product curves closer together or farther apart, which means in the former case that the technological change has engendered economies of scale.

The labour demand relation depends in a unique way on the production function; for each technological change (i)–(iv) there

† If all supply and demand elasticities are constant, then the second assumption would hold.

is a homologous change in the labour demand relation. Hence, changes in the labour demand relation can be categorized in terms of (i)–(iv). We can then measure the impact of technological progress on labour demand, and since we have output and relative factor prices as variables in the labour demand relation, it is possible to measure changes in employment attributable to technological progress separately from other factors influencing employment.

Before proceeding to our own analysis, it is useful to note some of the labour demand relations that have appeared in the literature. This is not meant as an exhaustive survey of the literature in the field of labour demand relations, but as an indication of the kinds of specifications that are relevant.

PRECEDENTS

In the Tinbergen tradition there is the work of Profs. Klein and Goldberger. Their model of the United States contains a 'wage fund' equation: total real wages as a function of current and lagged output. A trend term is also included which may be interpreted as an adjustment for productivity changes.[†] Their function is (roughly)

$$wN/p = \alpha_0 + \alpha_1 X + \alpha_2 X_{-1} + \alpha_3 t.$$

or

$$N = p/w(\alpha_0 + \alpha_1 X + \alpha_2 X_{-1} + \alpha_3 t).$$

In a later study, Klein and his colleagues used a set of three equations with these variables to describe a larger number of aspects of the labour market.[‡] One of these equations is

$$w - w_{-1} =$$
$$\beta_0 + \beta_1 \left[\frac{u + u_{-1} + u_{-2} + u_{-3}}{u} \right] + \beta_2 \left[\frac{\Delta p + \Delta p_{-1} + \Delta p_{-2} + \Delta p_{-3}}{u} \right],$$

where u is unemployment. But this is not a labour demand relation, since it embodies the total labour force variable (u is defined as total labour force minus employment); it shows up in

[†] L. R. Klein and A. S. Goldberger, *An Econometric Model of the United States, 1929–1952* (North-Holland Publishing Co., 1955), pp. 16–17.

[‡] L. R. Klein, R. J. Ball, A. Hazelwood and P. Vandome, *An Econometric Model of the United Kingdom* (Oxford University Press, 1961), pp. 74, 77, 79.

the wage rate via the supply side. In the latter study there is a wage bargaining equation, an hours worked equation, an equation specifying the spread between wage rates and earnings; the labour demand is embedded in these.†

Professor G. Tintner has experimented with a labour demand relation.‡ He offers a method which tests whether or not the demand for labour is homogeneous in prices. In the theory of the firm the demand for labour depends ultimately only on the real wage rate, although this strict form is rarely used. Professor Tintner does use this strict form, though, to test whether labour demand in the United Kingdom in the inter-war period depends on the ratio of wages to prices or upon the absolute prices.§ Using the method of weighted regression, he finds that the demand relation tends to be homogeneous.

A labour demand relation which suppresses relative price effects is embodied in the Leontief production system. Also, R. Ferber and P. J. Verdoorn specify the demand for labour only as a function of output.‖ They use an ingenious method of determining whether employment is a function of a distributed lag in output, or a function of a single lag, or a function of current output.

A more sophisticated labour demand relation which also suppresses the effect of relative factor prices is developed by A. Conrad. He relates labour demand to actual output, planned output and capacity output. Technological change is represented by a trend term and possibly by changes in the parameters in the system.¶ Another employment-output relation is developed by E. Kuh.†† He explicitly considers the important cyclical factors in this study.

For the most part, very little attention is paid to changing

† The Dutch planning model contains an unemployment equation which, again, contains supply and demand elements. See H. Theil, *Economic Forecasts and Policy*, pp. 53–4.

‡ *Econometrics* (Wiley, 1952), p. 143.

§ In a challenging article, Professor Tintner has demonstrated that the labour demand function is homogeneous of degree zero in prices for a great variety of market organizations. See his 'Homogeneous Systems in Mathematical Economics' *Econometrica*, vol. 16 (1944), pp. 273 ff.

‖ *Research Methods in Economics and Business* (New York, Macmillan, 1962), p. 374.

¶ A. H. Conrad, 'The U.S. Employment Dilemna and a Family of Employment Forecasting Functions', Netherlands Economic Institute, December 1961.

†† 'Profits, Profit Markups and Productivity', Study Paper No. 15, Joint Economic Committee (United States Government Printing Office, Washington, 1960).

technology in these studies.† In what follows, a method of treating technological progress in a labour demand relation in a systematic manner is developed and tested.

A general labour demand relation is used to illustrate the derivation of the relevant measures. Therefore, the method itself is applicable to any reasonable labour demand relation. We proceed first to the presentation of the labour demand model. Since it is based on the CES production function, its properties are familiar by now and we treat it briefly. The method of measuring technological employment and unemployment is then set out, followed by the empirical results of confronting the method by data on the private domestic non-farm sector of the United States, for the period 1890–1958.‡

THE DERIVATION OF THE LABOUR DEMAND RELATION

It is necessary to derive the labour demand relation explicitly. We start by assuming that production proceeds in a CES world:

$$X = \gamma[\kappa C^{-\alpha} + (1-\kappa)\, N^{-\alpha}]^{-v/\alpha} \qquad (11.1)$$

the relevant expansion path relation is

$$\rho = \kappa' u^{1/\sigma} \qquad (11.2)$$

where $\rho = q/w$, $u = N/C$ and $\kappa' = \kappa/(1-\kappa)$.§ From (11.2), we find

$$C = N(\rho/\kappa')^{-\sigma} \qquad (11.3)$$

which can be combined with (11.1) and solving for N, yields

$$N = h_1 X^{1/v}[h_2 \rho^{1-\sigma} + h_3]^{\sigma/1-\sigma}, \qquad (11.4)$$

where $h_1 = \gamma^{-1/v}$, $h_2 = \kappa\left(\dfrac{1-\kappa}{\kappa}\right)^{1-\sigma}$ and $h_3 = 1-\kappa$.

The parameters that enter the labour demand relation are γ, v, κ and σ and they are interpreted just as we did in Chapter 4.

† In the Klein–Goldberger labour demand relation a trend term is included which could represent the effects of technological change (*An Econometric Model of the United States, 1929–1952*). The Conrad model attempts to measure the effect of technological change on labour demand. The Kuh model includes a productivity index, but variations in it can be attributable to substitution, etc., i.e. to variables not directly associated with technological progress.

‡ The methodology and results are derived from M. Brown and J. S. de Cani, 'A Measure of Technological Employment', *Review of Economics and Statistics*, vol. 45.

§ w is defined as the cost per unit of labour employed. The capital rent per unit is the product of the price of capital goods and the sum of the interest and depreciation rates.

It is no surprise that the properties of the labour demand relation conform to neoclassical expectations.† Thus, a rise in output increases the demand for labour by an amount that depends on the degree of returns to scale v. If there are important economies of scale, then a given increase in output produces a smaller increase in employment than if v were small. As to the relative price factor variable, if the price of capital services increase *cet. par.*, i.e. if ρ increases, then employment rises depending on the size of κ and σ.

It is possible to employ the labour demand relation that is based on the Cobb–Douglas production function. In familiar notation, it is

$$N = \bar{A}X^{1/(\alpha'+\beta)}/\rho^{\beta'/(\alpha'+\beta)},$$

where $\bar{A}$ is a constant α' is the elasticity of production with respect to labour and β is capital's production elasticity. For certain purposes, this form may be adequate. However, it is subject to all the limitations that are associated with the Cobb–Douglas relation itself. Although the CES labour demand relation is much more difficult to estimate than the Cobb–Douglas labour demand form, its greater generality justifies the marginal effort devoted to it.

The expansion path (11.2) specifies an equilibrium condition. As discussed in Chapter 5, we would like a less restrictive specification, one that can also hold in a non-equilibrium situation. This is provided by

$$u = \kappa'^{\sigma(1-\lambda)}\rho^{\sigma}u_{-1}^{\lambda} \qquad (11.5)$$

where λ is the rigidity parameter. The reason for solving for u rather than ρ has been discussed above.

Having settled upon a labour demand relation, it is necessary

---

† The labour demand relation is homogeneous in output of degree $1/v$. It is homogeneous in prices of degree zero since a 1 per cent increase in q and w cancel each other in the variable ρ; this is an application of Tintner's theorem on the homogeneity of relative prices in homogeneous models.

We can express labour's marginal product equilibrium relation in terms of labour as follows:

$$N = [(1-\kappa)\,v\gamma^{-\alpha/v}]^{\sigma}\,(w/p)^{-\sigma}(X)^{-\sigma(1\alpha/v)}, \qquad (11.4a)$$

whence it is seen that the labour demand relation in its present form is linear in logarithms and can be estimated directly. The difficulty is that the neutral and non-neutral parameters are indistinguishable in the intercept of the logarithmic relation, i.e. they are under-identified. In other words, using (11.4a), it would be difficult to derive estimates of the two kinds of technological change in which we are interested. However, if only the total technological change effect on employment is required, then (11.4a) can be used to estimate the demand for labour. This is the approach followed in Murray Brown, *The Share of Corporate Profits in the Postwar Period*, U.S. Department of Commerce, 1965.

to divide up the overall time span into technological epochs. These are periods within which the parameters which represent non-neutral technology (i.e. κ and σ) are stable. If R epochs are obtained, then we can employ the finite differencing method (see Chapter 8) to determine the impact on employment of : (*a*) the change in output, (*b*) the change in the relative factor prices, and (*c*) neutral and non-neutral technological change. In symbols: ΔX refers to (*a*); $\Delta \rho$ refers to (*b*); ($\Delta \gamma + \Delta v$) is the neutral component and $\Delta \kappa + \Delta \sigma$ is the non-neutral component of (*c*). In sum, once the epochs are obtained, the method used in adding up the changes in the parameters to determine their influence on employment is precisely the same as that used in adding up their effect on output, which is employed in the previous chapter.

One can use this method for an industry or firm to find the effect on employment of technological change. But there is no way, using the available data, of quantifying technological unemployment at the firm or industry level. For an aggregate, however, a technological unemployment measure can be derived if one assumes that the unemployed workers are unemployed for the same reasons that the employed workers are employed.†
The reasons that the employed workers are employed are summarized in

$$\Delta N = \left(\frac{\Delta N}{\Delta X}\right)\Delta X + \left(\frac{\Delta N}{\Delta \rho}\right)\Delta \rho + \left(\frac{\Delta N}{\Delta v}\right)\Delta v + \left(\frac{\Delta N}{\Delta \gamma}\right)\Delta \gamma$$
$$+ \left(\frac{\Delta N}{\Delta \kappa}\right)\Delta \kappa + \left(\frac{\Delta N}{\Delta \sigma}\right)\Delta \sigma.$$

Let ΔL be the change in the labour force; then

$$\frac{\Delta L - \Delta N}{\Delta N} = 1 - \left[\left(\frac{\Delta N}{\Delta X}\right)\frac{\Delta X}{\Delta L} + \left(\frac{\Delta N}{\Delta \rho}\right)\frac{\Delta \rho}{\Delta L} + \left(\frac{\Delta N}{\Delta v}\right)\frac{\Delta v}{\Delta L}\right.$$
$$\left. + \left(\frac{\Delta N}{\Delta \gamma}\right)\frac{\Delta \gamma}{\Delta L} + \left(\frac{\Delta N}{\Delta \kappa}\right)\frac{\Delta \kappa}{\Delta L} + \left(\frac{\Delta N}{\Delta \sigma}\right)\frac{\Delta \sigma}{\Delta L}\right], \quad (11.6)$$

thus the percentage change in unemployed labour is decomposed into six components which exhaust the total. The last four terms in (11.6) combine to give us a measure of the percentage change in unemployed labour due to technological progress. Of course, this refers to the economy as a whole.

† The proper way to derive a measure of technological employment for an aggregate is to apply this method to the micro units, i.e. industries, and then aggregate the measures. This is analogous to the problem of finding an aggregate measure of technological change which avoids the problem of changing output mix.

Let me summarize the procedure before confronting it with an empirical situation.

(1) A labour demand equation is specified: employment as a function of output and relative factor prices. We have specified a completely general constant elasticity of substitution labour demand relation, since it is based on the CES production function. The parameters entering this labour demand relation are determined technologically on the assumption that the capital and labour markets are imperfect in the same degree.

(2) The overall time period to be considered is divided into technological epochs, i.e. periods within which the parameters of the labour demand relation are stable, and thus differ from the stable parameters of an adjacent epoch. The statistical method of isolating epochs is identical to the one used above in the analysis of output change.

(3) If R epochs are isolated, then $R - 1$ parameter changes are available. These, together with epochal data on output and relative factor prices, are used to implement the finite differencing method. The finite differencing method permits us to quantify the effect on employment of a change in output, a change in relative factor supplies and variations in neutral and non-neutral technological progress. A change in employment between any two arbitrary time points can be quantified with respect to neutral and non-neutral technological progress, variations in output and relative factor prices.

STATISTICAL PROCEDURES
AND EMPIRICAL RESULTS

A two-step procedure is used to derive estimates of the labour demand relation. In the first step, the expansion path function is fitted to time-series data for N, C, q and w. The fitting equation of (11.5) is

$$\log u = b + \sigma \log \rho + \lambda \log u_{-1}, \qquad (11.7)$$

where $b = \sigma(1 - \lambda) \log [(1 - \kappa)/\kappa]$. This yields estimates of κ and σ, and hence b, which can be combined with (11.4) to form a new time-series $[\hat{h}_2 \rho^{1-\hat{\sigma}} + \hat{h}_3]^{\hat{\sigma}/(1-\hat{\sigma})}$.

Then, the fitting equation of the labour demand relation is

$$\log N - \frac{\hat{\sigma}}{1-\hat{\sigma}} \log [\hat{h}_2 \rho^{1-\hat{\sigma}} + \hat{h}_3] = -\frac{1}{v} \log \gamma + 1/v \log X + \beta \log t,$$

$$(11.8)$$

which produces estimates of v, $\log \gamma$ and β. Notice that a trend term is added to the fitting equation (11.8). Its parameter β is interpreted as the rate at which neutral technological change proceeds. Since it displaces labour as well as capital, we would expect β to be negative in our estimates.

The short-run expansion path (11.7) is used in the first step to generate estimates of κ and σ, since it provides long-run as well as short-run estimates of the parameters necessary for the implementation of the second step. It is the long-run estimates in which we are interested in the present problem. To obtain them, single-stage least squares is applied to the expansion path function $(11\cdot7)$ using data on the private non-farm domestic sector of the United States.†

The periods of time over which the estimates of the parameters of (11.7) are stable are the technological epochs for the present problem. Within each epoch, there is no non-neutral technological progress. In the study by Brown and Popkin, three epochs are derived for the period 1890–1958. They are: $r(1) = 1890–1918$, $r(2) = 1919–37$, and $r(3) = 1938–58$. These are the epochs used in the present study. A variance analysis applied to (11.7) for three sets of estimates on the epochs reveals significant structural dissimilarities.

Inspection of the epochal estimates of the parameters of (11.7) indicate their differences. Column 1 indicates that there was a substantial reduction in the labour intensity of technology

† The data used for this and the following study are the preliminary estimates of J. Kendrick for the private domestic non-farm sector of the United States. They include fixed capital stocks, man-hours employed and gross output. The capital stock series was adjusted for under-utilization of capacity by the same method used on Kendrick's final estimates (see Chapter 10). Data for q and w were obtained as follows: annual estimates for w were constructed by splicing together three wage rate series for the domestic non-farm sector *Historical Statistics of the United States* (Department of Commerce, 1960), Tables D 696–707, D 685–695 and D 603–617. The series were transformed into a compensation per man-hour series by using Kendrick's preliminary data on man-hours worked and then made commensurate with Kendrick's labour compensation figures by using his bench-marks for 1899, 1919, 1929, 1937, 1948 and 1957. To derive a series for q, data from R. Goldsmith *A Study of Saving in the United States*, vol. 3 (Princeton, 1956), tables N-5 were used to interpolate between Kendrick's six figures for capital rentals (same years as for labour compensation).

These data are not presented for two reasons, first, they are based on Kendrick's preliminary figures (his final estimates and the adjustments are shown in Appendix D) Secondly, very crude methods were used to derive the q and w series. It is to be noted, in view of this, that our conclusions are highly tentative. In fact, the methodological rather than substantive aspects of the studies in the present chapter and in Chapter 12 should be emphasized.

between $r(1)$ and $r(2)$, but that labour intensity increased between $r(2)$ and $r(3)$. The movement of the short-run elasticity of substitution is traced in column 2 and the long run σ is traced in column 3. Apparently σ followed the time shape of $(1-\kappa)/\kappa$, falling from a high in $r(1)$ to a low in $r(2)$ and then rising again in $r(3)$. The long-run σ exceeds its short-run counterpart in all epochs since we built this relation into the model. Epochal estimates of the technological rigidity parameter λ are given in column 4; there appears to be a trend in rigidity which is not unexpected. For one would think that the kind of technology introduced in the 1920's would be much more rigid than the technology of the first epoch simply because of the increased roundaboutness of the former. Interestingly, the rigidity does not seem to have increased significantly from the second to third epochs. In terms of statistical significance, of the nine parameter estimates in Table 11.1, only two are not significantly different from zero by the two-standard error rule. These two are $\log(1-\kappa)/\kappa$ and σ for the middle epoch. Since we will deal with epochal changes, it may seem that the meaningfulness of our subsequent measures is reduced. To some extent this is true; yet the measures can be calculated in terms of changes from the first to third epochs, thus permitting us to draw inferences about the long-term forces (between the first and third epochs, say) affecting employment. However, since the middle epoch estimates do not throw off the long-term trend implications, we will include them in the measure.

The estimates in Table 11.1 are used to calculate the remaining parameters in the labour demand relation (11.8). These are presented in Table 11.2.

Since changes in v and γ are categorized together as representing neutral technological change (as is β) we do not require the decomposition of $1/v$ and γ in column 1 of Table 11.2. The coefficient on $\log X$ is $1/v$ and this is given in column 2. We see that returns to scale were extremely high in $r(1)$ and $r(2)$ and there appeared to have been decreasing returns in $r(3)$. Although the values of v are too high in $r(1)$ and $r(2)$, the time shape of returns to scale is not unreasonable from an *a priori* point of view. Were we really to test for returns to scale, we would of course employ the production function (1) rather than the labour demand relation. Again, we repeat that any constant elasticity of substitution production function such as the one

TABLE 11.1. *Parameter estimates of equation (11.7) for three epochs*

Epoch	(1) $\log\left(\frac{1-\kappa}{\kappa}\right)r$†	(2) σ	(3) $\frac{\sigma}{1-\lambda}$‡	(4) λ_r	(5) $\bar{R}^2$
$r(1)$: 1890–1918	−0·8865 (0·437)	0·3453 (0·123)	0·55	0·3764 (0·169)	0·8472
$r(2)$: 1919–37	−7·1660 (5·36)	0·0779 (0·098)	0·31	0·7462 (0·221)	0·7300
$r(3)$: 1938–58	−2·9275 (1·45)	0·1112 (0·038)	0·47	0·7623 (0·159)	0·8606

† Log $(1-\kappa)/\kappa$ has been corrected for the bias of a ratio estimate. q and w are index numbers. C is in millions of 1929 dollars. N is in millions of man-hours worked.

‡ This long-run estimate of σ has not been corrected for the autocorrelation of N/C. (See Ferber and Verdoorn, *Research Methods in Economics and Business*, pp. 374 ff.)

TABLE 11.2. *Remaining parameter estimates of the labour demand relation (11.8) for three epochs within the overall period 1890–1958*

Epoch	$-\frac{1}{v}\log\gamma$	$\frac{1}{v}$	v	β†	$\bar{R}^2$
$r(1)$	0·9912 (0·0481)	0·5867 (0·0420)	1·7044	0·1091 (0·1186)	0·9893
$r(2)$	1·9863 (0·0931)	0·6393 (0·0531)	1·5642	−0·0406 (0·00989)	0·9053
$r(3)$	0·8196 (0·0991)	1·2456 (0·1673)	0·8028	−0·1873 (0·0539)	0·9506

† In $r(1)$ β is not significantly different from zero. N is in millions of man-hours worked. X is in millions of 1929 dollars, and q/w is a ratio of two indexes; t is a time variable starting at 1 in 1890, 1919 and 1938.

used in the present chapter confounds the two sources of returns to scale, a pure scale change in output and a technological change. In any case, to assume that the economy operated under constant returns to scale in the period 1890–1958 appears to be inconsistent with our data.

Our task now is to use the information in Tables 11.1 and 11.2 to help us to quantify the forces affecting employment. In order to isolate the effects of the changes individually, we apply a finite difference analog of the total derivative, which is described in Chapter 8 and Appendix C.

TABLE 11.3. *Sources of changes in the logarithm of employment, 1890–1958*

Contribution to
$\Delta \log N$ of the percentage change in

Time interval	1 Log output	2 Log relative prices	3 Neutral technology	4 Non-neutral technology	Estimated $\Delta \log N$ columns 1+2+3+4	Actual $\Delta \log N$
Epochs 1–2	0·0944	−0·1193	0·8834	−0·8956	−0·0371	−0·0457
Epochs 2–3	0·4094	0·0027	−0·0945	−0·1319	0·1857	0·2088

Table 11.3 embodies the results of applying the finite difference measure of technological employment to the private domestic non-farm sector of the United States 1890–1958. It contains the contribution to the change in the logarithm of employment attributable to changes in: (*a*) the logarithm of the scale of output, column 1; (*b*) the logarithm of relative factor prices, column 2; (*c*) neutral technology, column 3; and (*d*) non-neutral technology, column 4. The sum of the first four columns add up to the estimated change in the logarithm of employment. In the last column the actual change in the logarithm of employment is presented. These changes refer to epochal differences in parameter estimates; with respect to variables, they refer to the changes in the average of the values for the last five years of each epoch.† It is clear by inspection that the estimated $\Delta \log N$ is very close to the actual $\Delta \log N$; in fact, they are as close as the log N estimated by the labour demand relation is to the actual log N.

The forces affecting $\Delta \log N$ can now be read off Table 11.3. In the first epochal change in $\Delta \log N$—i.e. the change in the logarithm of man-hours worked from 1914–18 to 1933–37— technological change had almost no effect, since neutral technological change offset the non-neutral change. The contribution of output was positive even though the terminal period was in a depression; this, however, was insufficient to compensate for the effect of the change in relative factor prices, and therefore

† The reason for this is that a 'long-run' labour demand relation is fitted, and thus the latter part of each epoch approximates the steady-state values more closely than the early values in each epoch. We hasten to add that this does not constitute an arbitrary facet in the method, since it is always possible to derive a measure between any given parts of an epoch, or between any given parts of any two epochs.

employment fell between the two epochs. Note that the effect of non-neutral change was of a labour-saving type.

Before proceeding to a discussion of the second epochal change in log N, we observe that technological change had almost no effect on $\Delta \log N$ between the first two epochs. The reason for this unexpected result can be seen on inspection of Table 11.2. There, returns to scale fell from $r(1)$ to $r(2)$ which would have the effect of increasing log N between $r(1)$ and $r(2)$; however, log γ increased, which had the effect of decreasing employment. Apparently, the fall in ν outweighed the effect of the rise in log γ and thus the total impact of neutral technological change on employment was to increase it. Coincidentally, the depressing effect of non-neutral technological change was sufficient to offset the compound effect of neutral technological change. In other words, non-neutral progress was of the same order of magnitude as neutral technological progress.

The relatively large increase in employment between the second and third epoch was almost entirely due to the scale change in output. Both neutral and non-neutral technological change provided a significant depressing effect on $\Delta \log N$, and, again, non-neutral technological change was of a labour-saving type.† The change in relative factor prices had almost no effect on $\Delta \log N$ between these two epochs.

Comparing the relative effect on the change in employment of the change in output and technological progress, the general picture that emerges is that output seems to have been more important. Put in another way, the labour that was displaced by technological advance seems to have been more than absorbed by the effect of the rise in output, although the displaced workers may not have been the ones absorbed. If we accept these crude estimates in broad outline, it appears that technological change has not been sufficiently powerful to form a 'surplus population' or an 'industrial reserve army' in the Marxian sense. The race between displacement and absorption of labour,‡ although close between the first and second epoch, was certainly won by the latter from the second to the third technological epochs. This conclusion is subject to serious qualifications, especially in view

† Yet in another study, when the last part of the 1950's are compared to the early part, we find non-neutral technological change to be of a labour *using* type. See M. Brown and J. S. de Cani, 'Technological Changes in the United States, 1950–1960', *Productivity Measurement Review*, no. 29.

‡ K. Marx, *Capital* (New York, Modern Library, 1906), pp. 689 ff.

of the inadequacy of the data.† Nevertheless, the methods developed here precipitate the hope that certain paramount propositions, for example, relating to the displacement-absorption problem, are susceptible to quantification.

Perhaps the major policy use of the results of applying our measure of technological employment (or unemployment, if an aggregate is used) is the following. We wish to know how much we must change the variables which we can control in order to effectuate a required change in employment. The forces affecting employment are technological progress, variations in output, and changes in relative factor supplies. Of these, perhaps output is the variable most susceptible to control at various policy levels. Hence, in order to achieve a given employment target, we require a measure of the effect on employment of output, holding the other forces constant. The measure proposed here goes a considerable way—at the very least, in principle—towards improving the treatment of this policy problem.

As an illustration suppose that we postulate a policy of offsetting every reduction in employment attributable to technological advance by a compensatory increase in output. How much must output increase in order to offset technological advance from the second to third epoch? Since $\Delta \log X$ is 0·4344, then 0·9422 ($= 0·4094 \div 0·4344$) is roughly the unit impact of output on employment from the second to third epoch. In order to offset the 0·2264 (0·0945 + 0·1319) per cent decrease in employment due to technological change, output would have had to increase 24 ($\approx 0·2264 \div 0·9422$) per cent more than it did. It is hardly necessary to emphasize that these are extremely crude numbers. But aside from the fact that there is little or no

---

† There is also a bias in the estimates that results from the absence of a trend term in the estimating form of the CES side relation (11·7). Recall that we are approximating the services of capital in (11·7) by a net stock series, which includes an obsolescence component. A trend term should then be included in the estimating form to depict the technological progress associated with the obsolescence component of depreciation. But the actual inclusion of a trend term proved to be unsuccessful, since its coefficient was not significant. Yet the first order correlation between $(N/C)_{-1}$ and a trend is sufficiently large—it is 0·78 for the overall period—to indicate that we are unable to distinguish between the distributed lag effect and the obsolescence component. We assigned all of the effect to the distributed lag term, thus biasing downward our estimate of technological progress. This deficiency could probably be remedied by a more sophisticated treatment of the distributed lag effect, a task that remains for future work. But even with the bias, the effect on employment (and on relative income shares, see Chapter 12) of technological progress is considerable.

probability content in this exercise there is the difficulty of implementing such a policy. For even if we had reliable estimates of the sort we have proposed, the problems associated with the mechanisms and timing of policy implementation would still plague us. Yet it is incontrovertible that for any initial step in this direction we must obtain measurements of the relevant forces affecting employment.

12

TECHNOLOGICAL CHANGE
AND THE DISTRIBUTION
OF INCOME

One of the problems facing economics is the explanation of the behaviour of relative income shares—the share of total income originating that accrues to labour relative to the share that goes to the owners of capital. Relative income shares are the resultant of all the forces that make up the motor of capitalism: technological progress, saving, the growth of the labour force, government fiscal policy, imperfect competition, and the business cycle. But the problem is not important for this reason, since these forces act on all economic magnitudes. Nor is it necessary to see its importance to call attention to the famous Ricardian dictum that economics should inquire into the laws governing the division of the produce, since a tolerably correct law can only be established with respect to proportions, not with respect to quantities.† Stated simply, the question of relative shares is important because it represents the relative pay-off to various groups that is usually associated with their relative contribution to production. It is the end result of all of their productive efforts; for once their productive efforts are established their relative remuneration is determined and only an extraneous force can alter the final distribution. In this sense a factor's relative income share is a variable of last resort. Hence, the question of shares is at the centre of controversy between certain pressure groups, and motivates the appeals to political bodies to effectuate policies that alter the functional (and size) distribution of income.‡ This in itself is sufficient justification for their examination.

† See J. M. Keynes, *The General Theory of Employment, Interest and Money* (London, Macmillan, 1949), p. 4.
‡ The introduction of the Treasury *Guidelines* in 1962 (which shortened the service lives of fixed assets for tax purposes, thus increasing reported depreciation charges and reducing corporate income taxes) was partly motivated by the desire to compensate the recipients of profits for their post-war reduction relative to the increase in the compensation of labour.

A further justification for devoting our attention to the problem is an intellectual one, for the behaviour of relative shares has been relatively stable compared to other economic variables such as technological progress, production, investment, etc. Thus, underlying the study of the problem is the desire to uncover the reason for the relative stability of income shares, and to determine whether the absence of marked changes will be characteristic of their future movements.

The explanation of relative income shares entails the explanation of the forces affecting them, but the measurement of the forces affecting income share is a first step in the development of such an explanation. The present chapter reports on a study[†] which attempts to quantify the effect on relative shares of two of these forces, non-neutral technological change and the relative supplies of capital and labour.

There are two propositions in the neoclassical tradition which hold that relative shares are the resultant of configurations of non-neutral technological change, the elasticity of substitution and the labour–capital ratio. The first holds that a factor saving innovation, *cet. par.*, reduces the relative share of income of that factor in all cases.[‡] The second maintains that if one factor increases in supply more rapidly than another, and if the elasticity of substitution (σ) is less than unity, then the relative share of the first factor decreases.[§] Of course if σ exceeds unity, then the relative share of the first factor increases; and if σ is equal to unity (the Cobb–Douglas case), changes in the relative supplies of factors will have no effect on the relative shares.

In connection with the second of these neoclassical propositions, our inquiry into the sources of non-neutral technological progress in Chapter 4 has taught us how changes in the elasticity of substitution and the capital intensity characteristic of an abstract technology may affect the distribution of income between capital and labour. Briefly, it is known that an increase in the capital intensity characteristic of a technology is labour saving, and thus augments the capital share in relation to the wage share. Moreover, a rise in the elasticity of substitution rebounds to capital's advantage only if capital is increasing more rapidly

[†] Based on the article by M. Brown and J. S. de Cani, 'Technological Change and the Distribution of Income', *International Economic Review*, vol. 4.

[‡] J. R. Hicks, *The Theory of Wages*, p. 122. For the most part, Hicks assumed competitive markets.

[§] Ibid. p. 115.

than labour. These relations as well as the neoclassical propositions are re-stated below.

Leaving monopoly aside, variations in relative income shares are taken to depend on changes in relative factor supplies and on changes in the components of non-neutral technological change.† Conceptually, the interaction of these forces may set upper and lower bounds within which relative income shares may be forced to move. To illustrate this consider the following model. Suppose that capital is advancing more rapidly than labour and that the elasticity of substitution is smaller than unity; this single set of relations tends to reduce capital's share of income. Now assume that the capital intensity of the ruling technology rises, thus counteracting the forces producing a fall in capital's share. If there is a fall in the elasticity of substitution, i.e. if there is a reduction in the second component of non-neutral technological progress, then the share of capital rises on this account also. Hence, there is an initial reduction in the labour share due to the technological change, but labour may recoup its relative loss through time if the labour–capital ratio continues to fall and provided no further labour-saving innovation occurs. Of course a different set of changes in the elasticity of substitution, the capital intensity characteristic and the relative factor supplies, may generate a divergent movement in relative shares.

In the present chapter, these propositions are brought to a test on data for the private domestic non-farm sector of the United States for the period 1890–1958. First, we briefly indicate how our analysis differs from some previous studies of the relative share problem. The model is then introduced and discussed. Finally, the results are set out.

PRECEDENTS

There are three types of theories of relative income shares: those based on neoclassical supply and demand mechanisms, on mark-up hypotheses, and on aggregative or neo-Keynesian type relations. Of course the classical Ricardian theory of distribution does not fit into any of these categories; its emphasis on a subsistence level of compensation negates its applicability to developed economies, and hence is not seriously considered in

† In the present study we also abstract from the effects on relative shares of changes in capacity utilization and the shifting of the corporate income tax.

contemporary literature. In any case the present section is not intended as a review of the prevailing theories of the functional distribution of income. It is offered only to provide a minimal amount of orientation for what follows.

In the neoclassical framework, changes in relative income shares are produced by shifts in the production function, changes in relative factor supplies, and variations in monopoly power. However, the framework is a general one—it embodies the mechanisms by which these various forces affect relative shares, but in order to *explain* the shares the mechanisms must be specified. The only specification in the neoclassical tradition that is currently discussed is the Cobb–Douglas theory. This assumes that disturbances to the interaction of the *competitive* supply and demand factors tend to derive from the supply side. Moreover, the elasticity of substitution is assumed to be unity, and non-neutral technological change is zero. Hence, relative income shares are constant no matter what movements occur in the labour–capital ratio. These assumptions are extremely restrictive. Although our analysis is in the neoclassical tradition, we assume nothing about the variation or level of σ or non-neutral technology. It is apparent that we are concerned with the measurement of the forces affecting relative income shares. The objective here is to obtain measurements that do not presume a special theory.

Still within the neoclassical tradition is the work of I. Kravis[†] and R. Solow.[‡] The Kravis study suggests that movements in relative shares may be attributable to the introduction of labour-saving innovations accompanied by a relatively more elastic supply of capital than of labour. This assumes that σ is less than unity, which he indeed finds by computing an arc elasticity. The major difference of this study with ours is that we utilize a more complete model whose relations are identifiable, and which permits direct tests of these propositions as well as the proposition that non-neutral technological change may cause σ to vary.

The Solow studies either assume no non-neutral technological change or postulate a capital-saving technological change;

[†] Relative Income Shares in Fact and Theory', *American Economic Review*, vol. 49 (December 1959), pp. 917–49.
[‡] 'The Constancy of Relative Shares', *American Economic Review*, vol. 48 (September 1958), pp. 618–31; and 'Capital, Labor and Income in Manufacturing', *Studies in Income & Wealth*.

moreover, he assumes that the economic system under discussion operates at constant returns to scale. His emphasis on the elasticity of substitution as a focal determinant of relative shares and his attempts to discover its value, by testing a complete model, is similar to the present approach. We differ on the matter of non-neutral innovations which is explicitly identified and measured in the present model, whereas it is presumed to be either non-existent or is specified *a priori* in Solow's work.

The mark-up theories—best exemplified by Kalecki—hold that the relative factor prices are, for the most part, independent of the demand and supply of the factors. Relative shares depend, then, on monopoly power, since demands and supplies of products and factors of production exert a negligible influence on their prices and quantities. (Of course the neoclassical system also recognizes the effects on relative shares of imperfect competition and thus is akin to the mark-up theory.) Kalecki adds the assumption that marginal costs are horizontal up to capacity output. Hence, in the short run, property income depends only on the mark-up price less marginal or average costs. The mark-up in turn is a function of diverse non-'market' phenomena such as union pressure, etc. The Kalecki type analysis has received considerable attention, yet has not been stated or tested in an acceptable manner.† The principle reason for rejecting the theory as a research strategy at this stage of our knowledge is that it presumes more than we wish. We would like a framework that is as general as possible so that if market forces do happen to be influential in determining shares, it will not presume their absence; conversely, we would also like to know when market forces are not relevant. In principle, tests of the neoclassical system will meet these research objectives.

The aggregate theories of distribution—associated with the names of Kaldor, Boulding, Robinson and Weintraub—focus on macro supply and demand relations. For the most part, these models are competitive with the neoclassical system, and since they form a different tradition it is not necessary to outline them here.‡

---

† See M. W. Reder, 'Alternative Theories of Labor's Share', in the *Allocation* of *Economic Resources* (Stanford University Press, 1959), pp. 181–206. This contains a discussion and critique of all three types of theories of income distribution.

‡ An interesting comparison of the Kaldorian model and a neoclassical type model is developed by A. K. Sen, 'Neo-Classical and Neo-Keynesian Theories of Distribution', *The Economic Record*, vol. 39 (March 1963), pp. 53–64.

THE MODEL

The model is based on the marginal productivity equilibrium relations derived from the CES production function. First recall that, for a two-factor model of production, the marginal product of labour, $\partial X/\partial N$, is equal to w/p, where w is the wage rate and p is the product price: hence

$$\frac{\partial X}{\partial N} = \frac{w}{p}, \tag{12.1}$$

or

$$\frac{N}{X}\frac{\partial X}{\partial N} = \frac{wN}{pX}, \tag{12.2}$$

where wN/pX is the share of labour in the value product. By Euler's theorem

$$1 - \frac{\partial X}{\partial N}\frac{N}{X} = \frac{\partial X}{\partial C}\frac{C}{X}.$$

Thus, we obtain

$$\frac{\partial X}{\partial C}\frac{C}{X} = \frac{qC}{pX}, \tag{12.3}$$

where q is the unit capital rent.
Taking the ratio of (12.5) to (12.2), gives us

$$\frac{\partial X/\partial C}{\partial X/\partial N}\frac{C}{N} = \frac{qC}{wN}. \tag{12.4}$$

By evaluating the partial derivatives in terms of the CES production function, (12.4) becomes

$$\frac{qC}{wN} = \frac{\kappa}{1-\kappa}\left(\frac{N}{C}\right)^{(1/\sigma)-1}, \tag{12.5}$$

Aside from Reder's article, a general review of the field, with special emphasis on the aggregative approach, is presented by T. Scitovsky, 'A Survey of Some Theories of Income Distribution', Conference on Research in Income and Wealth, *National Bureau of Economic Research* (April 1961), mimeographed.

The following selected sources contain explicit critiques of the marginal productivity theory: F. Machlup, 'On the Meaning of Marginal Product', *Readings in the Theory of Income Distribution* (The Blakiston Co., 1946); N. Kaldor, 'Alternative Theories of Distribution', *Review of Economic Studies*, vol. 22 (1955–56), pp. 83–91; S. Weintraub, *An Approach to the Theory of Income Distribution* (Chilton Co., 1958); N. Georgescu-Roegen, 'Economic Theory and Agrarian Economics', *Oxford Economic Papers*, N.S. 12, 1 (February 1960); F. Knight, 'On Diminishing Returns from Investment', *Journal of Political Economy* (March 1944); C. Hoover, 'On the Inequality of the Rate of Profit and the Rate of Interest', *The Southern Economic Journal*, vol. 27 (July 1961), pp. 1–12.

and $\kappa/(1-\kappa)\,(N/C)^{1/\sigma}$ is the familiar CES marginal rate of substitution of labour for capital. It will be convenient later to work with (12.5) in the following form, where π is the capital share

$$S = \frac{wN}{\pi} = \frac{1-\kappa}{\kappa}\left(\frac{q}{w}\right)^{\sigma-1}. \qquad (12.6)$$

THE FACTORS AFFECTING
RELATIVE INCOME SHARES

Using (12.6), we can explore the neoclassical propositions concerning relative income shares. If technology is unchanging, then (12.6) states that a relative rise (fall) in the wage rate— or a relative rise (fall) in the supply of capital—augments (reduces) labour's income share if σ is less than unity. This is Hick's second proposition that we noted in the introduction to the chapter. In other words, the income share of the more rapidly growing factor of production will tend to rise if the elasticity of substitution exceeds unity; a value of the elasticity smaller than unity tends to reduce the income share of the accelerating input under these circumstances.

The effect on relative income shares of non-neutral technological progress can be discerned from (12.6) also. However, we need only refer to the results in Chapter 4 to specify it. There it is established that a rise in κ was capital-using, which means that the capital share is increased. In terms of (12.6) a rise in $(1-\kappa)/\kappa$ indicates, of course, that labour's share is benefited. As for a change in the elasticity of substitution, it was observed that an increase in σ is labour-saving if capital is advancing more rapidly than labour, i.e. if $q/w < 1$, when all variables are in index number terms. Hence, in terms of (12.6), a rise in σ reduces labour's share if $q/w < 1$, but increases it if $q/w > 1$.

In addition to non-neutral technological change and the movement in relative factor supplies, relative income shares are affected by the degree of exploitation of one factor by another which we noted above, and, in a three-factor market, by the elasticities of supply of the various factors. That is when more than two factors of production are included in the analysis, the effect on one factor's relative income share depends not only on the partial elasticities of substitution, but on the elasticities of supply of the other factors. For a rise in the price of one factor may change the proportions in which the other factors are used; if these proportions change, then the substitutability with the first factor is affected, and so is its relative income share.† However, if the other factors continue to be employed in the same proportion, the relative share of the first factor is independent of their elasticities of supply. But this is a strong assumption and we are wise to avoid it by staying within a value-added framework in which only two factors of production, labour and capital are operative.

We are now in a position to prepare the model for estimation. However, no additional work need be done since we can use the estimating equation for the CES side relation developed in the previous chapter; it is repeated here:

$$\log u = a + \sigma \log \rho + \lambda \log u_{-1}. \qquad (12.7)$$

Estimates of a, σ and λ provide us with all we need to determine the effect on relative shares of changing factor supplies.

Equation (12.7) assumes that there are no non-neutral changes in technology, and such is the case with a technological epoch as we define it. By applying stability analysis we can isolate these epochs and obtain epochal estimates of κ, σ and λ. Finally, we can evaluate the effect on relative shares of changing technology and changing factor supplies by finite differencing the estimates of equation (12.7) between any time points in which we are interested.

PRELIMINARY RESULTS

The model has been tested on data for the private domestic non-farm sector of the United States for the period, 1890–1958— the same data used to confront the technological employment model in Chapter 11. The CES side relation is fitted to three epochs and the results presented in Table 1 of Chapter 11. These form the basis for our calculations in the present chapter. Recall that we found the labour intensity parameter had fallen from the first to the second epoch, but had then turned up from the second to the third epoch, although it displayed a downward long-term trend from the first to the third epochs. Moreover, the short-run and long-run elasticities of substitution traced a

† J. R. Hicks, 'Distribution and Economic Progress: A Revised Version', *Review of Economic Studies*, vol. 4.

time path that was similar to the labour intensity variable: from a high level in the first epoch they fell to a low in the second and then rose again in the third but did not achieve the same level as in the first epoch.

The qualitative effect on relative income shares of these non-neutral technological changes can be determined as follows. As noted above, the decrease in the labour intensity of a technology tends to reduce S, the labour share relative to the capital share. But, since capital is increasing in supply more rapidly than labour, a reduction in σ tends to increase S, thus partially compensating for the labour-saving aspect of the non-neutral technological change. Another force which compensates S for the fall in the labour intensity of the technology is the fall in the rental of capital relative to the wage rate, since σ is less than unity in all epochs.

Two of the forces that affected relative income shares—non-neutral technological change and the relative supplies of the inputs—executed significant variations over the time period studied. Yet relative income shares themselves displayed much more stability than each of the forces acting on them. Hence, we can tentatively conclude that a contrapuntal movement in the forces occurred, one that produced a stable or 'linear' time path in the relative income shares.

That labour acted rationally by attempting to reduce N, thus raising w, seems to be a proposition that holds only when $\sigma < 1$. But this is what happened in the period under discussion. Also, the technological change which made substitution of labour for capital more difficult, coupled with the relative scarcity of labour, permitted q/w to fall by more than the fall in N/C, thus improving the labour share. In this case labour would wish to see a reduction in σ, which is a conclusion that is not intuitively obvious. The capital sector, on the other hand, would clearly wish to introduce a capital-using technology, but would also like to see a rise in σ. Then all three forces affecting ΔS would be negative if capital continued to grow more rapidly than labour. Yet it is difficult to think of a technology which uses relatively more capital but at the same time eases the substitution of capital for labour.

Now we turn to a quantitative measurement of the forces acting on relative income shares.

THE RELATIVE IMPORTANCE OF THE VARIOUS FORCES AFFECTING RELATIVE INCOME SHARES BETWEEN EPOCHS

In Table 12.1 we present actual estimates of $\log S$ and S and compare these with the computed estimates of the same magnitudes, i.e. computed on the basis of parameter estimates of (11.7) which are given in Table 1 of Chapter 11. It is clear that, for each epoch our estimates have come close to the actual estimate of relative income shares, the largest percentage error is 10 in the first epoch. In the first and third epochs we over-estimated relative shares and in the second we under-estimated relative shares (recall labour's share is in the numerator). Although it is unsportsmanlike to blame the data, a better fit would probably have been forthcoming had the price data been more reliable and had we focused on individual sectors in the economy.

TABLE 12.1. *Actual and computed average of log S and S for the last five years in each of three epochs*

	Actual		Computed		Error in
	$\log S$				computed S
Epoch	$\left(S = \dfrac{wN}{qC}\right)$	$S\dagger$	$\log S$	$S\dagger$	(%)
1890–1918	−0·412	0·39	−0·365	0·43	+10
1919–37	−0·299	0·50	−0·324	0·47	−6
1938–58	−0·201	0·63	−0·184	0·66	+5

† Actually S is greater than unity. In computing, however, the price data were in index number form while N and C were not. The base year for the index numbers was 1929, so that in effect each of the S ratios given above has been multiplied by q/w for 1929.

Which of the forces affecting the change in relative income shares were most influential per unit of change? Table 12.2 shows the effect on $\log S$ of a unit change in σ, $\log [(1 − \kappa)/\kappa]$ and $\log q/w$ between epochs. Column 2 indicates the effect per unit change in σ; column 3, the effect per unit change in $\log [(\overline{1 − \kappa})/\kappa]$;† and column 4, the effect per unit change in

† $(\overline{1 − \kappa})/\kappa$ is the long-run estimate of $(1 − \kappa)/\kappa$.

$\log q/w$. Between epochs then σ has the largest per unit effect, $\log q/w$ the second, and $\log[(1-\kappa)/\kappa]$ the least. It is apparent that the maximum impact between epochs is obtainable from a per unit change in the elasticity of substitution, the least impact from a change in the labour intensity parameter.

TABLE 12.2. *Arc partial derivatives of* $\log S$ *between epochs*

Interval	$\dfrac{\partial \log S}{\partial \sigma}$	$\dfrac{\partial \log S}{\partial \log \left(\dfrac{1-\kappa}{\kappa}\right)}$	$\dfrac{\partial \log S}{\partial \log (q)/w}$
(1)	(2)	(3)	(4)
Epochs 1–2	−4·0871	+0·2116	−0·7884
Epochs 2–3	−5·3084	+0·0946	−0·8054

ACTUAL SOURCES OF CHANGE IN RELATIVE INCOME SHARES

We should like to know how the various forces we have been discussing actually affected relative income share over the period 1890–1958. That is, variations in σ, $\log[(\overline{1-\kappa})/\kappa]$, and $\log q/w$ affect relative income shares and we wish to quantify their separate influences. This measurement problem can be handled by the finite differencing method (Appendix C).

TABLE 12.3. *Sources of long-run changes in* $\log S$ *between epochs*

Interval	$\Delta \sigma$	$\Delta \log[(\overline{1-\kappa})/\kappa]$	$\Delta \log q/w$	Computed $\Delta \log S$	Actual $\Delta \log S$
(1)	(2)	(3)	(4)	(5)	(6)
Epochs 1–2	+0·399	−0·413	+0·055	+0·041	+0·113
Epochs 2–3	−0·106	+0·202	+0·044	+0·140	+0·098

The finite differencing method applied to the relative share equation for the three epochs yields the information in Table 12.3. It is possible to read off the forces influencing $\log S$ over the period 1890–1958. Adding column 2 to column 3 we can see how non-neutral technological change influenced $\Delta \log S$. From the first to the second epoch, non-neutral technological change was labour saving on net, since $\Delta \log S$ tended to be forced down by the sum of $\Delta\sigma$ and $\Delta\log\left[(\overline{1-\kappa})/\kappa\right]$. The opposite occurred from the second to the third epoch where the effect of $\Delta\sigma+\Delta\log\left[(\overline{1-\kappa})/\kappa\right]$ is positive, thus indicating a labour-*using* technological change.†

Interestingly, the effect of changing relative supplies of capital and labour, as embodied in the $\log q/w$ term, had relatively smaller effect on $\log S$ than non-neutral technological change in the first to second epoch, but relatively larger effect between the second and third. This is little better than a speculation, however, because we have not taken sampling error into account. In general, though, we can say that perhaps the principal finding in this study is that, according to Table 12.3, the effect of technological change on relative income shares was of the same order of magnitude as the effect of changes in relative factor prices.‡ If this result is supported by additional evidence, then any explanation of relative income shares must give technological progress a large role and also attempt to explain the relative contributions of these forces.

† We found this unexpected result in another study where our data were up-dated to 1960. See M. Brown and J. S. de Cani, 'Technological Changes in the United States, 1950–1960', *Productivity Measurement Review*, no. 29, *op. cit.* pp. 26–39. This is consistent with the results for roughly the same period reported in Chapter 10. There, a Cobb–Douglas production function is used to measure non-neutral technological progress.

† The conclusion would probably be more striking if the downward bias of the effect of technological progress is eliminated in the estimation of the CES side relation. See the footnote on p. 178.

APPENDIX A

THE DERIVATION OF THE LEONTIEF, COBB–DOUGLAS AND CES PRODUCTION FUNCTIONS

The CES production function, the Cobb–Douglas production function, and the Leontief function are derived here. All three assume a constant elasticity of substitution between capital and labour. Their derivation proceeds directly from the definition of the elasticity of substitution.

In a production function in which output Z is expressed as a function of the inputs x and y of two factors of production, the elasticity of substitution σ is defined as the ratio of the percentage change in the ratio of the inputs to the percentage change in the marginal rate of substitution when the inputs are changed in such a way as to hold output constant.† The elasticity of substitution is then a property of the isoquants of the production surface. To see this let the production function be given by a general expression

$$Z = Z(x, y). \tag{A. 1}$$

We can hold Z constant at some value, say Z^*, and solve (A. 1) so as to express y explicitly as a function of x, suppressing Z^* because it is held constant,

$$y = y(x). \tag{A. 2}$$

The marginal rate of substitution is the negative of the slope of (A. 2).

$$\frac{\partial Z/\partial x}{\partial Z/\partial y} = -\frac{dy}{dx} = -y', \tag{A. 3}$$

and σ, the elasticity of substitution, is given by

$$\sigma = \frac{d(y/x)/(y/x)}{dy'(x)/y'(x)} = \frac{-y'(x)}{(y/x)} \frac{d(y/x)}{-dy'(x)} = y'\frac{x}{y}\frac{d(y/x)}{dy'}. \tag{A. 4}$$

Now
$$\frac{d(y/x)}{dy'} = \frac{x(dy/dy') - y(dx/dy')}{x^2} = \frac{1}{y''}\left(\frac{xy' - y}{x^2}\right), \tag{A. 5}$$

since
$$\frac{dy}{dy'} = \frac{dy}{dx}\frac{dx}{dy'} = y'\frac{1}{y''},$$

† R. G. D. Allen, *Mathematical Analysis for Economists*, pp. 340–5.

and
$$\frac{dx}{dy'} = \frac{1}{y''},$$

$$y'' = \frac{d^2y}{dx^2} = y'\frac{dy'}{dy}. \tag{A. 6}$$

Substituting (5) in (4) and rearranging gives an ordinary non-linear second order differential equation

$$\sigma xyy'' = xy'^2 - yy'. \tag{A. 7}$$

The solution to (A. 7) will contain σ explicitly as a parameter and two arbitrary constants, and will be the equation of an isoquant, i.e. an explicit form of (A. 2). Having solved (A. 7) it is possible to construct production functions of arbitrary, though constant, elasticities of substitution and degrees of homogeneity.

We shall discuss the solution to (A. 7) in some detail because we are interested in three special cases, σ equal to zero, unity, and infinity, and in cases other than these special ones. The case of zero elasticity of substitution is easily disposed of. In this case, the left-hand side of (A. 7) becomes identically zero and we must have either

$$y' = 0 \tag{A. 8}$$

or
$$xy' - y = 0. \tag{A. 9}$$

The solution to (A. 8) is
$$y = c \tag{A. 10}$$

and the solution to (A. 9) is
$$y = cx, \tag{A. 11}$$

since
$$\frac{dy}{y} - \frac{dx}{x} = 0$$

or
$$\log y + \log a = \log x + \log b,$$

which gives (A. 11). We can eliminate (A. 11) as nonsensical. It says that as the input of one factor increases, the input of the other factor must also increase in order to hold output constant. This implies a production function that is homogeneous of degree zero. Equation (A. 10), which is a Leontief type isoquant, says that given output the input of y is uniquely determined. The factors of production combine in fixed proportions and substitution of one factor for another is impossible. The isoquant when σ is zero can be written as

$$\begin{aligned} y &= y_0, x \geqslant x_0, \\ x &= x_0, y \geqslant y_0, \end{aligned} \tag{A. 12}$$

i.e. they are right-angled curves which are concave upward and parallel to the axes.

Suppose, next, that σ is greater than zero and in (A. 7) make the substitution

$$x = e^u, \tag{A. 13}$$

where

$$du/dx = e^{-u},$$

$$d^2u/dx^2 = -e^{-2u}$$

and

$$d^2y/dx^2 = y'' e^{-2u} - y' e^{-2u}.$$

We have, after eliminating e^{-u},

$$\sigma yy'' + yy'(1-\sigma) - y'^2 = 0, \tag{A. 14}$$

in which the derivatives are taken with respect to u. Since (A. 14) does not contain u explicitly, we can reduce the order of (A. 14) by letting

$$p = y'. \tag{A. 15}$$

We then have, after cancelling a p,

$$\sigma y(dp/dy) + y(1-\sigma) - p = 0, \tag{A. 16}$$

since

$$\frac{dy'}{dy} = \frac{dp}{dy}\frac{dy}{du} = \frac{dp}{dy}y'.$$

Using $y^{-1/\sigma}$ as the integrating factor, the solution to (A. 16) is

$$p = y + cy^{1/\sigma}. \tag{A. 17}$$

Remembering the definition of p (A. 15) we have

$$dy/du = y + cy^{1/\sigma}, \tag{A. 18}$$

an equation of the first order. There are two cases to consider, σ equal to unity and σ different from unity.

If σ is equal to unity, the solution to (A. 18) is

$$y = ke^{u(1+c)}, \tag{A. 19}$$

because

$$dy/y = (1+c)\,du,$$

or

$$\log y = (1+c)\,u + \text{constant}.$$

Remembering (A. 13) we have

$$y = kx^{(1+c)}, \tag{A. 20}$$

as the equation of the isoquant. To construct a production function homogeneous of degree v, we write

$$Z = Z(x^{1+c}/y) = Z(w). \tag{A. 21}$$

From Euler's Theorem we have

$$vZ = x\frac{\partial Z}{\partial x} + y\frac{\partial Z}{\partial y} = (1+c)\frac{x^c}{y} x\frac{dZ}{dw} - \frac{x^{1+c}}{y}\frac{dZ}{dw}$$

$$= c\frac{x^{1+c}}{y}\frac{dZ}{dw} = cw\frac{dZ}{dw}. \qquad (A. 22)$$

This can be written as $\qquad \dfrac{dZ}{Z} = \dfrac{v}{c}\dfrac{dw}{w}.$

Its solution is $\qquad Z = k(x^{1+c}/y)^{v/c} = ky^{-v/c}x^{v/c+v}. \qquad (A. 23)$

Equation (A. 23) is the Cobb–Douglas production function

$$Z = kx^\beta y^\gamma, \qquad (A. 24)$$

in a somewhat disguised form, in which

$$\left.\begin{aligned} v &= \gamma+\beta, \\ c &= \frac{\gamma+\beta}{\beta}. \end{aligned}\right\} \qquad (A. 25)$$

Hence, homogeneity of the production function and unit elasticity of substitution imply the Cobb–Douglas production function in terms of equation (A. 18).

If in (A. 18) σ is not equal to unity, we have an extremely simple form of Bernoulli's Equation. It can be written as

$$x(dy/dx) = y+cy^{1/\sigma},$$

since $\qquad \dfrac{dy}{du} = x\dfrac{dy}{dx}$

or $\qquad \dfrac{dy}{y(1+cy^{1/\sigma-1})} = \dfrac{dx}{x}$

The solution in implicit form is given by

$$y^{1-1/\sigma} - kx^{1-1/\sigma} = \text{constant.} \qquad (A. 26)$$

As σ tends to infinity the isoquant tends to a straight line. In this case, the factors of production are perfect substitutes for each other. In general, this line should have negative slope, which implies that the arbitrary constant, k, is negative.

To derive a production function that is homogeneous of degree v, we use the same device as we used in equations (A. 22) and (A. 23), this time, however, setting

$$Z = Z(y^{1-1/\sigma} - kx^{1-1/\sigma}) = Z(w). \qquad (A. 27)$$

The resulting function is

$$Z = k_1(y^{-\alpha} - kx^{-\alpha})^{-v/\alpha}, \qquad (A.\ 28)$$

where

$$\alpha = (1/\sigma) - 1. \qquad (A.\ 29)$$

Aside from notational differences, (A. 28) is the constant elasticity of substitution production function which is used in the text.

Since (A. 26) is a solution to (A. 18), then so is

$$\kappa y^{1-1/\sigma} - (1-\kappa)x^{1-1/\sigma} = M,$$

where κ and M are constants. Using this in place of (A. 26) yields the form used in the text.

APPENDIX B

UZAWA'S GENERALIZATION OF THE CES PRODUCTION FUNCTION TO THE n-FACTOR CASE

This appendix indicates the generalizations of the CES production function to the n-factor case developed by H. Uzawa.[†] For their proofs the reader is referred to Uzawa's paper. Let X be gross output as before, $x_1, x_2, ..., x_n$ be inputs. The first generalization is

$$X = A(\alpha_1 x_1^{-\beta} + ... + \alpha_n x_n^{-\beta})^{-1/\beta}, \qquad (B.\ 1)$$

where A and the α_1 are constants, $\sigma = 1/(1+\beta)$, σ being the elasticity of substitution. This function is homogeneous of degree one, and embodies diminishing returns to all factors. It assumes that the ease of substitution between any pair of factors is identical to the σ of any other pair. This is a highly restrictive assumption which Uzawa relaxes in his second generalization. As an example of the latter, consider a production process with four factors of production; thus x_1 and x_2 can be substituted with ease up to σ_{12}; x_3 and x_4 can be substituted with ease up to σ_{34}; x_1 and x_3 have a partial elasticity of substitution of unity, i.e. $\sigma_{13} = 1$; also $\sigma_{14} = 1$, $\sigma_{23} = 1$ and $\sigma_{24} = 1$. The function representing these conditions is

$$X = \beta(\alpha_1 x_1^{-\beta_{12}})^{-\rho_1/\beta_{12}} (\alpha_3 x_3^{-\beta_{34}} + \alpha_4 x_4^{-\beta_{34}})^{-\rho_2/\beta_{34}}, \qquad (B.\ 2)$$

where β and the α_1 are constants as before,

$$\beta_{12} = -\left(1 - \frac{1}{\sigma_{12}}\right), \quad \beta_{34} = -\left(1 - \frac{1}{\sigma_{34}}\right),$$

and the ρ_1 have the property such that $\rho_1 + \rho_2 = 1$, which ensures constant returns to scale. The meaning of this function is as follows: x_1 and x_2 form a set characterized by a common partial elasticity of substitution; x_3 and x_4 form a different set with a different partial elasticity; the partial elasticity of substitution between variables of two different sets is restricted to unity. The function has the economic properties of constant returns to scale and diminishing returns to all

† 'Production Functions with Constant Elasticities of Substitution', *The Review of Economic Studies*, vol. 29 (October 1962), pp. 291–9. Also see V. Mukerji, 'Generalized SMAC Function with Constant Ratios of Elasticities of Substitution', *The Review of Economic Studies*, vol. 30 (October 1963), pp. 233–61.

factors.† The difficulty with the function is that the elasticity of substitution between variables of two different sets is always unity. However, equation (B. 2) is still the most general constant elasticity production function that has been developed.

How would one estimate the parameters of equation (B. 2)? Let $f_1 = \partial X/\partial x_1, f_2 = \partial X/\partial x_2, \ldots$, and p_1 be the price of x_1's services, p_2 be the price of x_2's services, etc. Then form

$$\frac{f_1}{f_2} = \frac{p_1}{p_2}; \quad \frac{f_1}{f_3} = \frac{p_1}{p_3}; \quad \frac{f_1}{f_4} = \frac{p_1}{p_4},$$

$$\frac{f_2}{f_3} = \frac{p_2}{p_3}, \quad \frac{f_2}{f_4} = \frac{p_2}{p_4},$$

$$\frac{f_3}{f_4} = \frac{p_3}{p_4}. \tag{B. 3}$$

We do not know *a priori* which variables belong in each set. Therefore, all of the equations in (B. 3) must be estimated. Let us write out one and examine it; take

$$\frac{f_2}{f_4} = \frac{p_2}{p_4}$$

or

$$\left(\frac{\alpha_2}{\alpha_4}\right)\left(\frac{x_4}{x_2}\right)^{1/\sigma_{24}} = \frac{p_2}{p_4}.$$

This can be converted to logarithms and the parameters estimated. Suppose that estimate $\sigma_{24} \neq 1$, then we know that x_2 and x_4 belong to the same set. Now estimate $f_2/f_3 = p_2/p_3$; if it is found that $\sigma_{23} = \sigma_{24}$, the x_2, x_3 and x_4 belong to the same set, and so on. In this way the sets are determined and in the process the capital intensity and elasticity of substitution parameters are estimated. These estimates can be inserted in the general function

$$X = \beta \prod_{S=1}^{S} \left[\left(\sum_{i \in S} \alpha_i x_i^{-\beta_s}\right)^{-1/\beta_s}\right]^{\rho_s} \tag{B. 4}$$

where S is the number of sets, and in our example, $i = 1, 2, 3, 4$. Equation (B. 4) can then be converted to logs and the remaining parameters—namely β and the ρ_s—estimated.

† It is easy to relax the assumption of constant returns by allowing $\rho_1 + \rho_2 = \rho$, where ρ is arbitrary. This can be derived by the use of Euler's theorem.

APPENDIX C

A FINITE DIFFERENCE APPROXIMATION TO A TOTAL DIFFERENTIAL

The purpose of this appendix is to explain the numerical method of approximating a total differential which has been used in this paper. The method is discussed in detail in terms of three independent variables at first, and the extension to n variables is sketched briefly.

Consider the function $Z = F(x_1, x_2, x_3)$ which has been fitted to data coming from two different universes and the quantities x_1, x_2, x_3 either estimated or observed in the data. Let $\hat{x}_1, \hat{x}_2, \hat{x}_3$ be either estimates or observations derived from the first universe and $\hat{x}_1 + h$, $\hat{x}_2 + k$, $\hat{x}_3 + e$ be corresponding quantities derived from the second. We can write

$$\hat{\Delta}Z = F(\hat{x}_1 + h, \hat{x}_2 + k, \hat{x}_3 + e) - F(\hat{x}_1, \hat{x}_2, \hat{x}_3). \qquad \text{(C. 1)}$$

We are interested in estimating the separate effect on $\hat{\Delta}Z$ of

$$\hat{x}_1 + h - \hat{x}_1, \quad \hat{x}_2 + k - \hat{x}_2 \quad \text{and} \quad \hat{x}_3 + e - \hat{x}_3. \qquad \text{(C. 2)}$$

Now introduce in (C. 1) some additional terms, which cancel.

$$\begin{aligned}
\hat{\Delta}Z = {} & F(\hat{x}_1 + h, \hat{x}_2 + k, \hat{x}_3 + e) - F(\hat{x}_1, \hat{x}_2 + k, \hat{x}_3 + e) \\
& + F(\hat{x}_1, \hat{x}_2 + k, \hat{x}_3 + e) - F(\hat{x}_1, \hat{x}_2, \hat{x}_3 + e) \\
& + F(\hat{x}_1, \hat{x}_2, \hat{x}_3 + e) - F(\hat{x}_1, \hat{x}_2, \hat{x}_3). \qquad \text{(C. 3)}
\end{aligned}$$

This in turn can be written as

$$\begin{aligned}
\hat{\Delta}Z = {} & \frac{F(\hat{x}_1 + h, \hat{x}_2 + k, \hat{x}_3 + e) - F(\hat{x}_1, \hat{x}_2 + k, \hat{x}_3 + e)}{h} h \\
& + \frac{F(\hat{x}_1, \hat{x}_2 + k, \hat{x}_3 + e) - F(\hat{x}_1, \hat{x}_2, \hat{x}_3 + e)}{k} k \\
& + \frac{F(\hat{x}_1, \hat{x}_2, \hat{x}_3 + e) - F(\hat{x}_1, \hat{x}_2, \hat{x}_3)}{e} e \qquad \text{(C. 4)}
\end{aligned}$$

Since (C. 3) and (C. 4) are identical and (C. 3) is easier to compute, we will use a modified form of (C. 3). Any of the terms involving a difference of a particular one of the variables, say Δx_1, can be written in four different ways.

$$
\begin{aligned}
(a) \quad & \frac{\hat{\Delta}Z}{\Delta x_1}\,\Delta x_1 = \frac{F(\hat{x}_1+h,\ \hat{x}_2+k,\ \hat{x}_3+e) - F(\hat{x}_1,\ \hat{x}_2+k,\ \hat{x}_3+e)}{h}\,h, \\[2mm]
(b) \quad & \frac{\hat{\Delta}Z}{\Delta x_1}\,\Delta x_1 = \frac{F(\hat{x}_1+h,\ \hat{x}_2,\ \hat{x}_3+e) - F(\hat{x}_1,\ \hat{x}_2,\ \hat{x}_3+e)}{h}\,h, \\[2mm]
(c) \quad & \frac{\hat{\Delta}Z}{\Delta x_1}\,\Delta x_1 = \frac{F(\hat{x}_1+h,\ \hat{x}_2+k,\ \hat{x}_3) - F(\hat{x}_1,\ \hat{x}_2+k,\ \hat{x}_3)}{h}\,h, \\[2mm]
(d) \quad & \frac{\hat{\Delta}Z}{\Delta x_1}\,\Delta x_1 = \frac{F(\hat{x}_1+h,\ \hat{x}_2,\ \hat{x}_3) - F(\hat{x}_1,\ \hat{x}_2,\ \hat{x}_3)}{h}\,h.
\end{aligned}
\qquad \text{(C. 5)}
$$

Equation (C. 4) can be written in 6 different ways depending on the order of the differencing—i.e. $3! = 6$; this yields 18 terms. Forms (a) and (d) above each appear twice in these 6 ways, and forms (b) and (c) above each appear once. Hence, a good estimate of $(\partial Z/\partial x_1)\,dx_1$ would be a weighted average of the forms of (C. 5) with (a) and (d) receiving twice the weight of (b) and (c). Forms similar to C. 5 (a)–5 (d) which refer to $(\partial Z/\partial x_2)\,dx_2$ and $(\partial Z/\partial x_3)\,dx_3$ are distributed among the eighteen terms.

Extension of this scheme to n variables is computationally difficult. With n variables, there are 2^{n-1} ways of writing any particular difference and $n!$ orders of differencing. We can reason as follows: we can write the function $F(x_i, x_j, \ldots, x_k)$ with n terms inside the parentheses. There are $n!$ ways of writing in the subscripts. We agree always to difference in the order in which the subscripts appear. Suppose x_j appears in the kth place. There are $(n-1)!$ orders of differencing in which this occurs. The $k-1$ variables which precede x_j are held at their lower levels x_i and the $n-k$ variables which follow x_j are held at their upper levels x_i+h_i. The $(k-1)$ variables which precede x_j can be arranged in $(k-1)!$ ways and the $(n-k)!$ variables which follow x_j can be arranged in $(n-k)!$ ways. Hence, a particular form of $(\hat{\Delta}Z/\Delta x_j)\,\Delta x_j$ with a particular set of $(k-1)$ variables held at their lower levels and particular set of $(n-k)$ variables held at their upper levels appears in $(k-1)!\,(n-k)!$ forms of $\hat{\Delta}Z$. Then, in averaging, each form of $(\hat{\Delta}Z/\Delta x_j)\,\Delta x_j$ with $k-1$ variables held at their lower levels and $(n-k)$ variables held at their upper levels receives a weight of $(k-1)!\,(n-k)!$. With x_j fixed, there are $\binom{n-1}{k-1}$ ways to choose the variables to be held at their lower levels, and

$$
\sum_{k=0}^{n-1} \binom{n-1}{k-1} = 2^{n-1}, \qquad \text{(C. 6)}
$$

which is the total number of ways of differencing with respect to x_j.

Example. Consider $F(x_1, x_2, x_3, x_4)$. There are 4! orders of differencing, and there are 8 ways of differencing with respect to x_1 (and each of the others). Let us write them out with their weights.

Form of difference	Weight
$F(x_1+h_1, x_2+h_2, x_3+h_3, x_4+h_4) - F(x_1, x_2+h_2, x_3+h_3, x_4+h_4)$	$0! \, 3! = 6$
$F(x_4, x_1+h_1, x_3+h_3, x_2+h_2) - F(x_4, x_1, x_3+h_3, x_2+h_2)$	$1! \, 2! = 2$
$F(x_3, x_1+h_1, x_2+h_2, x_4+h_4) - F(x_2, x_1, x_2+h_2, x_4+h_4)$	$1! \, 2! = 2$
$F(x_3, x_4, x_1+h_1, x_2+h_2) - F(x_3, x_4, x_1, x_2+h_2)$	$2! \, 1! = 2$
$F(x_2, x_1+h_1, x_3+h_3, x_4+h_4) - F(x_2, x_1, x_3+h_3, x_4+h_4)$	$1! \, 2! = 2$
$F(x_2, x_3, x_1+h_1, x_4+h_4) - F(x_2, x_3, x_1, x_4+h_4)$	$2! \, 1! = 2$
$F(x_2, x_4, x_1+h_1, x_3+h_3) - F(x_2, x_4, x_1, x_3+h_3)$	$2! \, 1! = 2$
$F(x_2, x_3, x_4, x_1+h_1) - F(x_2, x_3, x_4, x_1)$	$3! \, 0! = 6$

The sum of the weights is 24, which is the total number of ways of writing the difference, $\hat{\Delta}Z$. The remaining partial differences can be averaged in the same way. Since each of the $n!$ ways of differencing add to $\hat{\Delta}Z$, the sum of the weighted averages of the partial differences will add to $\hat{\Delta}Z$. If the fit is good in both samples, $\hat{\Delta}Z \approx \Delta Z$.

APPENDIX D

DATA ON THE UNITED STATES PRIVATE DOMESTIC NON-FARM SECTOR, 1890–1960

Time series on output, labour input and capital stock for the United States compiled by John Kendrick[†] on an annual basis provide the basic data for the tests executed in Chapter 10. The specific series are gross private non-farm product in 1929 prices, man-hours worked per year in the private domestic non-farm sector, and fixed capital stock in the same sector in 1929 prices (this includes plant, equipment and inventories). The Kendrick series were carried forward to 1960 by splicing them on to the relevant Department of Commerce series in 1954. Percentage changes in net capital stock were obtained from *The Capital Goods Study*.[‡]

The Kendrick series on man-hours worked per year represents the actual flow of labour services. Hence, the labour series assumes homogeneous inputs. This is consistent with the objective of permitting changes in the quality of labour services and changes in occupation mix to be reflected in changes in the coefficients of the production function.

A measure of capital services is approximated by using a net capital stock series (see Chapter 6). But a net capital stock series measures only available productive facilities, not the degree of use. Available capital has long been recognized to be an inadequate measure for the estimation of production functions, for it probably underestimates capital productivity. Hence, it is necessary to adjust the available capital stock series for capacity under-utilization as best as one can even though capacity utilization measures are suspect.

In Table D. 1, the data are presented on gross product, man-hours employed, available capital, and on the first approximation to utilized capital stock.

The first approximation to the capacity utilization series utilizes the Wharton School method.[§] Briefly, it involves plotting trend

[†] *Productivity Trends in the United States.*

[‡] See G. Jaszi, R. Wasson, and L. Grose, 'Expansion of Fixed Capital in the United States', *Survey of Current Business*, vol. 42 (November 1962), pp. 9–18.

[§] 'Index of Percentage Utilization of Industrial Capacity for the United States', Econometric Research Unit, University of Pennsylvania, 1960.

lines to the peaks of Kendrick's output series, thus assuming that capacity is fully utilized at peak output. Actual output for each of the interpeak years is then expressed as a percentage of the relevant trend value for that year, yielding the percentage utilization of capacity for that year.

Several shortcomings of this method should be noted. First, the index is based on movements in the total output series and thus assumes that all industries and firms reach their peak output potential at the same time. Ideally, the index should be built up from output series in each industrial sector and weighted by the importance of that sector in aggregate output. Secondly, the index, whether constructed on an aggregative or disaggregative basis, assumes that in any year in which output is at a peak, capacity is being fully utilized. Thirdly, the index is based on the assumption that a linear interpolation between output peaks is a good approximation of the rate of growth of capacity. Fourthly, the index does not evaluate changes in the machinery mix attendant on changes in the level of output. Declines in the level of output are usually accompanied by the shut-down of less efficient equipment rather than by reductions in the utilization of all grades of capital. This touches on the problem of deriving a capacity utilization measure for the various vintage capital items that enter the stock— a problem that has yet to be resolved at the theoretical level. Finally, the index is constructed on the assumption that no economies of scale or neutral technological change are present.

A second approximation to a capacity utilization index is discussed in Chapter 10. At the minimum, it avoids the last deficiency to which the first approximation is subject. Both approximations are shown in Table D. 2.

TABLE D1. *Gross product, man-hours employed, available capital stock, and utilized (first approximation) capital stock—private domestic non-farm sector of the United States, 1890–1960*

	Gross product (millions of 1929 dollars)	Net capital stock (millions of 1929 dollars)	Utilized capital stock (millions of 1929 dollars)	Man-hours employed (millions)
1890	18,536	65,869	53,778	39,532
1	19,405	70,952	60,072	40,915
2	22,370	76,844	73,898	42,773
3	21,057	82,391	74,514	41,845
4	19,988	85,984	74,128	39,386
5	22,867	90,343	88,164	42,968
6	21,706	94,422	81,851	42,743
7	24,043	97,667	88,813	44,579
8	24,214	101,382	86,686	44,771
9	27,306	105,093	95,557	49,471
1900	28,185	109,228	97,431	50,136
1	32,551	113,244	111,236	53,195
2	32,985	117,442	113,567	56,357
3	34,795	122,224	119,833	58,560
4	33,942	125,872	112,276	57,174
5	37,071	130,183	120,769	61,035
6	42,041	136,334	133,259	64,236
7	43,245	142,854	139,594	66,046
8	38,486	148,070	124,407	61,985
9	44,664	151,960	144,029	66,563
1910	44,910	156,810	145,971	68,831
1	47,195	161,332	153,217	70,102
2	48,226	165,156	155,898	72,786
3	51,937	170,652	167,904	73,839
4	45,886	175,916	150,029	71,210
5	46,676	179,412	153,573	70,859
6	56,293	182,944	181,178	78,007
7	52,695	186,901	170,961	79,459
8	56,365	190,488	183,374	78,283
9	58,985	193,927	192,208	75,422
1920	59,734	198,597	196,262	76,336
1	58,698	202,714	182,617	68,167
2	62,084	206,480	188,741	74,269
3	71,285	214,037	209,628	81,994
4	74,284	222,980	217,853	79,197
5	75,481	231,905	223,531	82,429
6	81,366	242,777	229,674	86,127
7	81,833	253,140	241,562	86,508
8	83,097	261,488	247,105	87,083
9	88,562	269,602	265,545	89,467

TABLE D I (*cont.*)

	Gross product (millions of 1929 dollars)	Net capital stock (millions of 1929 dollars)	Utilized capital stock (millions of 1929 dollars)	Man-hours employed (millions)
1930	79,817	275,514	244,430	81,854
I	73,021	275,724	224,878	72,386
2	60,665	270,177	184,815	62,069
3	57,772	262,117	171,212	61,248
4	65,041	256,151	187,276	62,366
5	74,221	253,032	209,962	66,023
6	83,278	253,260	234,236	73,426
7	90,884	256,519	254,890	77,568
8	83,743	257,976	217,606	70,460
9	91,530	258,073	221,746	75,131
1940	101,313	261,238	228,757	79,694
I	116,415	267,526	250,238	89,276
2	127,434	271,939	266,469	97,056
3	136,274	271,011	266,154	101,633
4	146,470	268,028	269,520	100,124
5	145,052	265,260	263,098	94,920
6	140,288	269,194	252,357	96,671
7	142,022	279,813	262,536	100,072
8	149,895	291,586	285,700	101,304
9	147,122	302,616	277,522	96,784
1950	163,620	314,695	307,946	100,352
I	173,398	330,176	322,436	104,801
2	178,864	343,826	334,878	106,168
3	186,264	356,394	350,110	109,195
4	183,526	367,734	346,097	104,477
5	198,759	382,076	374,905	109,878
6	205,298	396,213	378,491	113,141
7	206,773	403,345	397,780	112,383
8	198,419	401,732	378,387	109,068
9	216,475	409,483	393,440	114,445
1960	221,541	414,686	403,843	115,234

Notes:

Gross product: from Kendrick, *Productivity Trends in the United States*, pp. 298–301, Table A. III, column 7 minus column 8.

Net capital stock: from Kendrick, *op. cit.* pp. 320–2, Table A. XV.

Utilized capital stock: the product of a utilization factor (first approximation, see Table D2) and the two-year moving average of the available net capital stock series.

Man hours employed: from Kendrick, *op. cit.* pp. 311–13, Table A. X.

TABLE D2. *First and second approximations to capacity utilization series, United States domestic non-farm sector, 1890–1960*

First approximation to capacity utilization series obtained by Wharton School method				Second approximation to capacity utilization series obtained by iterative procedure			
1890	84·3	1925	98·3	1890	79·3	1925	96·0
91	87·8	26	100·0	91	83·8	26	100·0
92	100·0	27	97·4	92	100·0	27	96·4
93	93·6	28	96·1	93	90·6	28	96·2
94	88·1	29	100·0	94	82·8	29	100·0
1895	100·0	1930	89·7	1895	100·0	1930	84·1
96	88·6	31	81·6	96	82·1	31	72·6
97	92·5	32	67·7	97	87·0	32	51·8
98	87·1	33	64·3	98	79·6	33	48·1
99	92·6	34	72·3	99	86·4	34	56·3
1900	90·9	1935	82·5	1900	84·3	1935	67·3
01	100·0	36	92·5	01	100·0	36	78·5
02	98·5	37	100·0	02	99·8	37	100·0
03	100·0	38	84·6	03	100·0	38	74·5
04	90·5	39	85·9	04	85·5	39	74·6
1905	94·3	1940	88·1	1905	90·4	1940	77·1
06	100·0	41	94·7	06	100·0	41	85·0
07	100·0	42	98·8	07	100·0	42	89·5
08	85·5	43	89·0	08	76·4	43	89·4
09	96·0	44	100·0	09	89·4	44	100·0
1910	94·6	1945	98·7	1910	89·2	1945	99·8
11	96·3	46	94·8	11	91·3	46	94·2
12	95·5	47	95·6	12	91·2	47	94·3
13	100·0	48	100·0	13	100·0	48	100·0
14	86·6	49	93·4	14	78·4	49	90·3
1915	86·4	1950	99·8	1915	78·4	1950	98·7
16	100·0	51	100·0	16	100·0	51	100·0
17	82·5	52	99·4	17	88·7	52	99·9
18	97·2	53	100·0	18	94·7	53	100·0
19	100·0	54	95·6	19	100·0	54	93·7
1920	100·0	1955	100·0	1920	100·0	1955	100·0
21	91·0	56	100·0	21	86·4	56	100·0
22	92·3	57	99·5	22	86·6	57	99·9
23	99·7	58	94·0	23	96·2	58	91·9
24	99·7	59	97·0	24	96·2	59	95·9
		1960	98·0			1960	96·0

INDEX

Internal economies, 13–14
Investment, 187
  in: measurement of capital stock, 78,
    83–6, 89, 90, 91
  Salter measure of technological
    change, 106 n.
  Solow model, 78–81
  relation to: capital stock rigidity, 67,
    76
  innovation, 75, 76, 77, 78
Iso-outlay line, 166
Isoquant, 10–22 passim, 29, 30, 72, 166,
    192–5
Iterative estimation technique, 89, 133,
    135, 145

Jaszi, George, 202 n.
Johannsen, Lief, 64 n., 68 n.

Kaitz, Hyman, 83 n.
Kaldor, Nicholas, 184, 184 n., 186 n.
Kalecki, M., 184
Kamien, Morton, 44 n.
Kendrick, John, 1 n., 91 n., 96 n.,
    98 n., 100 n., 162 n.
  time-series data, 113 n., 202–6 passim
Kennedy, C., 21 n.
Keynes, John M., 165, 180 n., 182,
    184 n.
Klein, Lawrence R., 114 n.
  economies of scale, 33 n.
  labour demand function, 167, 169 n.
  production function estimates, 102 n.
Knight, Frank H., 34, 41, 185 n.
Konijn, H. S., 37 n.
Koyck distribution, 69, 69 n., 76
Kravis, I., 183
Kuh, Edwin, 168, 168 n.
Kurz, Mordecai, 45 n.
Kuznets, Simon, 82, 85 n.

Labour. See Factor supply, Factors of
    production, Inputs
Labour demand, 165–79
  forces affecting, 165–69, 170–2
  epochal quantification of, 176–7
  functions, 166–70
  fitting of, 172–3
  epochal estimates of, 173–7
  policy, 178
Labour intensity. See Capital intensity-
    labour intensity
Labour saving technological change.
    See Capital-saving–labour-
    saving technological change

Leibenstein, Harvey, 59 n., 136 n.
Leontief, W. W.
  capital stock measure, 81, 88
  concept of production function, 10 n.,
    43, 45 n.
  labour demand, 168
  production function derivation, 192–6
Levenberg, Kenneth, 133 n.
Levine, Herbert, 105
Long run
  defined, 65, 72, 75
  elasticity of substitution, 65, 67, 71–2,
    76
  equilibrium, 65
  labour demand function, 173, 176 n.
  production process, 63–76 passim
Lowe, A., 21 n.
Lucas, Robert E., 45 n., 129 n., 130 n.

McCarthy, Michael, 57 n., 80
McFadden, Daniel, 45 n.
Machlup, Fritz, 185 n.
McKinnon, Ronald I., 44 n., 129 n.
Managerial efficiency, 2, 78
Mansfield, Edwin, 74, 91
Marginal cost, 35 n., 52, 184
Marginal product, 35 n., 97 n., 98 n., 99
  capital intensity effect on, 16–17, 22
  elasticity of substitution relation to,
    18–20 passim, 23, 106
  neoclassical criteria for, 30–1, 41
  in: Cobb–Douglas world, 31–4, 41,
    126, 155
    CES world, 46–9, 50 n., 55–6, 61
    parameter estimation, 133, 135
    labour demand function, 170 n.
    net capital stock model, 82, 83, 84,
      89
    Solow embodied model, 78–80, 86,
      87
    Solow measure of technological
      change, 104
  theories of income distribution,
    184 n., 185 n., 185
Marginal rate of substitution, 12, 16–21
    passim
  role in: Cobb–Douglas world, 36–42
    passim
    CES world, 48, 49, 55–6, 61, 62
    parameter estimation, 133, 135
    derivation of production function,
      192
    expansion path, 64
    income distribution theory, 185
    labour demand function, 166, 167